On Brass

Reg
with best wishes
[signature]

Harry Mortimer on Brass

an autobiography
written with Alan Lynton

Alphabooks

Copyright © 1981 Harry Mortimer

First published 1981 by Alphabooks, Sherborne, Dorset
This book designed and produced by Alphabet & Image Ltd,
Sherborne, Dorset

ISBN 0 906670 04 7

Photoset by Photosetting & Secretarial Services Ltd, Yeovil
Printed and bound in Britain by Butler & Tanner Ltd,
Frome, Somerset

Jacket photograph provided by courtesy EMI Records.

The picture on page 1 shows a ceramic brass
band candelabra by Christine Poole. The picture
on pages 2-3 shows Harry Mortimer conducting
the band of the Boys' Brigade at Central Hall,
Westminster.

Contents

At rehearsal

Recitative

I was just settling down nicely into my seat in the dining car of the London to Manchester Inter-City train, when a young lady, laden with brief-case and all the other necessities of the long distance executive, breathlessly bustled in and took command of the opposite seat. As the train was delayed (again) we did a most un-British thing and started on a conversation.

Assessing me as a seasoned traveller on this line – quite rightly, as I must have bought British Rail several carriages by now – she asked if I knew Manchester at all. Encouraged by my positive response she ventured further and enquired if I knew Belle Vue.

'Just a bit,' I answered, and, entering into the spirit of the thing, I hazarded a guess. 'You must be,' I said, 'the advance bookings manager for a tour and are on your way to collect a large sum of money from the Belle Vue box-office.'

I was right on target. She was the business side of a forthcoming Andy Williams tour.

The flood-gates were open! Did I know the workings of Belle Vue? Had I been associated with that place for long? Did I know anything of the Brass Band Contests held there? I modestly answered yes to all three charges, and then came the big one. Her father had often talked of Belle Vue and had asked her to find out what she could about the Band Championships. 'In particular,' she said, 'he wanted me to find out about the characters of the past. For instance,' she went on, 'Is Harry Mortimer still alive?'

My face must have given the game away, as she immediately blushed right down to her elegant boots. 'Oh, no,' she stammered.

In case anybody else is in the slightest doubt, let me affirm here and now that, most of the time at any rate, yes I am.

The advantages of still being alive are enormous! The greatest of all is that I can look back over the last eighty years with a wonderful perspective. Hindsight is a tremendous advantage. To be wise after the event, with impunity, is the just reward for having stayed the course for so long. The BBC and I thought I had retired in 1964, but, thank heaven, that is not the case.

Let's take it from the top. I shall try to keep the tempo steady and you shall try to follow the downbeat. As Sir Thomas Beecham once remarked to a diffident young Harry Mortimer back in the twenties: 'You must keep your eye on me, and I will keep my eye on you. You have something which is very important: you temporarily live the part.'

So, for a while, live the part with me ...

1 The trumpet shall sound

1902 was a good year – the Boer War came to an end, Foden's Band was founded, Black Dyke achieved maximum marks at the National (and Empire) Championships, and I entered the world. My father's instant reaction to the news that he had a son was an excited, 'I'll make him the best cornet player in England.' So is one's destiny decided at birth!

I was christened Harry (not Henry) and my father, Fred, had no doubts about my future. Whether his ambition was ever fully realized or not is not for me to say, but even then he sensed that the future of our branch of the Mortimer family lay in music, and the sheer joy of being able to play an instrument is one which I have cherished all my life. My only regret is that 'stick-itch' – the desire to conduct – coupled with heavy administration responsibilities, took total precedence over my desire to play when I was in my fifties.

Most of the older generation of brass players know of my father, Fred Mortimer, and his immense contribution to the standards of playing and conducting which he brought to any of his bands. Not so many, though, know of grandfather Henry Mortimer. He had been a baritone player in the neighbouring Wyke Temperance Band, which was one of the most successful bands of the latter half of the last century, winning the coveted British Open Championship three times. From him Fred, the fourth of ten children, inherited a love of music. Of the five boys, Fred was the only one who decided against going into the family building business, and when he started his working life it was to the fustian mills at Hebden Bridge that he went. And it was at Hebden Bridge that my life started.

There is something about the Pennines which encourages music. The majority of bands of all grades come from the geographical area surrounding this great line of hills, and Hebden Bridge is as typical as any. Perhaps it is the sheer beauty of these hills which encourages men and women to get together to make music. By contrast, the average employment of the area is often tedious or dirty, or both, so perhaps we shouldn't be surprised that human nature, being what it is, finds an outlet which owes nothing to mills or mines except comradeship. Despite the noise and the rush of the modern world the Brass Band still holds its place in the lives of these people. You can still hear, on practice nights, the notes of the band on the night air: the warmth of the euphoniums, the insistence of the cornet and the

Hebden Bridge   9

steady throb of the bass. The quality of music and playing has improved almost beyond recognition in my lifetime, but the spirit has always remained the same. To be a member of the local band is as much an honour now as it has ever been.

But let's concentrate on Hebden Bridge for a while. Standing securely between Halifax and the Brontës' village of Haworth, its rows of back-to-back houses climbing up the steep Pennines, and its tall chimneys of the mills rising from the banks of the River Calder, leave the visitor in no doubt about his surroundings. This, even if bureaucrats mess around with borders and re-draw the map with strange-sounding, uneasy names, is the West Riding. Brass is not just a dialect word for money. Brass is music. It's a challenge. A way of life. Father – he shall be known as Fred from now on – was the bandmaster at Hebden Bridge, and one of the youngest of that breed, when I was born. His interest in music had, like many others, been fostered in youth by singing in the Birchcliffe Baptist Church choir. Although he had no illusions about being an Ernest Lough, he must have been very good, as he was singing the solos in 'The Messiah' before the age of eleven. When he was fourteen, probably when his voice broke, he started to play the cornet, and such was his success at this instrument that he was promoted to soprano cornet in the Hebden Band by the time he was sixteen. Banding, though, was and still is only a hobby rather than a means of livelihood for the average player, so Fred went into the local cloth trade, making fustian at a factory owned by a man with the typical Yorkshire name of Arthur Crabtree. This strange sounding cloth has made many appearances in the history of fashion, but its main function was always as an extremely hard-wearing fabric for heavy labourers. Thomas Hardy describes it well in *Under the Greenwood Tree*, where his agricultural workers would have a winter coat of fustian which, for added protection, they would oil. It kept out storm and tempest, and even had the dubious advantage, when not on the back of its owner, of being so stiff as to stand up by itself in the kitchen corner. Its main use in the North was by the great army of road and rail builders, mainly Irish. In this age of leisure, where it is the mark of great affluence to dress as casually and, sometimes, as scruffily as possible, it has once or twice challenged denim as the uniform of those who wouldn't dream of wearing a uniform!

Fred was undoubtedly a talented cornet player and ever keen to learn from others – a willingness which he followed all through his life – and it was for this reason that he would set off at least once a week, walking over the hills and moors to Queensbury where resided one of the most consistently 'top' bands this country has ever produced – the mighty Black Dyke Mills Band. Here he would be able to watch a master at work – John Gladney, then towards the end of a long and distinguished career. Gladney was born in 1839, the son of a military band conductor. His musical life encompassed more than just bands, though. He was a member of the infant Hallé Orchestra but, like so many of us, couldn't confine himself entirely to the concert platform, and returned to the earthier world of bands and contests. He could command four or five of the best bands in the

The great Black Dyke Mills Band early this century, with John Gladney, wearing a top hat, standing at the back.

country, Black Dyke among them, who would employ him on a professional conductor basis. His great mission in the scoring and conducting of brass was that the band should not be merely an accompaniment to a soloist, but a fully used 'orchestral' unit. Not for him the background 'chuck-chucks' of the basses, euphoniums and the tenors, whilst a proud cornet took all the glory. He wanted to hear the full sound of twenty-five instruments all adding their individuality to the depth of sound which, to we devotees of brass, can only be made by a band. It is this sonority which is the distinguishing feature of our art. Every time a second row player finds himself confronted by an interesting and challenging score, he should offer up a silent thanksgiving to John Gladney.

When Fred's moorland wanderings took him in another direction it was often to his father's old band – Wyke Temperance Band – where the professional conductor was another great figure, and a rival to Gladney, Edwin Swift. Swift was born four years later than Gladney and had an equally distinguished career. The lasting record he left to the twentieth century was in his arrangements of Beethoven, Berlioz, Wagner, Meyerbeer and Rossini, which were to be standard band classics for many years.

A third member of this fellowship of deadly but friendly rivals was Alex Owen, whose memorable path I myself was to cross in my youth.

11

Rival giants: John Gladney (left) and Edwin Swift.

By the time Fred was twenty-one he was appointed bandmaster at Hebden, a position he held with much pride, and great honour. The bandmaster is the man who trains the band in readiness for the professional conductor to come along and add his own coat of polish to the performance when it comes to the important contests. It was not unknown, in those days, for the bandmaster to be solo cornet as well, and this was the case with Fred. It left him, a perfectly dextral man, with a permanent preference for left-handed conducting. The cause of this was that he stood in the middle of the band, playing and conducting at the same time. As he needed his natural right hand for the cornet valves it meant that the conducting had to be done by his left. Many years of this practice rendered him uncomfortable if he tried to change. Even when the cornet was packed away for good it was too late to change. His tobacco hand, though, was never affected, and he continued to fill a charred pipe bowl to capacity right-handed all his life.

Another point worth noting about those early years is that the band would stand to play in a square with the conductor in the middle, unlike the picture we are used to today where the band sits in a semi-circle. It was to be many years before this square formation was abandoned, and then it was an Australian band who were to lead the way.

Single minded in his love of brass bands Fred may have been, but like the best of us, he gleefully embraced the idea of romance when the right opportunity presented itself.

The Liberal MP Simpson Hinchcliffe sits in the centre of Hebden Bridge Band, of which he was President. My father stands immediately behind, wearing the distinguishing bandmaster's cap.

Employed as a 'mender' in the woollen mill which employed Fred was a small, dark, curly-haired and immensely attractive girl called Sarah Midgeley. Her quiet life as the daughter of the local sexton must have contrasted sharply with the busy life at the appropriately named 'Nursery Nook', the house of Grandfather Mortimer and his ten children, but, undeterred, her bright blue eyes alighted on Fred and decided that he would do very nicely. They were married at the age of twenty-one and settled down to live on thirty shillings a week. If that sounds a meagre budget on which to start a lifetime of bliss I imagine that my arrival, a year or so later, did nothing to increase the family fortunes.

My earliest memories of childhood and, for that matter, music, are the sounds of Father's cornet. Brass players are notoriously unpopular as neighbours. The band may well be the town's pride and joy at Christmas and fêtes or in the park – but *not* next door. This inexplicable attitude still persists amongst unappreciative neighbours to this day. I can't think why. To avoid any unpleasant encounters Fred would take himself off to the moors in the summer when folks wanted to leave their windows open, and practise his cornet whilst perched on a stony outcrop on the side of a hill. As soon as I was able to make the short journey without recourse to being carried or pushed it was my delight to accompany him. Later, Alex, my younger brother, would tag along as well. Apart from the buzzards and the hovering kestrels we were his sole audience. I don't suppose we sat still and behaved ourselves all the time, but in an age when children were required to be

13

seen and not heard I daresay we gave him little trouble. Besides, we occasionally caught a glimpse of an illicit cock-fight – something we would never mention to Mother as it was this very activity which caused us, in the normal course of events, to be forbidden access to the wild moors.

Behind the farm cottage where we lived was Cockhill Moor, and adjoining this moor was an area of several acres which my Uncle Matthew had rented to graze his horses when they had earned a rest from pulling the cartloads of building materials used in the family business. The moorland air had a distinctive clarity and aroma on hot summer days and, if we were lucky, we would catch a glimpse of the other local pastime of 'billeting', played with a ball and a long, pointed stick rather like a billiard cue. The details of this game seem to be lost to memory, as by the time I was old enough to enjoy such perilous pleasures I lived miles away from the moors and, besides, I have a feeling it was outlawed.

Those days at Hurst Farm were possibly my only period of true childhood as an ordinary small boy, playing in the fields and eventually going to Stubbings School down the hill. I also attended Sunday School, but never managed to sing in the choir, not being blessed with Fred's talent for singing.

The winters were bleak and the north-east wind would howl down through the moors. The summers stand out in my memory, as I suspect is the case with everybody, with the annual Sunday School treats, where each child was presented with a small oval 'school-bun' for tea, and the smell of the sharp home-brewed beer which we took out into the fields at harvest time for the refreshment of the Irish labourers, who took a week or so off from their normal tasks in order to help with the harvests and the hay-making. Mother must have worked as hard as any of them. Day and night, it seemed, she was baking enormous quantities of pasties and 'oven-bottom' cakes for the extra workers, as well as her normal day-to-day chores of poultry and family, which by this time had grown still further. As well as Alex and me, there was now a baby sister Nellie. What splendid names children were given in those days. Before everybody wanted to be different and bless their children with such modern names as Daren and Wayne or Karen, we had some wonderfully unpretentious names. In the family Bible which recently came back into my keeping the names of Fred's brothers and sisters are all listed with their dates of birth. Just before the Gospel of St Matthew, chapter 1, verse 1, we can read of John Herbert, Matthew, Evelyn, Arthur, Fred (not Frederick), Luther, Annie Evelyn, Florence Edith, Mary Eliza and Nelly (with a 'y').

Next to haymaking in terms of hard work was Christmas. To swell the family income Mother would supply, pluck, dress and prepare poultry for a large number of Hebden Bridge families. In her kitchen on these occasions she was the unchallenged monarch, and we were wiser to do as we were told without argument or delay. Until the Christmas before she died at the age of ninety, this was her domain, and her annual pleasure.

Grandmother Mortimer is not even a memory. She died, after bearing ten

14

children, in her fifties the year after I was born, but grandmother Midgeley, my mother's mother, was a different matter. When things got too hectic in our small cottage, Alex and I were often sent across to see grandmother Midgeley, who would sometimes manage to find in her purse three half-pence each for us to go and buy a small meat pie at a shop a few doors down from her in Woodbine Place. Sometimes we would go a little further along the road and visit great-grandmother Rogers, my mother's grandmother, a little Welsh lady to whom my mother bore a remarkable resemblance later in life. From there we would invariably return with a bag of currants, or a quarter pound bag of tea, for Mother's almost empty store cupboard.

Family holidays or excursions were unknown. A ride on the tram which rumbled through the valley provided a thrill, or a visit to Hardcastle Crags, real Brontë country, where we were allowed to paddle in the shallower reaches of the river. Sometimes Alex and I would simply sit and watch the trains rumbling across the viaduct which spanned the valley at Whiteley Arches, between Todmorden and Hebden Bridge – the plumes of smoke disappearing over the horizon on their way to the faraway legendary cities of Manchester or Liverpool, another world away. Life was simple – but good, and certainly happy. And, despite the absence of such wonders as radio or television, filled with music. Indeed not a day went by without music from one source or another.

When I was about five Fred decided that it was time to start my music lessons, and taught me a few simple tunes such as 'In my Cottage near a Wood' on his cornet. I don't think I was ever asked if I wanted to learn – it was as much a matter of course as cleaning my teeth or polishing my boots. There was no music room in the house and Fred had always practised with his back to the kitchen range, where the fire which coped with our cooking and hot water seemed to be perpetually alight: a delight in winter, but uncomfortably warm in summer. My early efforts at playing will always be associated with a warm seat to my trousers and the appetising smell of a rabbit stew.

We eventually moved to a slightly larger house in Foster Lane, down in Hebden Bridge itself, which was probably just as well, because my second sister, Marion, was soon to arrive, and the old cottage was beginning to bulge at the seams. Fred had an increasing number of pupils who came regularly to the house in the evenings, and, as often as not, the last sounds I would hear before dropping off to sleep would be those of the cornet or euphonium. This constant bombardment appears to have encouraged me rather than put me off, because I was always willing, even eager, to accompany Fred to the band room at Hangingroyd on practice nights. I vividly recall the solo cornet player, William Ellison, a dapper young man in a smart suit and a wing collar with bow tie, and the magnificent cornet which he owned. It had a beautifully engraved bell and mother-of-pearl tops to the valves – I don't think it ever occurred to me that, one day, I might own anything so grand.

William Rimmer, pictured here wearing the uniform of the Southport Military band which he conducted after retiring from the contest field in 1909. He handed over the conducting of such bands as Irwell Springs, Wingates Temperance, Black Dyke, Hebden Bridge and Fodens to his friend William Halliwell, shown right.

Back at home, I was still continuing my lessons with Fred, where we would play simple duets. My favourite was a little piece called 'Martha' in which I took the legato melody while Fred accompanied it with a cheerful little counter melody. It's just possible that this 'Martha' set the pattern of my playing career. I was at my happiest with a melody which flowed and allowed for individual expression. Fred, never one to lavish praise, must have felt that our lessons were bearing fruit as, at the age of seven, I was allowed a cornet from the band store to take home and treat as if it were my own. The entry, as far as I know, is still to be seen in the Hebden Bridge Committee Book: 'Master H. Mortimer is to be provided with a cornet on which to learn.' This was indeed an honour. There was no Junior Band at Hebden, and even if I had shown the precocity of an infant Mozart there was no earthly way that I could have taken a place in the band for many a year. Apart from any other consideration it would have meant paying out for a special pint-sized uniform at the astronomical sum of at least 17/6d (87½p).

About this time Black Dyke changed their professional conductor. John Gladney was coming to the end of his long career, and his place was taken by a new man who was to achieve even greater fame: William Rimmer. This was a name that was to shape the destiny of we Mortimers for Hebden Bridge, not to be outdone amidst so many wonderful bands in that corner of the world, quickly seized the opportunity to follow suit, and thus I first came into contact with one of my lifetime's heroes. We had already seen the great Rimmer at work over the moors at Black Dyke, and I had, by this time, taken to tagging along behind Fred on his walks across Midgeley Moor. The band room at Queensbury was full of fascinating

16

pictures and trophies. Black Dyke had been founded as long ago as 1815, which made them nearly a hundred years old by the time I was old enough to take an interest. What was more, they had recently returned from a tour of Canada – something indeed to be marvelled at. To me, Manchester seemed to be as far as anybody could ever wish to travel. Canada was simply another world. To sit and look at these ordinary-looking men and think that they had been as far as that ...

When William Rimmer accepted Hebden Bridge's invitation to become their professional conductor they were all overawed, and spoke of it in almost hushed tones of reverence. Fred, of all people, could never be accused of being a sycophant, but William Rimmer's word was, to him, sacrosanct and to be treated with the utmost respect. One unfortunate trombonist found this out the hard way. On leaving a practice one night, Rimmer said to Fred, 'You know, Mr Mortimer, the trombonist can't play that section. He should be made to practise it at least five hundred times before my next rehearsal.' Out came a slate and a piece of chalk. Fred took this instruction literally! The poor chap played through the offending section and was chalked off. He played it again – another chalk mark, and so on. Five hundred times. No more, no less!

I wonder if Fred could ever, in all but wild daydreams, have imagined that in future years two of his sons, Alex and myself, would both follow in Mr Rimmer's footsteps and enter the Black Dyke band room as conductors?

And what of Mother's part in all this music-dominated household? Quite simply, she was the one who made it possible. 'Our Sarah', as she became known to a generation of bandsmen from all over the country, encouraged us, consoled us, cajoled us and sometimes even scolded us. She possessed infinite patience, which no doubt owed something to her agricultural background, and an unsung wisdom. Her opinion on matters musical was seldom, if ever, sought, but was sometimes offered nevertheless. Her opinion on the running of the household was, on the other hand, undisputed. On the odd occasion when she would venture a comment

'Our Sarah'. The wife of a great bandsman had to combine many roles, which my mother did with ease.

17

on some point of musical interpretation it was usually opposed by Fred, or else apparently ignored. Strange to relate, her comments often found their way in at the next rehearsal but, of course, they were by now Fred's opinions. Her real value, though, lay in her extraordinary kindness and sympathy. No bandsman ever made it to the top without a great deal of patience and understanding from his wife, and Fred in marrying 'Our Sarah' struck a rich vein. In the next decade or so the Mortimer family were to up and move more than once and, as far as I can remember, however trying the circumstances, she was always prepared to throw the full weight of her backing into the venture.

Her kindness wasn't confined to us, either. The first time I came into contact with the Salvation Army was as a boy at Hebden Bridge. This organisation, with which I have been happily associated ever since, was then still in comparative infancy. Consett, in County Durham, was the first established Corps Band, and Salvation Army Headquarters were busy trying to establish strongholds in every town and village where they felt there was a need for them. The bands were of secondary importance, as the main preoccupation was to establish their special brand of practical Christianity. To Hebden Bridge, indeed to Foster Lane, came two young lady officers straight from training college. Armed with only their faith and a tambourine each they set about their mission. If we thought we were poor in our busy house, we had only to look at the plight of those two young officers to keep our lack of worldly goods in proportion. The frugality forced upon them would be unacceptable these days. I believe it was this early introduction to such dedication which endeared the Salvation Army to me for the rest of my life. I am happy to say that 'Our Sarah' always managed to have some soup left over which went their way – just 'to save wasting it'!

William Halliwell succeeded Mr Rimmer and was already the rising star conductor, with many other bands under his leadership. One was the oddly named Southern Band, Luton Red Cross, which had for some time been the Champion Band of the South, and despite the fact that it was north of Watford it *was* a Southern band, a fact which surprises, even today, many a Londoner. Halliwell was quick to spot Fred's talent as a band trainer and, when a vacancy occurred at Luton, recommended Fred for the job. I suppose there must have been many hours of soul-searching and questioning at home, but I was not aware of it at the time, and the outcome was that in 1910 we moved south. There were now four children to cope with and another very much on the way. As Mother was in no fit state to keep two boys and two even younger girls in control on what was, in those days, a long journey, Fred's sister, my Aunt Florrie, was pressed into service to keep us all in order. Her special charges were Nellie and Marion, whilst I as the eldest was given the job of helping Mother. Presumably Alex, although not big enough to be given a special job, was considered old enough to look after himself. Father looked after the goods and chattels, such as they were. Dressed in his best bowler hat, he supervised the whole exodus – first by local train to Manchester, and

In 1913 Fodens sported striking hussar-like uniforms, with cockades. Mr Halliwell, in the centre, sticks to his top hat. Behind the bandmaster, Tom Hynes, is Edwin Firth, the famous cornet player of that era.

then on to a great steaming monster to Luton, passing on the way such sights as the Peak District and all sorts of wonderful countryside, all of which was wasted on us. We were far too excited by the journey and the train to look at scenery.

Poor Mother spent most of the day leaning, pale and perspiring, out of the window, whilst I did my best to make consoling noises and to raise her flagging spirits. Part of the romance of steam that tends to be largely forgotten is that if you felt the worse for wear on those bumpy tracks, you had the choice of staying still and feeling really ill, or leaning out of the window and receiving half a ton of coal smuts full in the face. Furthermore, the soot had an amazing knack of hitting you unerringly right in the eye when you were feeling at your lowest ebb.

I left Hebden Bridge with mixed feelings: on the good side was the adventure into the unknown south, but on the debit side I couldn't help reflecting on all the treasures left behind – my cornet, Miss Geddes the local teacher who, though formidable, was kindly (and a member of the Esperanto Society, no less), and Phyllis Westerman, whose father kept a photographic shop and whom I loved dearly, if distantly. On my way home from school every day I would peer into the shop window, past the pictures of befrilled babies, wedding groups and local dignitaries, in the hope of catching a fleeting glimpse of the beautiful Phyllis who, I am sure, had no idea of the existence of her faithful admirer. So far as I know, I never saw her again and, at the time, it was a bitter gap in my life. What could this place Luton possibly have to compensate me for the loss of all this?

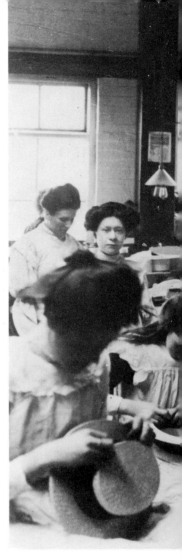

The girls in the Luton hat factory, 1911. They made straw hats for everyone, from Eton scholars to tramdrivers and bandsmen.

2 Luton

The move was accomplished. We settled into a pleasant little house in Talbot Road, and Rex was born – the first Lutonian from the Hebden Bridge branch of the Mortimer family.

Fred exchanged fustian-making for hat-making – what else in Luton? Even the tram conductors wore straw caps in this, the capital of the hat industry. The Luton Band caps were also made of straw in those days, which complemented their unusual uniform of lounge-style blue jackets with white waistcoats. This, remember, was before the days of even the military-style mess jackets, when most bands wore high-collared, high-buttoned tunics.

I started at the Old Bedford Road Boys' School, an education which culminated in the passing of a Labour Examination, a passport to the adult world at the age of thirteen. My Headmaster at Old Bedford Road was Mr G. Wistow Walker (a never-to-be-forgotten name to me), who later made his mark as an early leader of

the Teachers' Association. We all, in fact, settled down quickly and I have to admit that even Phyllis soon took her place as nothing more than a memory.

As part of the inducement to come south, Fred was to be paid a fee of two pounds a week as bandmaster; this on top of his earnings at the hat factory. In theory we were financially better off than we had ever been. Unfortunately the band committee had overspent in getting us all there and the first week's two pounds was slow in arriving. A few committee pockets were dug deeply into and the money was found. Just as well, really, for we had rather burnt our boats and there was no going back.

Fred found a band in good heart and needing no drastic reorganization, and, despite the temporary shortage, financially fairly secure. Luton had a certain advantage over other similar bands in the shape of a patron (or should it be patroness?). The local stately home was Luton Hoo and its owner was Lady Zia

On Saturday nights we played on the corner of George Street, seen here from the Corn Exchange in 1910.

Wernher, who took a great interest in the welfare of the band and sponsored it to the tune of £100 a year. A considerable sum in those days, and one which almost covered Fred's fee – obviously a great help, but it meant that money had to be raised throughout the year by any other means available. 'A Mile of Pennies' was, in 1910, what the ubiquitous 'coffee-morning' is today – a reasonably safe means of opening up the purses of the public. Once a year the 'mile' would be started, usually by a local dignitary, and passers-by would be invited to add their coppers to the chain. By the time the coins had stretched a measured mile, there was a pleasant amount of money to go to the bank. How the bank cashiers must have groaned when they saw the heavily laden money-bags approaching!

More regular finance was provided by the shilling a week subscriptions demanded of every bandsman, and by the Saturday night open-air concerts at selected pitches, summer and winter alike. Wellington Street, Bute Street, George Street and the Market will for ever mean a circle of bandsmen for me: warm summer evenings, misty autumnal nights, sometimes with the rain lashing down, and freezing winter when the breath would turn to ice and hang over the instruments in a cold, vaporous cloud. The dark evenings were illuminated by our travelling lighting-system – four acetylene lamps mounted on poles, which gave a brilliant light and an obnoxious smell. If you don't know what an acetylene lamp was, let me attempt a scientific explanation. A container held carbide (obtainable from the local hardware shop), and water from an egg-sized chamber at the top dripped on to the carbide which then gave off a gas. The burner was ignited and, with the aid of a reflector, the light was more than ample to read the small print of the music. Out we went with our lamps and our army of knobbers every Saturday.

For those who didn't aspire to any musical talent, the occupation of knobber was a keenly fought for honour. You didn't just become a knobber, you had to go on a waiting list, and even then you stood a better chance if you could take over your position from a retiring relative. Whole families of knobbers would appear every Saturday night. Their job was to extract money from the ever moving audience, and they had an uncanny knack of not covering the same ground twice. Any passer-by who stopped for more than five minutes was sure to be invited to donate to the band funds. It was all very good humoured and very few customers failed to put something in the pot. Luton Salvation Army Corps, unlike their colleagues in Hebden Bridge, had a thriving band, and they used the same pitches the following morning. Their knobbing was for a much higher purpose, though, and they had no need of our 'professionals'.

The business of money-raising has given rise to many good stories, but my favourite is the old chestnut:

A bandsman was calling from door-to-door with his collecting tin, and not doing particularly well. Walking all the way up a long garden path he reached a front door and knocked. After much shuffling and grumbling from within the front door was opened an inch and an old lady peered through the aperture. 'Yes? What do you want?'

'We're collecting for the Horwich Railway Mechanics Institute Public Subscription Silver Prize Band,' announced the caller.

'What's that you say?' asked the old lady, cupping her ear.

'We're collecting for the Horwich Railway Mechanics Institute Public Subscription Silver Prize Band,' repeated the man, fortissimo.

'You what?' shrieked the old dear.

'We're collect... Oh, never mind,' and set off down the path again.

'Mind you shut the gate,' she bawled.

'Oh, bugger the gate,' mumbled the bandsman.

'Aye, and bugger the Horwich Railway Mechanics Institute Public Subscription Silver Prize Band an' all,' cackled the triumphant old lady.

I have to admit that I cannot personally vouch for the truth of that story, but it would seem to be fairly likely.

Fred had great ambitions for his new band. Of paramount importance was to get it 'match-fit' and to this end he set about seeking new contests to test them. The journey from Hebden Bridge must have whetted his appetite for travel, because in 1913 he came up with an ambitious scheme to take the band to Paris for the French Championships. Although the French representative had advised him that he should enter the second section contest, Fred rejected the idea and pressed on with his intention of going in at the deep end in the Grand Premier class. A salutary experience! When they arrived (I was too young to go) they were handed the band parts for the sight-reading test and were mortified to see that the arrangement was scored for a band of eighty-six. What was Fred to do with his standard British band of twenty-five members? Well, not a great deal, as it turned out. Despite Fred's desperate midnight oil attempt to re-score the parts, there was obviously little chance of matching the French bands of flugel horns, seventeen trombones, countless cornets and other instruments which he had never even seen before. They got through but, not unnaturally, came nowhere. The test-piece was 'Overture Characteristique' by Bailé, the musical director of the famous La Garde Republicaine, and was not forgotten by Fred. Despite coming so disastrously unstuck with it himself, he realized that it was a piece of music worth remembering, and so it was, for many years later in 1953 the organizers of the National Contest were at a loss for a test-piece and Fred was consulted from his sick-bed. He remembered the piece and suggested it to Frank Wright, the arranger. Frank immediately set to work and it reappeared a short while later as 'Diadem of Gold'. This time it was scored for a British-sized band, and the circle was completed very neatly when Foden's won the contest – and I conducted it! Fred's revenge, perhaps?

Back in 1910 the future was something which occupied Fred's thoughts considerably. It is probably no more than a guess, but I think that one of the reasons which contributed to his acceptance of the Luton job was that he saw a chance to create a subsequent platform for his young family. Moving to a new band he would more easily be able to promote a junior band than would have been the case at Hebden Bridge. A strong junior band is the best insurance policy for maintaining the standards of playing. There is a ready source of new talent waiting to take the place of any senior player who gives of anything less than his best, or who should retire. These days, Hebden Bridge has a thriving and talented junior section, but this was certainly not the case in 1910. A short classified advertisement in the *Luton News* which called for any lad who was interested in learning to play a brass instrument ('Some knowledge of music preferred') brought an enormous response. The band room was packed on Saturday morning with butcher boys, baker boys, apprentice hatters and schoolboys, all craving to be given a chance, and all (well, nearly all) wanting to play the cornet.

'What's your name, son?'

'Smith, sir.'

'What do you think you'd like to play?'

'A cornet, please, sir.'

'Well, I don't know ... you seem to have long arms. Go over to that corner and see how you get on with a trombone.'

And so on. It was more a case of matching the stature to the instrument than anything else. Big boys to the basses and euphoniums, medium sized boys to the horns and trombones, and the lucky ones to the cornet. On being given their instruments, the lads were all instructed to go home and, for a week, practise just the open notes (those playable without use of valves or slides). This was obviously not exciting enough for one of the lads who had been given a trombone. He came

Hebden Bridge: the background remains the same, but the Junior Band, non-existent in my day, is proof of the growth of youth bands everywhere.

back the following week and demonstrated his new skill by sliding up and down, playing a sort of 'elephant-call glissando'. Fred soon dealt with this, and he was sent home for a further week with the slide tied up with string, firmly sealed with sealing-wax. That soon cured him! Thus was a junior band formed. As I was getting my playing practice with the senior band as well, I was handed the baton. Alex, although he later became one of the best euphonium players in the country, was unable to fill this position with the band and had to settle, initially at least, for the percussion. He had started to play the euphonium at an early age, but a bout of rheumatic fever left him with a weak heart so he had to temporarily abandon his first love. It goes almost without saying that a musician of Alex's undoubted talent was equally excellent on this enforced second-choice instrument. Brother Rex's euphonium was to join us later.

With plenty of timely guidance from Fred we were left to get on with it. From such humble beginnings came some of the best servants that Luton Band ever had, maturing into senior players who formed the nucleus of the band which went to Crystal Palace in 1923 and won the most coveted trophy of them all – the thousand guinea trophy of the National Championships. *Still* the only Southern band to do so.

Fred's £2 a week bandmaster's salary and his earnings from the hat factory, when combined, were not the earnings which would keep a large family in the lap of luxury, but we managed. Mother's housekeeping must have been immaculate – almost a lost art. It was largely due to her prudence that, one Saturday morning, Father and I boarded the London train with a firm object in view: we were to go to the Besson's showroom and factory at Euston and, I hardly dared believe it, I was to have a brand new cornet.

Besson's at Euston was a mecca for all bandsmen arriving from the North. One of the best instrument makers, they occupied a building directly opposite the station. You couldn't miss it. Hanging from the front of the building was an enormous (about five times life-sized) E flat bass. It was a landmark for miles around, but from the exit to Euston it looked like one of the seven wonders of the modern world. Especially to a ten-year-old boy. In we went, and were faced with rows of gleaming brass in all shapes and sizes. A dazzling Aladdin's cave. After preliminary discussions with the salesman a cornet was brought forth. And what a cornet! It was silver plated with gold embellishments; mother-of-pearl tops to the valves, and all presented in a crocodile skin case lined with rich blue velvet – if anything, it even surpassed the instrument I had so admired as a small boy at Hebden Bridge.

I still have this fine piece of work, and it is still a good instrument. In the following forty or fifty years it went with me to Africa, Canada, Australia, New Zealand, Scandinavia, Europe ... even West Hartlepools. The case is still perfect as well. It now resides at home in a cupboard from whence it is occasionally dragged when I want to remind myself of the meaning of the word craftsmanship. The price when I was ten? Incredibly only ten pounds! In the interests of economy and production such an instrument could not be bought today. If it could, it would cost £500.

Now equipped with the tools of my trade, I started 'pot-hunting' in earnest. I was entered for a solo contest at Dunstable, not far from Luton, but the fare to get Fred and me there was five shillings, which was really more than we could afford. I mounted the platform with all the other hopefuls and, when it came to my turn, went through my piece – probably 'Softly Awakes my Heart' from Samson and Delilah, as that was my party piece at the time – and to my great joy and Fred's relief I won. The first prize was *five shillings*, so, if I was never really able to repay him for all he did for me, this, at any rate, was one debt paid in full.

Our Junior Band was making great strides by now and the repertoire was becoming increasingly wide and varied. The staple diet was undoubtedly selections from the 'hit' London shows. Our band room reverberated to such innocent pleasures as *The Arcadians* and *The Quaker Girl*, Lionel Monkton's two whimsical shows made famous by the Gaiety Girls of George Edwardes' famous theatre in the Strand. Gertie Millar was the toast of the last years of elegance before the Great War came along to turn all previous values upside down. Side by side with these 'modern' works were Mr Rimmer's arrangements of 'Gems of Sullivan'. Lovely word, gems. Nobody arranges gems these days, only selections or medleys. Gems belong to another age and whenever I see the word on an old arrangement it immediately conjures up those blissful days when the summers always seemed to be warm and the winter hearth was inevitably cosy.

It was in those warm summer days that the Junior Band really came into its own. Sunday School treats were the thing. Such was the demand for our musical presence on these treats that, in desperation, we split the band into three units of eight players on days when demand exceeded supply. This small but valiant band of miniature players would arrive at the venue on a wagonette on which were placed two benches. Four players would sit on either side facing inwards until we reached the town or village square. There we would alight and, with a final polish on our cuffs or trouser legs, form up into marching order. Three in the front, two in middle and three at the rear. Off we would go to the lilt of some martial tunes and arrive at the appointed meadow or park in time for the treat, where we would put away our marching tunes and exchange them for the new, modern, selections. If the playing wasn't always brilliant nobody ever seemed to notice and it was invaluable practice. After all, if you could get away with such ambitious music with a band of eight, how much easier it would be with the full complement of twenty-four or five.

For some obscure reason or other, these treats almost invariably fell on a Wednesday afternoon, and amongst the popular venues were two local spots. Sorry to keep harping back to the phrase 'innocent pleasures', but the only requirement for a treat in those days was an open space where any childhood exuberance could be given a relatively free rein. It was not considered necessary to have any elaborate entertainment laid on, and the buns which were handed out like gifts from the wise men were treasured and devoured with more relish than any modern equivalent. Of these popular venues there is no doubt that top of the list was Wheathampstead and Ayot, the home of George Bernard Shaw, and it was on one of these occasions that I first met the great man, G.B.S. I don't think that I can fairly claim that our Junior Band influenced him at all, but he was always interested in brass and for years I treasured a postcard from him in which he requested an explanation of a baritone. Not, perhaps, one of his great letters, but an interesting keepsake nevertheless. He was to remain an interested, and not uncritical, observer of bands for the rest of his life. One of his greatest plays, *Major Barbara*, owes a debt to this interest. Whilst keeping his tongue firmly in cheek, it is an affectionate look at a

Sir Edward Elgar dedicated his Severn Suite to Bernard Shaw. In the picture above he is shown at Bernard Shaw's garden party in 1932, standing next to Mrs John Drinkwater. On the right is the young J. B. Priestley.

Salvation Army band, with more warmth and truthfulness than many subsequent attempts on the subject. Twenty years later he was to write to Sir Edward Elgar, whose *Severn Suite*, dedicated to G.B.S, had just burst on to the bandstands. His suggestions, though not to be taken too seriously, had the stamp of what can only be described as the cynical enthusiast. Shaw offered his opinion that the usual Italian score markings should be altered for bandsmen and replaced with something in their own language. 'Remember the Minuet is a dance and not a bloody hymn', or 'Steady up for artillery attack', or 'Now like Hell', are just three of the more vivid instructions which should appear on the score, according to Shaw. He could be right.

Along with the 'sunday school treat' there is another, equally outmoded and equally memorable phrase – the P.S.A. or Pleasant Sunday Afternoon orchestra. Fred thought that a spell in this company would benefit my general musicianship and, as usual, he was right. On my £10 cornet I was required to play all the brass parts which were not otherwise covered. I found myself playing French horn cues, trumpet cues and even the odd trombone part. These soirées took place, as the name suggests, on Sunday afternoons, usually in chapels and churches. The experience was invaluable for two reasons. Firstly, it concentrated my mind on the matter in hand, namely music, and secondly it introduced me to a young man of my own age with whom I shared a friendship which lasted until his death in 1976. His name was Arthur E. Davies (always with the 'E'). Despite the fact that we lived

28

in the same road, it was not until the P.S.A. brought us together that he and I realized that a fruitful partnership could be formed between us. At that time he was an accomplished pianist and boy soprano. Our first engagement together was at the Luton Salvation Army Citadel number one, and from that day we performed as a duo right up until 1925 when our family left Luton.

To radio buffs of the forties and fifties he will be remembered as the leader and founder of the Luton Girls Choir, a broadcasting phenomenon of those years, but to me he will be simply the best accompanist it was ever my privilege to know. He was instinctively always right. We both knew what we wanted from a piece of music and, after the necessary preliminary discussion, both worked towards the same goal. This may not seem a startling recommendation, but it is a rare gift and one confined to a rare breed of musician. It was not surprising, then, that he took this talent further and founded the Luton Girls Choir. He gave birth to the choir and it all but died with him. During the years of its existence it raised over

'Scarlet and Blue' was the series which I produced with members of the Luton Girls' Choir and the band of the Irish Guards, photographed here in Eamonn Andrews' programme 'This is Your Life' for Arthur E. Davies, seated centre with his wife. I am standing behind, next to conductor 'Jiggs' Jaeger, but Arthur is looking at the pianists Rawicz and Landauer who so often appeared in our programmes.

£100,000 for charities. Not a startling figure now, but a vast sum in an austere wartime Britain between 1930 and 1950. His personal dedication to his girls was reflected by every member of the choir. The original girls would, later, provide daughters to fill their places, the mothers branching off into the Festival Choir. It was one vast family which did more to put Luton on the map than could ever be achieved by 'Lu'on Airport' package holidays, or even the M1. Arthur's lifetime habit was to conduct the choir from his piano stool, a facility which owed something to our youthful endeavours. Long after our duet days were over, our paths continued to cross. When I was a producer at the BBC the choir was in great demand, and there Arthur would sit at his piano not only conducting, but adding his sotto voce baritone to the proceedings as well. A fact not always received with much enthusiasm by a frustrated sound engineer who could not work out where the extra voice was coming from.

Just before his death he was presented with the freedom of the town by the Corporation of Luton. I couldn't help remarking, when asked to speak at his funeral service, that they had left it a bit late! The M.B.E. he received from the Queen, though, was more timely. A statue now commemorates the life of Arthur E. Davies and all he did for music and Luton. It was my great privilege to unveil that bust which stands in the Public Library, Music Section.

And so life continued – the Junior Band, the P.S.A., contests, concerts, and, of course, school. The senior band, under Fred and the professional conductor, William Halliwell, progressed and attended contests up and down the country. It must be said that they were more successful in local surroundings than at the National but, still clinging to the title of Champion Southern Band, they continued to look beyond their own region and try their hand against the Black Dykes and the Irwell Springs of the band world. Then, in 1913, my never-to-be-forgotten moment arrived. I was to play in the senior band at the Crystal Palace in the National.

This year, 1913, was remarkable for two reasons: first, on a purely personal note, it was because the eleven year old Harry Mortimer was so much shorter than his colleagues (don't forget that this was still in the days of standing to play) that a ginger beer crate was provided. By using this extra twelve inches I was able not only to look less incongruous, but also to see the conductor. What an introduction to the National! Of far more lasting importance was that 1913 saw a new age of band music emerge. Instead of the usual brass adaptations of classics a piece was written specifically for bands to play – 'Labour and Love' by Percy Fletcher. In itself this is not important, but the far-reaching consequences of such a step were not even guessed at in that year. Band music was to go from strength to strength as a musical entity in its own right, instead of its cloth-cap image of a working man's orchestral shadow. It was an inspired move by the greatest showman ever to enter into the realms of banding – John Henry Iles – who inaugurated the National in 1900, and who was to guide it and nurse it right up to the Second World War.

John Henry Iles, the great impresario – the man who brought brass bands to the notice of the world at Crystal Palace.

What was, and is, this thing called the National which, with its Northern counterpart, the British Open at Belle Vue, so dominates the lives of bandsmen?

The story of the National, which was born only two years before I was, is the story of John Henry Iles himself. You cannot talk about one and ignore the other. On a casual visit to Manchester in 1898 John Henry was invited to Belle Vue to see the British Open Brass Band Championship. Knowing nothing of bands and imagining that he was about to witness a competition between several German Bands who would, in all likelihood, be marching up and down, he reluctantly agreed to go along. Far from being bored, he found himself staggered by what he saw. In his own words:

> Inspired by what I had heard, I returned to London with a clear-cut vision at the back of my mind. I resolved to make the wonderful musical achievements of these Northern pitmen, and other comparatively poor men, known to the whole world, and from these humble beginnings to widen the scope of the Brass Band Movement until its benefits could be enjoyed by other working men musicians all over the country ... . Back again in London I got in touch with Mr Samuel Cope, one of the Grand Old Men of the Brass Band world. I bought the *British Bandsman* – a periodical then published monthly, but devoted mostly to military bands.

To this acquisition he soon added the publishing business of Richard Smith & Co., a company which specialized in the publication of brass band music. With these imposing tools he now had the means to influence the whole world of brass players and their organization, and he wasted no time in making his influence felt.

31

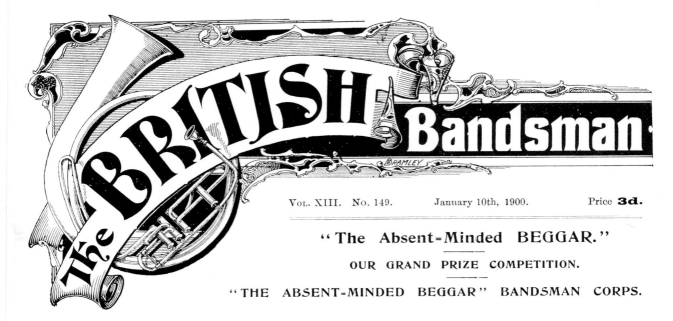

Vol. XIII. No. 149.   January 10th, 1900.   Price **3d.**

" The Absent=Minded BEGGAR."

OUR GRAND PRIZE COMPETITION.

"THE ABSENT=MINDED BEGGAR" BANDSMAN CORPS.

1900, the beginning of a new century and the beginning of the rise of John Henry Iles. By way of a little historical perspective, it is worth remembering that this was the year when Mafeking, Ladysmith and Kimberley were all relieved, and the British Empire was secure for ever. It was also the year in which Mr Rolls and Mr Royce joined forces, and Sherlock Holmes was every reader's hero. In January of that year John Henry presented his concert at the Albert Hall. Guest conductor was to be Sir Arthur Sullivan who, as a respected musical figure, would guarantee to fill the hall with his followers, no doubt curious to see what he was up to in such company. Dame Clara Butt, Madame Albari, ten brass bands, a full corps of Guards drummers and the band of the Royal Engineers from Chatham were all engaged for the night. John Henry was never one to do things on a small scale. The fact that the concert was advertised as being in aid of the widows of our 'Glorious Boys in Africa' was a further insurance against a financial disaster, should such a thing be needed. Of course it was a sell-out, and people were even recorded as standing outside the Albert Hall offering vastly inflated amounts for the privilege of a ticket. John Henry Iles, master showman, was on his way! The programme for that concert – known as the 'Absent-minded Beggar concert' after a popular current work by Sullivan - is worth remembering.

PART ONE

1	Hymn:	ONWARD CHRISTIAN SOLDIERS Cond. Sullivan Clara Butt accompanied by Bands, Drums, Organ	Sullivan
2	Selection	MOSES IN EGYPT St Albans City Band. Cond. A. R. Seddon	Rossini
3	Selection	BEAUTIES OF ENGLAND Arach Griffin – Wales. Cond. H. Bentley	E. Newton

4	Song	HEARTS OF OAK Mr Andrew Black		Boyce
5	Selection	WORKS OF MENDELSSOHN Hucknall Excelsiors. Cond. John Shadrey		Godfrey
6	Song	THERE'S A LAND Clara Butt		Allitson
7	Overture	WILLIAM TELL	Wyke Temperance. Cond. Swift (winners of over £7,000 in prizes)	Rossini (arr. Swift)
8	Irish Ballad	THE MINSTREL BOY Edward Lloyd		Moore
9	Selection	OBERON	Besses O' the Barn. Cond. Owen (winners of over £10,000 in prizes)	Webber (arr. Owen)
10	Aria	NON MI DIR (Don Giovanni) Madame Albari		Mozart
11	March	THE ABSENT-MINDED BEGGAR Massed Bands, Drums, Grand Organ. Cond. Sullivan arr. J. Ord Hume)		Sullivan

Interval

1	Fantasia	RULE BRITANNIA & GOD SAVE THE QUEEN Cond. Pearce	Pearce (arr. J. Ord Hume)
2	Welsh Airs	MEN OF HARLECH Sung by London Welsh Ladies Choir. Cond. Miss Frances Rees	
3	Selection	HEROIC West Hartlepools Band. Cond. Alex Owen	Webber (arr. Owen)
4	Song	THE GAY GORDONS Sung by Andrew Black. Liddle at the piano	Liddle
5	Selection	ELIJAH Black Dyke. Cond. John Gladney (winners of over £10,000 in prizes)	Mendelssohn
6	Song	THE LOST CHORD Clara Butt. Organ obligato Dr Pearce	Sullivan
7	Selection	WALES Nantle Vale Band. Cond. Owen	J. Ord Hume
8	Song	THE DEATH OF NELSON Edward Lloyd	
9	Selection	THE WORKS OF BALFE Clydebank Band. Cond. T. Sutton	W. Rimmer
10	Songs	(a) THE BLUEBELLS OF SCOTLAND (b) L'ETE Madame Albari	
11	Selection	GEMS OF VICTORIAN MELODY Kettering Rifles. Cond. Owen	
12	NATIONAL ANTHEM GOD SAVE THE QUEEN Soloists: Albari & Clara Butt with Massed Bands, Drums, and Grand Organ. Cond. Sullivan	Setting by M. Costa

I have never seen anything like it before or since – it took over 15,000 people to fill all the transepts in the Crystal Palace, and to have to play 'The Last Post' to that audience was the most terrifying experience in my whole life.

Inspired by the success of this first major venture into the brass band world, John Henry wasted no time in setting the wheels in motion for his ambitious scheme to stage a major contest in the South. The inspiration of Belle Vue was still driving him and he looked around for a suitable hall in the London area, and found the perfect setting at Crystal Palace in the Victorian suburb of Norwood in south-east London. The building had not always been there, of course, as it was originally conceived as the central showpiece of the Empire Exhibition of 1851, and was erected at Hyde Park. It was in later years that the idea occurred to the authorities to move it, lock, stock and barrel – an ambitious project as the building was vast and almost entirely made of glass. It was enormous – big enough, in fact, to house seven different section contests all under the same roof. Again it must be said that

John Henry never dealt in trivia. He had the plan and he had at his disposal the means to publicize it; he had the building – all he needed now was to attract the bands and induce them to make the long journey to London. What could be more appropriate than a thousand guinea trophy? This wonderfully impressive piece of work is still in existence today and, as a matter of fact, came out on display at Belle Vue Granada Championships as recently as 1980. It has lost none of its glamour nor its magic. If ever a trophy was worth fighting over, this must be it.

Continuing his successful link with Sir Arthur Sullivan, the test-piece for that first National in 1900 was announced as 'Gems of Sullivan, number one' and the music was plugged unmercifully in the columns of the *British Bandsman* for months. No piece had ever been so musical and no arrangement so masterly. What

J. Ord Hume was a great character; he once gave a very bad tenor horn player the medal for the best trombone!

is more, no concert was complete without it – or so the *British Bandsman* claimed. It even went so far as to suggest that any discerning, patriotic audience would not accept a concert without this or 'The Absent-minded Beggar'. History has proved it almost right; the Sullivan selections are still in use today, or are, at least, in every band's library. They were, indeed, works of enduring quality. The fact that they were the publishing property of John Henry no doubt had some bearing on his concern for their regular performance. The arrangements for these 'Gems of Sullivan' scores were all by our old friend J. Ord Hume, who added another equally long-lasting credit to his name about this time – 'B. B. & C. F. MARCH', a title which has intrigued many a young bandsman over the years. Most older bandsmen know its origins, but just in case any of you younger ones are puzzled let me put the matter right. Not long after John Henry bought the *British Bandsman* periodical, his acquisitive eye fell on another, more obscure, magazine called *The Contest Field*. The second of these was more of a brass bands publication, concerned, as its name suggests, with the many contests up and down the country. *British Bandsman* had previously been more of a military bandsman's magazine. The two together became known, for obvious reasons, as B. B. & C. F. and the march was commissioned by John Henry to celebrate the amalgamation. It is said that Ord Hume was a little tardy in its completion and John Henry had to literally stand over him while he finished it.

Even with all this cajolery and a glittering prize the first National only managed to attract twenty-nine bands for the Championships. The contest, though, was established. Not only the contest either. John Henry's great love and pride had found an outlet in the concert which was to follow the contest. Here was soon established an annual event which was as eagerly awaited as the contest itself. John Henry's great ambition and mission in life was, once a year, to mount the conductor's rostrum and lead the massed bands in 'Abide with Me' and one other suitable piece – probably the finale from the *William Tell* Overture. The extraordinary amount of emotion he was able to pour into his performance of 'Abide with Me' threatened, year after year, to bring the hymn to a grinding halt. Due to this surfeit of passion it grew slower and slower with each performance, and it became the irreverent habit of bandsmen to make bets as to when it would finally stop altogether in a welter of tears. Poor John Henry, he loved his moment. His 'Night of the Year' was completed by *William Tell*, when his pace would become just the opposite. With arms going like pistons, he never quite managed to keep up with the band, and in his exertions his waistcoat and trouser waistband would slowly part company. Topped by a very red face (and not from embarrassment either) he was, indeed, a formidable spectacle.

From a slow beginning of twenty-nine bands in 1900 (when the first winners were a band called Denton Original) the National grew to attract an incredible one hundred and forty entries in the years leading up to the Second World War – seven sections, each containing twenty bands. The passing of the Crystal Palace put paid to such an unwieldy number as there was no other hall capable of holding so many.

This, then, was the National. At the age of eleven, with the aid of a £10 cornet and a ginger beer crate I was to join the men and compete for the big prize. How

Only four medals on the tablecloth when this photograph was taken in 1915, but how proud I was, holding the £10 cornet. On the right: the whole family in Talbot Road. The babe in arms is my youngest sister Louie, and my father is holding my brother Rex.

37

The band of the 36th Division of the Royal Irish Rifles contains all seven members of the Luton band who joined up with my father – and they all came back. Fred, solo cornet, is on the extreme left. He wrote me the postcard from the Front, to enquire about the Junior Band.

romantic it would be to report that Luton won and I became a celebrity overnight. Unfortunately that was not the case; it was another of William Halliwell's bands which took the thousand guinea trophy. Not, mind you, that we disgraced ourselves, but, like Thursday's Child, we had far to go. Our day was yet to come – and mine was to come sooner than I thought.

The junior band was fast improving and Fred arranged that we should enter our first contest – at the Bedford Eisteddfod. The test piece was 'Dawn of Spring' by F. De Luc, whom I later discovered to be William Rimmer under one of his many assumed names. For a first contest we did reasonably well, coming a creditable third – mind you, there were only four competitors. Never mind, I had at last conducted a band in a real contest!

And then an obscure terrorist, who desired to free the Slavs from Austrian oppression, went for a stroll on 28 June 1914 and put a bullet through Archduke Francis Ferdinand. Sarajevo was the name on everybody's lips and the German Army was goose-stepping all over the continent of Europe.

Life did not immediately change but it was never to be the same again. I had been privileged to see both worlds.

Europe had enjoyed an uneasy peace for a hundred years and war was, to most people, something which happened in Africa and an excuse for any amount of flag-waving jingoistics. It was an affair for professional soldiers, adventurers and sentimental song-writers. But this was something different. A quick burst of activity followed by months of stalemate gave rise to a new industry – recruitment. From every music-hall stage the cry was repeated, 'Come on, lads, take the King's shilling and make us proud of you. Your country needs you,' or the grim 'We don't want to lose you, but we think you ought to go.' The pre-war wit of the halls and the charm of the Gaiety were replaced by crude cajolery or, worse, the implication of cowardice to any man not in uniform.

Caught up in this fervour, the military-aged members of the band – eight of them, including Fred – volunteered for France. Mind you, it was as a band that they offered their services and for which they were accepted. They were drafted into the 36th Division of the Royal Irish Rifles as such. Once in France, though, the realities of the war were soon impressed upon them and they found that music was not very high on the list of priorities. They were instead pressed into service as stretcher-bearers. It could be that the name of the band – Luton Red Cross – had something to do with this decision, but if so, the War Office must have been disappointed. The reasons for the Red Cross part of the title are lost in obscurity, but certainly it had nothing to do with first-aid. Nevertheless, it was as stretcher bearers that Fred and his band made their initial impact on the war effort.

As bandmaster, albeit to a silent band, Fred was offered a sort of 'Morton's Fork' arrangement, whereby he could be made either sergeant unpaid, but enjoy the privileges of his rank, or corporal paid. He may have lived in Luton for some time, but he was still a Yorkshireman and he opted for corporal *paid*. The rank of unpaid sergeant was quickly snapped up by an organist of loftier ambition who had been drafted into the same squad. As the war ground on and sank deeper and deeper into the mud of that winter so the stalemate in the game of human chess became more and more moribund. Morale needed lifting, so the band were given back their instruments and allowed to get on with the job which they had come to do in the first place. The snag was that Fred was no longer in charge. Corporal Mortimer had to take his orders from sergeant unpaid organist. Despite advice to the contrary the first parade was reduced to a shambles by this good man's insistence that the trombones should march in the rear – thus giving the horns of the front row an uncomfortable time. I have it on good authority that this same man, after his discharge, took to teaching and was given the care of the school band. It was not long before he wrote triumphantly to the instrument manufacturers with the joyous tidings that he had 'put a stop to all that nasty leaking business in the brass instruments'. He had soldered up all the water keys!

While Fred was away harassing the Kaiser he managed to achieve one private little triumph, his own personal family get-together. Two of my uncles on my mother's side, and aunt Eliza, Fred's sister, who had joined the Women's Service, somehow managed amongst all that chaos to meet up for a brief reunion. It was the last time the two uncles had any family contact, as they were soon to be yet another two digits in the lists of the fallen. Letters home were an infrequent pleasure. There was something for everyone. To Mother he kept up a good façade of cheerfulness which must, at times, have strained his resources of invention. To me he wrote detailed letters packed with advice on conducting, playing and the general running of the band which, due to the absence of so many of the senior members, was largely made up of my ex-juniors. The public demand for entertainment grew in relation to the depression of the war. Ivor Novello's new song 'Keep the Home Fires Burning' suited the mood of the country and became, with 'When you come Home' and 'Little Grey Home in the West', the most requested items. The need for diversion was never more acute and we seemed to be out performing at one function or another every available hour.

My life, too, had undergone a fundamental change. At the age of thirteen we sat what was known as a Labour Examination which, if passed, meant that we had completed our education and were fitted to take our place in the world as young men and women. Few managed actually to fail the examination – certainly not me – and out I went to work. Getting a job was easy with all those men away, and I was quickly snapped up by the Great Northern Railway Company. And what a bargain they had! To accommodate the band, the P.S.A., the solo contests and all the other extramural activities to which I was prone, I came to an amicable arrangement with the stationmaster, Mr T. H. Few, to take my annual seven days' holiday in fourteen half-days. Never a brilliant mathematician I seriously miscalculated, and when the half-days were totted up at the end of the year it was discovered that I had had eighteen, and so I was invited to choose between the band and the railways. The railways, needless to say, lost. Over the next sixty years, though, they have managed to recoup from me any losses they might have suffered, so my conscience is clear. I was sorry to leave them at the time, Luton was a fascinating railway town – a sort of Crewe in miniature, but spread around. From London to Luton was the property of the Great Northern Railway, and then north from Luton it became the London North-West Region, via Dunstable and up to Rugby. This complicated arrangement required all sorts of staff duplication which would be the envy of most unions these days. Just to confuse matters further, the line from Luton to Leighton Buzzard ran on privately owned land at a place called Stanbridge Ford. To pass this single line stretch the driver had to stop at a signal box and, on the end of an outstretched pole, hand a permit to the signalman. No wonder they say the romance has gone out of the railways.

My next employer was the Vauxhall Motor Company, whose main attraction was that it had its own orchestra. I was a clerk again, and the work was not too demanding, if a little tedious. My outside activites were quite absorbing enough, though, so I could dream my days away until the evening hooter sounded.

It was one evening in winter. I was teaching a pupil at the time, for which I charged the exorbitant sum of sixpence, or 2½p if you prefer. There was a knock on the door and a breathless messenger informed me that the local theatre was a brass player short for tonight and, with the manager's compliments, could I come – now. Stopping only to strap my precious cornet to the crossbar I dashed to the rescue like a hero of the silent movies I was about to get to know so well. The theatre orchestra consisted of ten players – two trumpets, one trombone, a cello, a bass, drums, three violins and a piano which was played by the conductor. On my cornet I was expected to play most of the brass cues: if it was meant to be a French horn the technique was to cover the bell with your hand; trumpet cues called for the use of an A shank, basically like adding an inch or two of tubing to change the pitch and character of the cornet, something which Fred had been doing for years in local *Messiahs*. Thank goodness for those hours spent with the Pleasant Sunday Afternoon Orchestra.

Thrown in at the deep end with this U.M.N. (Unpleasant Monday Night) orchestra was not the hair-raising experience it might otherwise have been. I was used to coping with the unexpected and I must have given them cause for hope as I became a regular member. Of all the acts we accompanied I think Marie Lloyd was my favourite. Apart from anything else, her band parts would always be immaculate, which is more than can be said for many of the 'turns'. Some of the lesser lights of music-hall had the unpleasant habit of handing out scraps of dog-eared paper with so many alterations, cuts, arrows and strange rune-like signs on them that the notes were hardly visible. The jugglers were the worst, because not only did you have to read the notes, but you had to watch the performance and your conductor at the same time, and the crash on the drum which accompanied every successfully caught ball or plate began to jangle on the nerves – just a little bit!

41

Apart from the excellence of her band-parts and her performance, Marie Lloyd also had the endearing habit of giving the band an extra five bob each at the end of the week which, when you think that I was only getting thirty-five shillings for the week, made a substantial difference.

The Elliott Savonas Saxophone Band were another eagerly awaited act. Not only were they good classical musicians and beautifully dressed, but they were also one of the few performances we could sit back and watch since they provided all their own music, which was 'straight-sax' and not jazz.

The average weekly fare at the Palace Theatre was four variety acts, one feature film (silent, naturally) and a Pathé Gazette accompanied by the pianist only, which afforded another welcome break from playing, which was just as well because our sagging music stands were already laden to breaking point with literally dozens of excerpts and complete scores. There was the Introduction to Schubert's Unfinished – most effective when the screen depicted a fire; a gallop for chase scenes which were the feature of nearly every film (as they still are, but now accompanied by the screech of rubber and a swirl of dust as monster cars battle it out on the streets of New York or Los Angeles), and, of course, dear old 'Hearts and Flowers' for the love scenes. It makes one realize how little the film industry has changed over the years. The job of conducting and playing the piano was highly skilled, as is the modern equivalent of writing and conducting an original film score – but at least that only has to be done once. Our poor conductors had to work out a new sequence, and perform it, twice nightly every week. Every Monday I would cycle from Vauxhalls to the theatre for the weekly band-call during my lunch break, then turn round and cycle back again. All good, exhilarating stuff, but hell for the digestion.

It was during this period that I first became aware that there was such a thing as a musician's union – not that it was called anything so formal in its infancy.

With my wages from Vauxhalls and the extra thirty-five shillings a week from the theatre, I had managed to keep things going at home reasonably well as the main bread-winner. It had not entered my mind that I was being underpaid, until one night a gentleman appeared during the interval and asked each member of the orchestra what his payment was. When I proudly told him he looked grim and turned to walk up the aisle to the manager's office. The manager, as it happened, was busying himself with the queue at the door. Our visiting gentleman insisted that he leave the queue and step into his office, and when the manager protested he was told firmly, if not politely, that if he did not come and talk there would not be a show that night. That was enough for the manager. As a lamb to the slaughter he preceded the union man into the office and shut the door. A few minutes later they emerged, one looking determined, the other shaken. At the end of the week, and from then onwards, I opened my pay packet and found that my value had risen to four pounds. It felt like a fortune.

If you are thinking that all this is a far cry from brass bands ... well, you could be

From the soprano sax (extreme left) to the bass, all members of the Elliott Savonas band were classical players in their own right, and would have graced any orchestral platform today.

right, and you would be in good company. Father returned at the end of the long war, eager to get back to his band, and was not altogether pleased to see me going out every evening, wasting precious time, and that was nearly the end of that. Anything other than the band was of secondary importance, and whilst I think he was secretly pleased that I had managed to keep the family coffers, such as they were, ticking over, it wasn't the band! He had been away for four frustrating years, and was anxious to get back to work. Even so, the experience I had gained in that orchestra pit was invaluable. Nothing sharpens the wits like panic, and I had learnt the hardest lesson of all – to keep going whatever the adverse circumstances. Variety theatres are, unfortunately, of another age, so I can hardly recommend the experience to present-day young players, but if there were any modern counterpart of the old pit orchestra with a new set of band parts every Monday, I would encourage any youngster to try his hand. Whether it was Marie Lloyd, a juggler, or the local operatic society presenting *Floradora*, it made no difference. Every week presented its own new challenge. There was never time for boredom. Like the old actor's mournful lament for the passing of the old weekly repertory theatre, where do you gain that sort of experience these days? The cocooned atmosphere of the weekend workshop or experimental theatre is no substitute for having to get out there and turn in a professional performance week in week out.

Thinking that he had brought me as far as he could, Fred decided that I needed a change of teacher and arranged for me to visit William Rimmer, miles away in his home at Southport. William Rimmer, you may remember, was our professional conductor for a while at Hebden Bridge, and although retired from conducting was considered to be still the best teacher in the country.

A long train journey finally broght me to Southport and I once again made the acquaintance of the great man. It might have been in Fred's mind that I was becoming just a little conceited and needed to be brought back to earth. If that was the case he could not have sent me to a better teacher. Winning local competitions was all very well (by the time Fred returned from the war I had amassed something like three hundred medals and prizes), but I needed to test my strength against fiercer opposition.

Arriving at Mr Rimmer's house I confidently presented myself and the well-wishes of Fred. And then straight down to work. 'Softly Awakes my Heart' had done very nicely for me over the last two or three years, so that was my first offering to him. At the end of the piece he was silent for a few seconds, then, thoughtfully asked, 'Er ... have you got a tongue?'

'Oh, yes,' I replied, somewhat puzzled.

'Well, show it to me.'

I did so without too much show of enthusiasm.

'Do you know how to use it?' he asked gently.

I replied that, yes, I thought I did. What did he want, I wondered. Conversation perhaps?

'I haven't heard you use it once in the entire piece,' he said. My ego, if not my confidence, was jolted. I had always imagined that my tonguing, the articulation of brass playing, was reasonably good. Nobody had criticised that aspect of my playing before. In all fairness, I still don't think it was that bad, but that was Mr Rimmer's way. Observe the style, if any, of the pupil, and eradicate any fault which hinders the free expression of that style. I had always, right from those fireside early duets with Fred, had some sort of feeling for lyrical playing. Perhaps I had unconciously neglected the more precise articulation which comes from good use of the tongue.

Mr Rimmer was the ideal teacher for me. Strange how, even now, I only think of him as *Mister* Rimmer: a mark of the respect he claimed from all who came into contact with him. His philosophy of teaching was so simple as to be obvious. No tricks. Never impose your own style on a pupil if he has one of his own. If he has no style, give him one, but be sure that it is a style which suits him, and not a carbon copy of the teacher's. Do all you can to encourage the pupil's own individuality.

Easy, isn't it? But how many teachers follow this advice? All too often you can tell the teacher by listening to the pupil. Not only in brass playing, but in any form of music. Apart from the physical technique, music teaching is the same for any instrument or even the voice. BBC television presented a series of master classes by

Taken in a park at Luton, this photograph shows me wearing the wing collar, bow tie and brown shoes which I later wore down the pit at Mansfield Colliery. No wonder I was called the Duke of Portland!

the great French 'cellist Paul Tortelier a year or so ago. It was a superb demonstration of the art of teaching. A brilliant stylist himself, he never sought to impose his own style on the pupils, but was content to encourage their own interpretation, within the limits of the music. Such teachers are a rare commodity.

Another simple fact of life expounded by Mr Rimmer was advice to a conductor. If your soloist is having a struggle with a particular passage, especially one full of semi-quavers, alter it so that he *can* play it and enable him to get on with the business of making music. As he said, 'The composer won't mind – he's probably dead anyway!' I have often availed myself of this good advice. Many a time I have arrived in a band room ready to take over the baton, only to find the soloist struggling away at a phrase which, in the context of the whole piece, is infinitesimal. The relief on his face when I simplify it, and the freedom with which he then attacks the work is, to say the least, gratifying.

After that first encounter, Mr Rimmer became the opposite of the tyrant I first thought him. He became a true, and lifelong, friend and guide. Indeed, the only other occasion I can ever recall being alarmed by the stern exterior of the man was much later. He was a prolific composer and he had taken to placing his latest work on my music stand to see what I would make of it. My copy was completely devoid of any markings, apart from the notes – no crescendo, diminuendo, rallentando (nor even Shaw's 'Now like Hell') blemished the virgin score. He simply counted me in and off we would go, he at the piano and me on the cornet. It usually worked quite well, particulary on one occasion, when I was feeling very pleased at my effort. At the end of the music he picked up his ebony ruler and slowly advanced upon me. What had I done to his piece to deserve his wrath?

'What a pity,' he sighed, 'that I can't knock it into your head that God has given you something which you fail to understand. I had not put one mark of expression or tempo on this piece of music, and yet you play it exactly as I had envisaged it. I shall now mark it just the way you played it.' I glowed with pleasure and relief at this accolade.

Back home in Luton I was growing restless again. The days of the orchestra pit were still fresh in my memory, and I missed the excitement (and the money) of this semi-professional life. When another emergency arose, this time in the new full-length feature film industry, I jumped at the chance and became, for a while, the Bedfordshire 'Apocalyptic Trumpeter'. The average melodrama or silent comedy needed only the assistance of a sympathetic pianist to give the right atmosphere of excitement or pathos, but, every now and again, a film came along which called for something on a grander scale. Rudolf Valentino, the first international sex-symbol (or so my lady-friends advise me), in *The Four Horsemen of the Apocalypse* was one such case. At various intervals throughout the film, the four horsemen would rend the sky in their quest to right all wrongs, and when they appeared they had to be accompanied by a stirring trumpet fanfare. That was where I came in. I travelled all over Bedfordshire in the wake of Valentino, shattering the peace of Leighton Buzzard or Stony Stratford. The orchestra, or often only a piano, would be playing the standard tunes of the day – 'Hearts and Flowers' and the like – but whenever those horsemen appeared I had to be ready, preferably in the same key as we were currently in, to blast the fanfare. It was not unlike following the jugglers at my previous theatre engagement. You had to be ready to stop whatever you were playing in order to give the special effect, but instead of a cymbal crash or drum roll it was my clarion call.

The Luton Band was progressing very well by now, and most of my junior bandsmen had graduated to the senior ranks where they were acquitting themselves with distinction. Alex was gaining a reputation as a fine euphonium player, Rex also learning to play the euphonium ... and I was once again restless!

Thus began a brief, but inglorious, spell at Mansfield Colliery Band working at the Crown Farm pit. It was not a question of running away or leaving home, just a period of self-assertion or, to put it more plainly, bloody-mindedness. I exchanged the comforts of Talbot Road for the discomfort of working down the pit. Anybody who has never experienced the terrifying drop of the cage as it hurtles the men down the shaft, and then a journey to the coal face, can have no idea of what Hell is like. The bottom falls out of the world at every descent. I daresay that miners eventually become immune to such feelings and accept them as part of the working day, but to me, having propped up a desk in the rarified atmosphere of the railways or the car factory, it was a feeling which I shall never forget. Crown Farm pit at Forest Town, incidentally, held the unofficial record at that time for speed in drawing the cage up and down the shaft full of 'Tubs', as they call their fall of coal. My job, although in the realms of Orpheus, was not too demanding. I was not required to look like Eugene Stratton (Lily of Laguna) and emerge black-faced at the end of the day. Quite the reverse, in fact. I worked in the underground office to which I would report every day with shiny shoes, a suit and, believe it, a wing collar and tie. My natty appearance earned me the more or less affectionate title of the Duke of Portland amongst the other bandsmen. The real Duke owned the mine in those pre-nationalization days, but it was not he who controlled my destiny for the following few weeks; it was Alex Owen, the professional conductor of the band. On my first appearance in the bandroom I was introduced to this man who had become a living legend. He was one of the original three pioneers from the previous century and was revered as a daunting conductor and a fearsome enemy. I was introduced as 'the young man from Luton'. 'Luton, eh ...' he mused ominously. 'One of Rimmer's men. I see ....' It was to be made abundantly clear to me during my short stay at Mansfield that one of Rimmer's men need not think he could lord it in Owen territory. When Fred arrived to put a stop to this nonsense and take me home to Luton he encountered little opposition.

The name of the great Alex Owen was linked in my mind with Besses o' the Barn, the band which took its name from the inn where it originally practised.

47

With " Besses o' th' Barn " Band to Windsor & through France. Published by "BRITISH BANDSMAN." 188, Strand, London, W.C.

No. 14. DISTRIBUTING THE MEDALS TO THE BANDMASTER AND BANDSMEN.

Before their world tour in 1906, Besses o' the Barn under Alex Owen played at Windsor.

Not that my time had been wasted. To work under Alex Owen was, in itself, an education. Although he was by then in the declining years of his career, his presence and authority were still a force to be seriously reckoned with. He had, after all, been the first conductor to take a band (Besses) on a world tour – a fact which in itself was enough to gain the respect of all but the most unaspiring of young bandsmen. He led a band to a contest in nearby villages like Hucknall and Brinsley with as much organization and attention to detail as he had employed in taking Besses to the other side of the world. Mansfield Colliery Band was the proud possessor of a touring coach, a long, open-topped affair with a folding roof for bad weather, rather like a giant pram which transported us and all our instruments from contest to contest, sometimes as many as three in a single day – and, what's more, it was not unknown for us to win all three. The only problem with this wonderful contraption was that, every now and again, the folding roof would refuse to budge, and always when we needed it most. The picture of Alex Owen standing all the way in lashing rain, rather than sit down and get the seat of his trousers wet, is one which will always come to mind when I think of those days. He stood like a proud charioteer out of *Ben Hur* while we lesser mortals cowered for shelter behind the seat in front. For him, any discomfort was preferable to presenting a wet behind to the audience. Conditions generally did not improve on arrival at the venue, as few of the villages had a hall and the bands, as often as not, played in the open air.

The village of Brinsley was mentioned as one of these venues, which serves as a

Mr Owen refused to sit down in the Mansfield Colliery band bus lest he got the seat of his trousers wet, and later exposed them to view at a concert.

timely reminder that this was the home of George Hawkins, another successful conductor of the day and a composer of, amongst others, a delightful programme piece called 'A Day in the Alps'. He was the conductor of Harton Colliery and, later, CWS Glasgow – two highly successful bands. It also calls to mind the fact that he was an adjudicator at Belle Vue in 1941 and 1947 – two years when my bands were privileged to win the Championship.

The other undoubted plus of my stay at Mansfield was that I met and became friendly with another young player of my own age and ambition who accompanied me back to Luton, where he stayed, more or less, for the rest of his playing career. His name is Albert Coupe and he came back to live with us at the crowded Talbot Road house, where he quickly became one of the family. To this day he still refers to my parents as Mother and Father. What's more he is a valuable source of information. Time after time, whilst putting these memories on to paper some point of detail has escaped me and we have invariably ended up by phoning Albert. Fortunately his memory has often proved more reliable than mine.

Now, with my temporary lapses behind me, at least for the moment, it was back to work with a vengeance at Luton. The immediate target was the National Contest at Crystal Palace and our conductor, William Halliwell, was faced with the most promising band Luton had ever had. As well as the now resident Albert Coupe there was another young man who was to give Luton excellent service – E. S. Carter, or Ted Carter as he was better known. The test-piece we were working on was another specially commissioned work, this time from Hubert Bath, called

'Freedom', and it was a piece for which we had high hopes. It was Fred's kind of music – symphonic by the standards of 1922 and a challenge. Although Fred was not to conduct the band in the contest, it was his training which brought Luton to the high standard required to make any impression on the London judges. Halliwell's record in the National was second to none. He had conducted the winning band at the previous five contests and no doubt expected to make 1922 the sixth. It was not to be so. He was beaten into second place by his rival John Greenwood, conducting the wonderfully named Horwich Railway Mechanics Institute Band – Horwich RMI is the more usual and certainly more accessible name. Dear old Hebden Bridge came third.

So our band, Luton Red Cross, was becoming a force to be reckoned with, and if any doubters of the day put this down to a flash-in-the-pan they were made to eat their words. Encouraged by coming so close, Fred set to work with renewed energy, bringing into our repertoire all the best new music he could find, so that when the test for 1923 was announced as 'Oliver Cromwell' by Henry Geehl, he was ready to meet it half way. Geehl was typical of the composers of that time, in that his music was descriptive and called for imaginative playing – just the stuff for Fred and the band. We tackled the piece like men who had been starved of music

The only Southern band ever to win the National thousand guinea trophy was Luton Red Cross Band of 1923, in which I played with my brother Alex. He can be seen in this photograph just behind my father, who holds the baton in his left hand. Behind Alex is Ted Carter, who threw his flugel horn out of the train window on the way home.

for centuries. It was discussed, pulled apart, put back together again and lived in every available minute of the band's time. I thought then that no piece could have been so conscientiously prepared, and time was to prove me right on that count as well.

As in all the best moral tales, the hard work was rewarded when Luton Red Cross emerged as the winning band at the end of the day's contest. Nothing in banding can equal the feeling of winning the National for the first time. We were jubilant. No, more than that, we were in another world. For most of us the journey back to Luton would be unbearably slow to meet the reception we knew would await us. Only Ted Carter had other ideas, and his idea of a celebration was unorthodox to say the least. For the sake of the music Fred had prevailed upon Ted to forsake his favourite cornet and play a flugel horn, an instrument rather larger than a cornet, nowadays very popular in dance bands and light orchestras. Ted was disgusted, but being a good bandsman did what was right for the sake of the contest. But he made an apparently light-hearted vow: if Luton should win he swore to throw 'this damn coffee-pot', as he lovingly called the flugel horn, under the first train he saw. To everybody's speechless amazement he did precisely that, on the way home from Crystal Palace to Luton.

A small, personal triumph of our performance that day was the opening of the piece. At the best of times it is not easy to play a perfect octave with a colleague. To have to open the performance, with all the attendant nerves and shakes and the atmosphere of the big day, with such a delicate task is to make it almost impossible. Fred had foreseen this in his painstaking preparation and had given the job to two of the youngest of his players – Albert Coupe and me. Remember we were both living in the same family home and had practised it every day until it was as safe as could be hoped, but he had no idea how the big occasion might affect us, or whether it would negate the weeks of practice. Fred need not have worried. We were as steady as seasoned campaigners – or perhaps I should say steadier, as some of the most experienced soloists came unstuck in those few bars. They still rank as some of the most difficult opening bars ever written for a test-piece.

Our arrival back in Luton was triumphant. In those days the returning champions were treated in much the same way as the winners of the FA Cup. A civic reception was quickly arranged (as I imagine that our victory must have taken the town Council by surprise). Lady Zia Wernher, our patron, added another £100 to the band coffers as well as regally entertaining us at Luton Hoo. Our own small family house was re-named 'Cromwell Villa', and a newly acquired cat christened Oliver as the Mortimers' special celebration. The celebrations, however, were not to divert Fred from his purpose. No sooner had the furore died down than he was sifting through piles of music to find the concert piece for the following year. It was the custom for the winning band and its soloist to feature in the concert which followed the day's business in the next year's festival at Crystal Palace. This was to be our opportunity to show the band world that we were here to stay and, accordingly, he selected a showpiece for me called 'Shylock', which allowed me full rein to put into practice all I had learnt in my years of contesting all around Bedfordshire. 'Shylock' went into the repertoire immediately and not a day passed without me practising at least some part of it. By the time the contest came round again I could play it in my sleep – and probably did.

As the day approached it became known that another band had also been booked to appear in the concert. It was the champion band of Australia, Newcastle Steel Works, which featured their top cornet player, Arthur Stender. The news-hungry press cottoned on to this fact and were billing it as a contest between the champion of England and his counterpart from Australia. Of course, this was just overblown journalism – we were merely to be featured in the same concert and it was in no way a competition. This did not deter the press, however, and the hall was packed to the chandeliers on the night.

Arthur Stender was brilliant. His style was full of showmanship, with the notes literally flying from his cornet in a dazzling display of fireworks which was the hallmark of his playing. There was nothing of the element of competition between us which the public had come to expect, and Arthur Stender and I finished the evening as firm friends expressing the unlikely hope that the event could be repeated some time. (We were, in fact, destined to meet in Australia some twenty-five years later.)

Instead of getting straight back to work this time I once more set off on one of those strange tangents which were to lead nowhere, but which seemed a good idea at the time. This time it was to the bright lights, as Albert Coupe and I joined the ranks of the once famous Commodore Orchestra in London's Hammersmith. My stay was a short one before I once again trailed home, but Albert stayed long afterwards.

As soon as I got back to Luton I was off again, but this time not because of restlessness. Arthur Laycock, the cornet soloist of the great St Hilda Band, had burnt his face trying to put out a fire in a chip pan. He had ignored the golden rule and attempted to put the flaming pan outside the door. Of course, all the flames blew back into his face and left him unable to play. Arthur Laycock was the star of the day and – an honour indeed – I was to go and live with him and temporarily take over his duties with the band. Arthur was known as an immaculate, if pedantic, man and his painstaking attention to his appearance was reflected in his playing. As his deputy I was expected to imitate him in all matters. Every detail of life was ordered and timed to a precision which made Father Fred's discipline look positively lax. His routine started from the moment of his rising from his bed, and breakfast was as much of a ritual as a concert. Whilst I was eager to get on with some practice he would slowly go through his routine of eating, clearing away and preparation for the forthcoming day. After breakfast we would listen to some records from his collection, but not until each one had been inspected, wiped and carefully placed on the turntable. Even the winding of the gramophone was done to a carefully planned pattern. It was not till eleven o'clock that I could get down to any cornet playing, after which we would take a stroll. On the first of these strolls I was nearly sent packing. Thinking it right and proper to accompany him I made to leave the house, only to be arrested by his imperious 'Where do you think you're going?'

'Out for a walk with you, Sir,' I said.

His face registered a mixture of horror and distaste. 'Not dressed like that,' he said. 'You're out with Arthur Laycock, my boy. Where's your hat?' (I had never worn one in my life, except a straw hat at Luton's.)

I later learnt that he suffered from a heart complaint and forced himself into this steady routine to save his health, but even with this knowledge his eccentricities were not easy to bear. When he was fit enough to start playing again we were placed side by side at a concert for a farewell duet, which is where I committed the cardinal sin. The fact that I fluffed a note was accepted – my mistake was to turn and look apologetic. He was furious. 'Never admit to the audience that you have made a mistake,' he thundered. 'It is unprofessional conduct.' He was quite right, of course, and it is good advice.

Returning once more to Luton and the family there was a different atmosphere.

The greatest euphonium player I have ever heard quit the
family nest in 1924; Alex Mortimer left Luton and went to Fodens.

Claustrophobia was the order of the day. The committee which had been so ambitious in 1910 had given way to a new body who, having tasted success, wanted a greater share of the glory and a larger say in the running of the band. To say that Fred was adamant in his opposition to them is probably an understatement. He could undoubtedly be stubborn, but he was nearly always proved right by events. A growing source of discontent was the fact that Brother Alex, having matured into a really fine euphonium player, was not allowed to take the principal euphonium seat. Too many Mortimers in charge looked like a bad scheme to the committee, so he was constantly held back. This waste of talent was bitterly opposed by William Halliwell, who felt it right to tell the committee that if any of his other bands needed a good euphonium player, he would have no hesitation in recommending Alex, as he was wasting his time at Luton. No idle threat. A few weeks later, Foden's needed just such a player and Alex found himself invited to fill the position. Alex was not a confident young man, his youthful illness had left him permanently weakened and with a natural reticence. He must have found it harder to go out on a limb than any of us, yet he made his decision. Before the National in 1924 he had joined Foden's, and played in opposition to us that year. Looking back on those days, I feel that Fred must have had an inkling of the future. I am almost sure that Alex went to Foden's with the promise of reunion before long, but this can only be surmise. The facts are that after six months we all followed, and Foden's became the band of the Mortimers for many happy and successful years.

Of course, when we left Luton it was not without regret and many backward glances. To most of the young Mortimers it had been the cradle of our infancy, more so, perhaps, than Hebden Bridge. We had lived there for fifteen exciting years which saw the growth of the family to six (with the addition of Rex and my youngest sister, Louie), as well as the growth of the band, but at least we were leaving it in good hands. Ted Carter (without his flugel horn), another young player called Ernie Davies who served in the Junior Band with me, and, incredibly, is still playing and comes to Belle Vue every year to lend a hand, and after a brief absence my old friend Albert Coupe who served them as bandmaster for thirty valuable years.

But for us it was a fresh challenge, and a new life in Cheshire with a promising band called Foden's.

Albert Coupe, conductor of Luton until 1975.

3 Rejoice greatly

Indirectly it was the Relief of Mafeking which led to the formation of Foden's Band.

Such a bald statement needs some elucidation. In 1900 the sun shone high on the Empire and patriotism was an acceptable word. To the vast majority of the people Queen Victoria was the only monarch who had ever sat on the throne and must have seemed immortal. The Boer War was regarded as a just crusade and our glorious boys were only doing what was right and proper. The good people of Elworth certainly had no misgivings – and when the papers screamed of the relief of Mafeking it was a cause for celebration. A celebration called for a procession, and a procession called for a band. Unfortunately Elworth did not possess such a thing – but nearby Sandbach did! And Sandbach, whether through a lesser sense of patriotism or lethargy on the part of the council, had not planned a celebration. An emissary was sent immediately from Elworth to Sandbach and an exchange was contrived. The band would march through Elworth at the head of the procession and then go on to perform a similar function on their own patch at Sandbach.

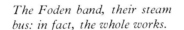

The Foden band, their steam bus: in fact, the whole works.

Having accomplished this they were to turn again and complete the celebration in Elworth as a final flourish – a round trip of several miles. Everybody seemed delighted with the proposals and the Sandbach Volunteer Band polished up their buttons and their patriotic marches in readiness for the great day.

The events started wonderfully well, with the weather playing its part to perfection. The Empire was duly celebrated in Elworth and the band, as arranged, marched on to Sandbach for the second part of the bun-fight. Having acquitted themselves here as well, they right-wheeled again to return to Elworth, but after they had got a half-mile or so down the road the more observant revellers noticed that the sound of drum and bugle had faded out of earshot sooner than should have been the case. In fact it had ceased altogether. The Sandbach Volunteer Band had refused to volunteer any longer. They had had enough, and the waiting crowd at Elworth would just have to wait! In the fury which ensued in the Elworth camp it was decided there and then that Elworth would do without their fickle neighbours in future and have a band of their own. And so the Elworth Public Subscription Band was born amidst much 'hurrahing' and nose-thumbing. A second-hand set of

In profile on the right, in the billycock hat, is Edwin Foden, founder of the firm and saviour of the band. His two sons, William and E. R. Foden, are pictured standing fourth from right and, on the bus, standing second from the left. Both brothers had to leave the band when Mr Rimmer came; he said they made a sound like a saw.

58

Outside the house in Clifton Road, Sandbach: sister Nellie, Alex, myself and Rex.

instruments was bought from nearby Knutsford, and the precious cargo arrived on the evening train some weeks later. Enthusiasm greatly outweighed ability at first, but no matter. The streets of Elworth that night rang to the hellish sound of twenty-five good men, all trying to bludgeon a sound out of several hundred feet of brass tubing over which they had no control at all.

At a cost of three guineas a year Mr Samuel Charlesworth was engaged to bring some order into this chaos, and such was the goodwill and the enthusiasm of the village that in a matter of only two years the band was being booked to appear all around the area. Whilst the nation mourned the passing of Queen Victoria, the Elworth lads, looking into the immediate future, foresaw a lucrative time ahead at the coronation of Edward VII. The committee, however, had higher ideals and felt it more fitting for the band to appear as a labour of love. Such stormy scenes ensued that the committee, rather than face up to defeat on such a point of principle, called in all the instruments – and that was the end of that. Or very nearly.

The main industry of the area was provided by a company called Foden's, for whom most of the bandsmen worked. Mr Edwin Foden himself was a keen band supporter and offered to take over. A brand new set of instruments were ordered from Besson's and the Foden's Motor Works Band made its debut. Out of the ashes of discord came harmony – in every way!

By the time we Mortimers all arrived, Foden's had won the British Open Championship at Belle Vue no less than five times and the National at Crystal Palace once. Their conductors read like a list from *Who's Who*, following the tradition of the top bands of the day: John Gladney, Alfred Grey, William Rimmer and, currently, our mentor from Luton, William Halliwell, who led them to four of the Belle Vue successes. The instrumentalists were of an equal stature and I had to follow in the footsteps of such heroes as Edwin Firth and my immediate

Edwin Firth and Harry Mortimer. When these photographs were taken, both were eligible bachelors.

predecessor, James Thorpe, the winner of the Empire Cornet Championship – a competition in which I had failed to get through the preliminary rounds. Despite their good record the last real success of Foden's had been in 1915, ten years ago, so it was obvious that there was work to be done. And Fred was the man to do it.

One less fortunate tradition which should not go unmentioned was the unwitting fault of Edwin Firth. An elegant young bachelor when he arrived at Foden's he was quickly spotted by the Foden family as a good match for one of the daughters. He was a willing accomplice and soon was married. Edwin Foden was pleased as it achieved his aim of getting a daughter off his hands – the ambition of most fathers in those days – and Edwin Firth was happy with his future secured. When I arrived at the age of twenty-three I was considered equally eligible and, for a while, found my path strewn with one or the other of the misses Foden wherever I went. Fate and my natural trepidation rescued me, though, and we both avoided such a lifelong entanglement. I couldn't see my future as a maker of heavy goods vehicles, despite the obvious attractions of the social elevation. Besides, I was far too engrossed with playing the cornet, not only at Foden's, but with dozens of smaller bands who would pay for the services of a soloist. However, at the age of twenty-five I *did* take off from the Mortimer family nest in Clifton Road when I met and married an attractive local girl, Anne Blissett. Extensive tours with Foden's, my work as a cornet and trumpet soloist and later the Hallé involved travelling all over the country, and when our two daughters, Brenda and Margaret, arrived, they saw less of their father than we would all have wished. Although a good wife and mother, Anne was not one to fit happily into this busy and increasingly hectic musical life. However, as I remarked earlier, I have always been a lucky man and despite a later parting of the ways in 1942 when I came to London, we have all remained good friends.

After a year of Fred's unique mixture of cajolery, bullying and encouragement the band was beginning to sound the way he wanted it. An injection of a few new players and a tactful invitation to one or two lesser lights to seek pastures new was beginning to pay off. By 1926 there was a new confidence and harmony in the band which enabled us to go to the British Open at Belle Vue and take the first prize – the first of the elusive three-in-a-row hat-trick so coveted by bandsmen. With this first success behind us we boarded the London train in October with high hopes of repeating the victory at the National. We were to be sadly disappointed, but never mind, our engagement book looked healthy and we were, after all, the British Open Champions.

Something else happened in 1926 which, while not earth-shattering, had far-reaching consequences.

It is often forgotten that until the mid-twenties bands stood in a square block to perform, with the conductor in the middle. It was the Australian Commonwealth Band which came to do battle at Belle Vue that September which made everyone think twice about the tradition of standing to play. A few old diehards had apoplexy, and one or two traditionalists showed distinct signs of disgust when these Australians arrived on the platform carrying chairs which they proceeded to place in a semi-circle facing the conductor. Worse was to come. They then actually sat down to play! What sort of new-fangled idea was this? It would be nice to say that the Australians won the contest and so created a new fashion overnight, but that was not the case. Actually they came fourth – a creditable enough result – and the new formation did not catch on immediately. But the precedent was created and it was only a matter of a year or two before all the leading bands played sitting down.

The test-pieces for that year (1926) and for the following two years – all of which were won by Foden's – were by Dr Thomas Keighley, an imaginative composer who took for his inspiration in all three cases the plays and characters of Shakespeare. The first was *A Midsummer Night's Dream*, the second (1927) *The Merry Wives of Windsor* and the third *Lorenzo*. Dr Keighley's style obviously suited us. It was colourful, imaginative and, above all, orchestral. The descriptive passages were made for us. Whilst there may have been better technical bands, I doubt if any other band at the time could have taught Foden's much about interpretation. Our style, under Fred's leadership, became so individual that William Halliwell, still our professional conductor, had difficulty in moulding us the way he wanted. It wasn't that we were unwilling to go along with him, it was simply that we had developed beyond his experience. When I first went to William Rimmer from Luton I asked him why he had retired early from conducting. His reply, typically far-sighted, was being proved by Halliwell now:

'If you have four or five top bands under your control it becomes impossible to treat them all in the same way. Sooner or later one or two will need a different approach which you will be unable to give, because you have come to the rehearsals with your own preconceived ideas of interpretation.'

By 1928 Fodens had won the Open three years in succession, and had become outright winners of the Challenge cup (far right). All the bandsmen wear gold Belle Vue medals to celebrate the occasion. My brother Alex sits to my father's right, my brother Rex sits to the left of E. R. Foden.

Fred, as bandmaster, went to great lengths to ensure that his interpretation was not only the correct one, but the one which best suited his band. A degree of freedom was allowed to me in the solo passages, especially where the Merry Wives poke fun at poor old Falstaff. In order to get full value from the writing I was allowed by Fred to take liberties with the tempo and generally express myself (and Falstaff). Poor Mr Halliwell found this difficult to accept and tried, vainly, to bring the piece back under his more rigid control. It could not work. Fred had been too thorough in his training to allow things to get out of control and when we played for him we all knew exactly what we were doing. This led to a frustrating band practice during which Mr Halliwell tried to change our whole approach. It was no good, we had to play it Fred's way – the right way. Halliwell, great man as he was, was big enough to appreciate this and at the eleventh hour relented. Even as we were mounting the steps to the platform he whispered to me to play it as I wanted and he would follow. As the composer was one of the judges, and in the light of the fact that Foden's won, Fred's interpretation was obviously vindicated. Without any rancour whatsoever Mr Halliwell conceded that we played better for Fred and that he would recommend to Foden's directors that Fred should take over full responsibility for training and all conducting. 'They play better for you, Mr Mortimer,' was his final word on the subject. The changeover was not to happen straight away, indeed the records show that William Halliwell conducted Foden's to success for the last time the following year at Belle Vue in 'Lorenzo', the third

part of the hat-trick. Success at the National was still eluding us and, as three times winners, we were barred from Belle Vue in 1929. We were to wait till 1930 before feeling the real benefit of having one conductor – Fred – but the moment, when it came, was all the sweeter for waiting.

On a more personal note, for several years (since I was about nineteen) I had been pursuing the well known practice of appearing with other, smaller bands as guest soloist both in concerts and contests. Now this business of playing for smaller bands on an *ad hoc* basis was a common practice in those days. Many an unknown band won the lesser contests by resorting to this dubious method. The hired soloist was known as a 'borrowed man' and I found my services much in demand – a lucrative source of extra income. Whether this practice was a moral one or not never entered my head. If those bands were ambitious enough and their funds could run to it, who was I to question the ethics of the situation? Until, that is, a trip to the Isle of Man.

It is often said that an eavesdropper hears very little good about himself, and that was certainly the case that day bouncing up and down on the Irish Sea. Feeling somewhat the worse for wear I had taken refuge under a big green tarpaulin – a colour which blended perfectly with my complexion. This, incidentally, took place on the return trip from a contest at which my adopted band for the day and I had done rather well, with a first prize and a medal or two to show for our efforts. Whilst hiding from the world in general and the sea in particular in this manner, two hardier, but disgruntled bandsmen strolled past. Their conversation went something like:

'Hey, Charlie, who's that under the tarpaulin?'

'I don't know,' was the reply, 'But I hope it's that bugger Mortimer. He deserves to drown, playing against us little bands the way he does!'

I was feeling sorry for myself as it was. To be further reviled by my fellow bandsmen was a mortifying experience. I resolved there and then never to be a 'borrowed man' again and, what's more, my 'Road to Damascus' conversion was not forgotten the moment I recovered from my temporary malaise. The next month I sent a letter to the *British Bandsman* recommending that the practice of other such mercenaries be curtailed, and that more honest methods were needed to make all contests fairer. A band should stand or fall on its own merits and not resort to such shady manoeuvres to gain prizes.

To: The Editor, The British Bandsman
      Issue dated 4th August, 1928

Dear Sir

Borrowed Players

Will you spare me space in the *B.B.* to announce my decision regarding the 'Borrowed man' question, that is, I do not intend to play with any band at contests other than my own (with the exception of Knutsford, whom I have been teaching now for almost two years, and consider it quite in order for me to play and conduct them at any contest where the rules permit).

The three band secretaries who wrote to me during the last few weeks will understand now why I did not accept the offer to play with their bands.

I feel that playing with everybody and anybody at contests has caused bad feeling and even enemies amongst 'fellow bandsmen'. I use this phrase in all sincerity, for I claim to belong to the brass band world, because I love the work, not from a monetary standpoint, for any player with average ability can, if he so desires, earn much more by going into other musical channels, but they do not, presumably for the same reason as myself, because banding has become part of their life and they cannot leave it.

Very well then – when I refuse to go and play at contests with various bands someone else will go and take my place – good luck to them! The friendship and good-feeling of 'bandsmen' mean more to me than the £.s.d. derived from being 'borrowed' and I certainly do not intend the pleasure being taken out of my banding through that.

This letter is not intended as an object lesson or advice to other players on the 'borrowed man' question – merely a conclusion arrived at after some years of being 'borrowed' and a decision that it is not worth it!

Harry Mortimer
(Solo Cornet, Foden's Band)

Looking at it now, it sounds embarrassingly pompous. I must have been a rather earnest young man! Seventeen years later it was introduced as a hard and fast rule in all the National Contests, that players had to be registered with a band in order to be eligible. The Belle Vue rules followed suit and the practice quickly died. It is now one of the most strictly applied rules in contesting.

At this time, a new phenomenon was looming on the horizon, and the most exciting development in my career so far.

Any person born since 1940 can have no idea of the importance of radio in the thirty years between 1920 and 1950. What we now take for granted, and what has since become background music to accompany the ironing or wallpapering was, then, the wonder of the age. In the same way that the fifties saw families and friends gathering round the television set to watch 'What's my Line?' and 'Muffin the Mule', so, in the twenties, a similar group gathered round the 'wireless'.

When we first moved to Cheshire broadcasting was in its infancy, and to play on a broadcast came second only to winning one of the major contests. For an appearance on the wireless one was required to dress formally, which meant best uniform for the bandsmen and dinner suit for the announcer. Nobody questioned this rule. Nowadays people appear on television dressed far more casually than we would have dreamed of when nobody ever saw us. A studio was usually little more than a room which seemed to be decorated with miles of cable, and into this room a band was squeezed, where it would gather round the one microphone suspended in front of it. For this reason, the BBC preferred a soloist. The microphone was better able to cope with the sound of one than with twenty-five, and soon proved that bands, like orchestras, were better recorded in a concert hall. There was also the question of expense. A soloist's fee of two guineas was greatly favoured by the accounts department, especially as the soloist was required to pay his own travelling expenses.

Local radio then, as now, tried to reflect the life and people of the district and so it was quite early in my career at Foden's that I was summoned to play at Radio Stoke-on-Trent. As this was more than fifty years ago I am afraid that I cannot remember what I played for my first solo on the air, but I do recall most vividly the congestion in the studio. I was to share the honours of the programme with a local choir – the Potteries Choral Society – and their conductor, Carl Oliver, a local celebrity. This meeting with Carl was to be the first of many in the succeeding years, for Foden's often played in the Society's popular concerts at the Victoria Hall, Hanley. Fred and Carl became great friends, a friendship which has continued through his son, John, a band enthusiast and Music Correspondent of the *Staffordshire Sentinel*.

The announcer on that programme presented himself to us and was, as expected, immaculately dressed and with an accent quite unfamiliar in Stoke-on-Trent. He was, like most of his colleagues, an Oxbridge man – a necessary qualification for an aspiring BBC announcer. He was also the Station Director and, I suspect, did almost every other job on Radio Stoke as well. His apprenticeship in the Midlands obviously did him no harm, for he was to become probably the most familiar voice

At Radio Stoke on Trent I sit next to the young John Snagge, with the Potteries Choral Society and their conductor Carl Oliver. Right: Wilfred Pickles, with Violet Carson at the piano.

on the radio in the following fifty years, setting a standard by which others were to be judged. His name – John Snagge.

Another early acquaintance in the field of presentation was made in the Manchester studios which, although a major regional station, maintained an air of a family party.

Eric Fogg, a musician and composer of some stature, presented recitals and conducted orchestras but was, perhaps, even better known as 'Uncle Eric' on Children's Hour where he also established himself in the minds of countless young listeners as 'Grizzle the Dragon'! Wilfred Pickles was a young man who was to become a national institution. He was born in Halifax, not far from Hebden Bridge, a Yorkshire identity which was part of his public image. He did character parts and introduced programmes of all kinds. Most people, I suppose, think of Wilfred Pickles as the presenter of a show which toured the country inviting the locals to 'Have a Go', a sort of Light Programme 'Down your Way' in which a few relatively simple questions were fired at willing victims. If you remember this, then you will most certainly remember Violet Carson, who played the piano. Violet was also part of those early Manchester Studio days, and one of the most versatile. Her broadcasts ranged from being Auntie Vi in Children's Hour, where she would sing such gems as 'Hush, Hush, Whisper who Dares – Christopher Robin is saying his Prayers' to her own programmes, 'Songs at the Piano'. In between these two she would, as often as not, be accompanying another artist in a recital. You had to be versatile in those days. Whilst we all appreciated the talent of these two, nobody could have guessed at what the future was to hold for them. Wilfred as a film star and national broadcaster, and Violet as the immortal Ena Sharples. The first night that Wilfred Pickles read the nine o'clock news the listening public, always resistant to change, were fairly evenly divided between the outraged and the approving when he cheerfully signed off with an informal and characteristic 'Good Neet'.

One of the keys to Fred's success was his discipline, both in playing and in behaviour. Though strict, he never tried to impose any greater hardship on others than he himself would be willing to bear. The hours of painstaking rehearsal were all to the common good, and every single member of the band appreciated this. When on public display we were all expected to uphold the highest of ideals – he hated the 'beer an bacca' popular image of the bandsman. His men were to be respected amateur musicians. Nothing less would do. On one famous occasion we were fulfilling a long-standing engagement to appear at Newhall Temperance Weekend, which meant that both Saturday and Sunday afternoons were to be spent in a huge field with the sun (which always seemed to shine in those days) beating down mercilessly on us while we played. Most of us were billeted as guests with local families, but three of the men were put up in the local hostelry, which seemed strange for a Temperance Weekend. Sunday lunchtime on a hot day proved to be too much temptation for two of them, and they refreshed themselves rather too liberally with the 'national beverage' and arrived at the concert somewhat worse for wear. After the sun had been at them for ten minutes or so they gave up the unequal struggle and lapsed at times into innocent sleep. Their behaviour had not gone unnoticed by Fred who, nevertheless, said nothing – until later, that is.

On the Sunday evening we were due to go to Belfast for a week's engagement and the train journey, inevitably, was to be broken at Crewe. As we stood on the platform waiting for our connection to North Wales and the Irish Sea, Fred quietly informed the miscreants that they, in fact, were not coming the rest of the way with us, but were to catch the next train to Sandbach and were to report at the works the following morning, and inform their superiors of the reason. No more was said and it never happened again.

That reminds me of a similar story concerning J. Ord Hume. As a young man he was conductor of the Brampton Total Abstinence Band, from which sprang Carlisle St. Stephens. The little known Brampton Total Abstinence Band was to travel across the Pennines to do battle with Black Dyke and Besses. As they came away with the first prize it was no wonder that the men found cause to celebrate. The trophy was filled and emptied several times before they reached home again. As the train pulled to a halt the men spilt on to the platform, still celebrating. The trophy was dropped and fell in two halves at the feet of Lady Carlisle who was there waiting to greet her heroes. As a keen supporter of the ideals of temperance and also president of the band, she was, like her monarch, not amused. The instruments were recalled and the band was no more.

I mentioned, on the subject of Dr Keighley's style of composition, that his imaginative and orchestral approach suited Foden's talents particularly well. This was not merely a brass band transposition of standard classics, nor was it the stereotyped sort of band writing. Ever since 1913, when John Henry Iles first commissioned a piece specifically for a band contest, good composers were continually learning more of the brass idiom and how best to write for it. They were discovering, for instance that an imaginative and sometimes lyrical quality could be extracted from the best bands, and that their efforts would not be wasted if they introduced a new subtlety in the composition.

The three basic requirements for the best results were a conductor who understood what the composer wanted; a band willing and able to embrace the greater musicianship necessary; and, perhaps most importantly, a leader who could lead – who could discover and play exactly the right nuance for the sections to follow. The leader's role, even more exacting in a band than in an orchestra, cannot be over-emphasized. A successful band may well do without a brilliant soloist, but I think it true to say that no band ever did well without a strong leader.

My forté, if I can claim such a thing, was lyrical playing. A style which, in those days, was very much an English hallmark. Brilliant players came over from as far away as Australia – Arthur Stender was the classic example – and dazzled audiences with a shimmering display of rapid-fire cadenzas and brilliant top notes. Superb, but they were very much soloists and not necessarily good leaders. To play the sort of music which was, by this time, becoming the accepted standard, required the whole band to be involved as one voice, not a solo and backing group. Even today, listening to some of those old Foden's broadcasts and records, the quality which stands out, and which was to make Foden's the undoubted champions in the following decade, was the ability to play as one voice.

A few years after leaving Luton to go to Foden's I met up with an old colleague from my former band.

'That's a good band you've got now, Harry,' he said, 'But, you know, you don't stand out there like you used to with us.'

Unconscious compliments are always the best.

A great deal of the credit for our ensemble sound must go to Fred. It is not often remembered these days, but Fred's arrangements were of the highest quality. True to form, they were never flashy, but catered for the band under his care. The solo, from me if cornet, or from Alex if euphonium, never was allowed to dominate the piece completely. Listening to an old broadcast tape of the lovely old tune 'Passing By' which, incidentally, was Mother's favourite tune, and Fred's gift to her, one cannot help noticing the sensitivity with which the ensemble is treated. Almost every line had its own melody, each one adding something to the beauty of the simple tune. Uncluttered arranging at its best, and the sort of writing which put Foden's at the very peak of their trade.

But it was this style which ultimately made Foden's unique, and style, as I said, comes from the leader. To accuse me of blowing my own trumpet is far too obvious

Fodens band outside the BBC, Savoy Hill.

a jibe and unworthy of the sort of intelligent people who, I hope, are going to be reading this book, so I shall abandon all pretence of modesty and concentrate on why this style came about. The achievement of this style occupied most of my playing career. In the first place, of course, I had excellent teachers, beginning with Fred and then William Rimmer. The fundamental technique was so much a part of me that it was second nature: only when the basics of playing an instrument are mastered can the player be free to express himself. Scales, repetition and practice may be a bore to young players, but without them you will never develop. If you have to worry about where to put your fingers, or whether you can make the next note without splitting, you will never be free to interpret the music and never be a musician. Not that the two always go together. There are plenty of wonderful readers of a score who will faithfully play every dot and semiquaver put in front of them, but who will never make music. For some reason, these people are often found in choirs. The choir leaders, often grateful to have a singer who can be relied on to keep going no matter what the odds, tend to retain these singers, and often elevate them to a position of command where they can do harm, often belittling the efforts of those who have more musicianship but less speed in reading. Because of their imagined superiority, they will usually try to sing louder than those about them, feeling that they are hereby leading. The same can be said of instrumentalists. They are to be avoided like the Black Death. The inevitable result of their endeavours is a spiral where everybody around them tries to play or sing that much more loudly in order to balance the overall sound. This becomes a challenge to the *self-appointed* leader who then becomes even more strident. And the worst part about it is that the only person apparently unaware of the cacophonous escalation is the culprit himself. As leaders, whether of bands, orchestras or choirs, they are a recipe for disaster. Leadership must come from style and musicianship, and the leader must be worthy of the respect of his colleagues.

So why do I claim, immodestly, to have had these qualities? What gives me the right to preach on the subject?

Experience! That and the fact that what we were doing worked so well. Fred and I knew each other's moods so intimately that we had to be a good partnership, each with his own clearly defined territory. Having trained me so thoroughly as a youngster, he was, on the whole, content to let me now look after my own interpretation, whilst he conducted and made sure that the band all played towards the same end. On the odd occasion when I tried to impose my thoughts on tempo by foot-tapping or head-nodding, I was firmly put in my place.

'I know you think it should go faster, but this is the tempo it's going!'

In front of a thousand people, that was a pill which took some swallowing.

By 1927 I had already made a semi-professional entry into the real musical world by appearing not only at performances of *Messiah* but also at Celebrity Concerts (so-called in that era) playing cornet solos, the post-horn, the long Bach Trumpet, a tiny pocket-cornet and featuring my famous Echo cornet. This is a remarkable instrument which has never been used by cornet players as much as it should be. Older generations must remember bands playing in the park with the soloist on the bandstand playing an 'echo' tune, and another player hiding in the adjoining bushes to play the echo. This was not always effective – the soloist might well play 100 per cent but the echo player sometimes would be only 75 per cent with a few slipped notes. The Echo cornet – which some people might think of as a trick instrument – was designed in a simple manner. Attached to the main body of the instrument there was a small conical second outlet for the sound. By putting down an extra valve the air was directed through this smaller aperture – rather like a torpedo – producing a very soft sound quite different from that produced by using an ordinary mute. On this instrument I played a tune – with which I was identified almost universally – called 'Alpine Echoes', written for me by a great friend, Eli Smith, a teacher of music in Manchester. Realizing that his real name was hardly one with which to make a name as a composer, he called himself Basil Windsor. The instrument was obviously a god-send to me at Celebrity Concerts, when of course there was no band (and no assistant cornet) to accompany me, since more often than not I was accompanied only by a piano. Even Sir Thomas Beecham recognized the usefulness of this novelty and requested its use for the off-stage call in *Carmen*. He was quick to spot the fact that it avoided the often run risk of the off-

70

From the ridiculous to the sublime: Jimmy Edwards plays his own pocket cornet at the Victoria Palace; I am conducting. Below: the echo cornet of 'Alpine Echoes' fame. In the bottom picture I am playing the long Bach trumpet.

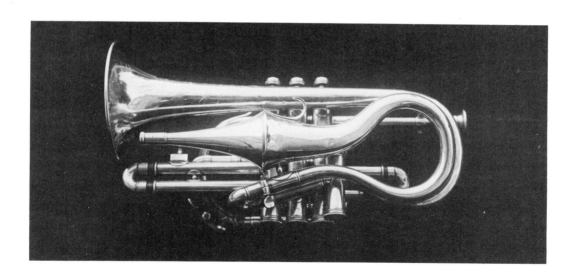

stage 'double' losing his way or even, as once happened, being locked in the lavatory – a favourite place, as the acoustics were excellent. During a concert in a large Methodist Hall, where the administrative offices are situated to the rear of the platform, the player performing one such off-stage call ('Leonora') was suddenly forbidden to play by a Reverend Gentleman, and when the cue came all we heard was 'They won't let me play it!'.

This, then, became a sort of travelling act and in the days before I owned a car, an extremely cumbersome one! One of my memories is of a concert in High Wycombe – an annual affair – at which I was invited to play. In the stalls were the local gentry in furs and dinner jackets, and when I appeared on stage with my selection of brass instruments some of the faces which I could see in the front rows registered surprise, which in the circumstances probably disguised incredulous horror! However, I was booked for a return visit.

About this time, there was in existence in Manchester a very enthusiastic crowd of amateur musicians who carried the intriguing name of Double Fisters. In their ranks were several players who afterwards graduated to the world of the symphony orchestra. The conductor was Maurice Johnstone (who in later years became secretary to Sir Thomas Beecham, and subsequently Head of Music at the BBC in Manchester, before moving up to be in charge of Sound Music output in London). From one of these rehearsals of the Double Fisters – which I had now joined – came a meeting with a notable teacher of singing in Manchester, Constance Astington. 'What are you doing wasting your time in brass bands if you can play a trumpet like that?' she asked. Wasting my time? Had she never heard of Foden's?

'Well,' I said, somewhat ungraciously, 'If you can get me a better job I'll take it.' This was 1927 and a job – any job – especially in the North, was hard to come by.

'I can!' she replied, and there and then wrote a note to Sir Hamilton Harty, the celebrated conductor of the Hallé Orchestra. The incident soon went out of my mind, dismissed as pure fantasy. It seemed unlikely that the celebrated Sir Hamilton Harty would take much notice of a postcard extolling the virtues of a young man practising at the back of a post office and stores. The Hallé was, after all, the premier orchestra in that part of the world, whose every concert was treated like a gala occasion with every seat sold well in advance. It was more than just an orchestra, it held a unique position in the social life of the North. A Hallé concert was not just for the rich enthusiasts. Row upon row was filled with men and women from every walk of life – most of them subscribers who took out a season ticket for the whole series of concerts at the beginning of the season, and had occupied the same seat in the hall for years. The one bright spot in the gloom of those depression years was, for so many, an outing to the Manchester Free Trade Hall where they would be treated to the greatest names in music. It was an informed audience too. They would sit enraptured through the most difficult modern works which were at that time finding their way into the orchestra's repertoire, often against the will of the more conservative, but influential, minority. The Hallé's great working-class audience would absorb all this along with the standard symphonies and concertos, and their critical approval was regarded as a thing to be sought.

That journalist and cricket lover, Sir Neville Cardus, in the affluent sixties, wrote of Manchester and the Hallé as it appeared to him as a younger man in the depressed twenties and thirties.

A Hallé concert was an event, an experience. I remember ... when the mills of Lancashire were closing down bankrupt. At Hallé concerts I would see worn men and women listening with closed eyes to Schnabel as he played the D Minor Concerto of Brahms.... The Hallé was a mirage of refreshment to mind, ear and spirit ...

And so it was. The Hallé was the pride of the people of the North. And Harty was as unique as his orchestra. He *did* take notice of the postcard, and a week or so later I received an invitation to an audition. On the appointed day I set off armed with a briefcase of music, an armful of trumpets (and, of course, my constant companion, the £10 cornet) and the confidence of youth.

Sir Hamilton Harty was accepted throughout the country as a great man of music, but in Manchester he was second to none. To the music-lovers of the North-west, Sir Hamilton and the Hallé were the very personification of music. The moment you were in his presence you knew that you had met a man worthy of his reputation. Tall and broad with silver hair, his physical appearance alone gave the impression of a man who knew what he wanted and had the means to achieve it. I later found him to be one of the politest men I ever knew – as long as he was getting the right response from his orchestra. If he was crossed or frustrated in his purpose he was, on the other hand, a tyrant with a fearful Irish temper which was signalled by a reddening of the neck and face. If these symptoms occurred, watch out. It is a dual personality characteristic which has been the hallmark of great conductors since their genre was invented: perhaps it is the outcome of a thwarted desire to be down there with the musicians, playing every instrument.

Harty's career began as a pianist. He soon found that his special talent was as an accompanist and it was in this capacity that he met a great singer of his day, Agnes Nichols, another forceful personality. He married her, and his later success as a conductor owed much to her influence and persistent encouragement. As a conductor he had a tremendous feeling for rubato playing, perhaps because his earlier life had been spent with singers, and would introduce this into orchestral works at every conceivable moment. Not for him the strict constraints of tempo. In the Hallé we became so accustomed to his gentle shaping of rubato passages that we invented a new musical term. Nobody wrote the usual 'rall' or 'rit' on the score at rehearsal, as is the normal case with musicians. In Manchester we had our own word – 'Hartify'. To Hartify was to extract the last ounce of music from a passage and, most importantly, keep your eye on the baton. Some of those early Hallé recordings, especially of Elgar, despite their scratchiness bear eloquent testimony to 'Hartification'.

*Sir Hamilton
Harty, my first
orchestral
conductor.*

I learned many things in my wonderful years with the Hallé, but this was, perhaps, the most important: not to be afraid of the emotion in music. Extract it to the last ounce. It will never topple over into sentimentality as long as you concentrate on giving the music full rein.

I was to learn this as time progressed, but at this moment my chief concern was to play my best and be accepted into the orchestra. As Foden's were currently rehearsing Rimmer's arrangement of Handel's *Water Music* I decided to make the last movement of that work my audition piece. It was good and showy. Sir Hamilton appeared to be reasonably pleased with what he heard and invited me to play something on the long D trumpet which, apart from its dramatic looks, gives a splendidly brilliant tone. 'Let the Bright Seraphim' was my offering this time, at the end of which I was asked if I knew the B Minor Mass which, of course, I did.

The audition was going well, if exhaustingly. It was with a certain amount of relief that I followed this, at his request, by a piece on the cornet. Less lip pressure is needed for the cornet and, besides, it was the instrument I had been brought up with.

After the cornet solo, Sir Hamilton disappeared into the music library – a welcome respite – as I had played four pieces by this time. The holiday was soon over, however, as it seemed no time before he was back, this time bearing a score of the Brahms Symphony Number Two, which he placed on my music stand. Up till now I had been playing music which I knew, almost from memory. This was to be the big test.

'Play me the second movement,' he said, a note of challenge faintly detectable in his normally authoritative voice.

I looked it over for the normal signposts – time signature, dynamics and, most importantly, key. Everything was clearly marked except the key. All it said was 'Trompete en H', which meant nothing to me.

'Well,' I said, admitting defeat, 'If you will tell me what key it's in, I will try to play it.'

'Ah,' he exclaimed, scarcely able to control a note of triumph, 'Now I know what sort of musician you are.' By which, I suppose, he meant that I lacked a formal college training. Having discovered to his satisfaction what I could and could not do he expressed himself happy with me, and I was offered the position of third trumpet and first cornet with the Hallé Orchestra at a fee of twenty-nine shillings a concert. It was only my native Yorkshire prudence which stopped me offering to pay the orchestra twenty-nine shillings a concert, in return for the privilege of playing in their ranks!

No doubt my two colleagues in the trumpet section would have agreed to this suggestion. Life in the orchestra was not going to be made comfortable for this young upstart from a brass band! Whilst I gained many friends in the other sections my two fellows on trumpet went out of their way to be unhelpful at first. If there was a musical pitfall to be negotiated, as there is in almost any orchestral piece, they could always be relied on to leave a metaphorical bar of soap in just the right place. Perhaps I lacked a proper modicum of respect for their age and senior position, or maybe they were, like many professional men coming to the end of a career in which they had never achieved the fame and fortune which they felt was their right, simply jealous of my youth. Who can say? Whatever the cause, they gave me an uncomfortable year with their note-passing and conversations which blatantly excluded me.

Matters were brought to a head in London where the orchestra had gone to record Elgar's beautiful *Enigma Variations*. There are many subtle differences between a trumpet and a cornet, the most obvious of which is the better breadth of tone in the lower notes which can be achieved on the cornet with its wider bore. Without consultation and, admittedly, in error, I played one small passage during the recording on my cornet instead of the trumpet as marked. Nobody, least of all

75

Sir Hamilton, would have known anything about it if my two colleagues had not made a point of informing him. During the break I was summoned to his room and asked to explain myself. My protestations that the line sounded better on the cornet failed to impress him and I was deservedly reprimanded.

'You must always remember, Harry, that a cornet is a sentimental instrument while a trumpet is a noble and magnificent one. Now, can you get a trumpet for tonight's recording?'

'I can get ten,' I said, knowing that Messrs Boosey and Hawkes just around the corner would oblige.

'One will do,' was the crushing reply. Why have I never learned to say the simple 'yes' or 'no'?

As a matter of fact I do not believe he was entirely right about the cornet, although I'm glad I did not carry the argument any further at the time. I have always maintained that a cornet, in the right hands, can be made to sound every bit as brilliant as the trumpet, whilst the reverse is much more difficult.

Some years later, this difference of opinion was resolved by the manufacture of a strange hybrid known as a trumpet-cornet, which embraced the qualities of both instruments but which had few of the disadvantages of either. It was an instrument which I was to use on many occasions. At that time, though, I had to be content to do as I was told. A mere fortnight passed before I was to have the last word. After a Manchester concert Sir Hamilton sent a note inviting me to the 'holy-of-holies', the Arts Club, which was the sanctified preserve of the conductor, section leaders, visiting soloists, and any other person of sufficient importance. The note requested that I should bring with me my armoury of instruments. By the time I had hung up my tails and collected my belongings the Arts Club was in full session. Awaiting my arrival was Sir Hamilton himself and a room full of other more or less important persons.

'Now, Harry,' was my greeting, 'I want you to settle an argument for us. When we were in London, you as good as said that a cornet was equal to a trumpet, and, in fact, better for certain pieces, and that nobody would know the difference anyway. Now I want you to go into that room and play the 'Leonora' Call six times, using both instruments, and we shall try to decide which was cornet and which was trumpet.'

The 'jury' consisted of leading orchestral members and other knowledgeable experts.

The end of the story is, of course, obvious. Not one of them got it right all the time, and the majority were wrong every time. As a matter of academic interest I played it five times on the cornet and only once on the trumpet. It is all a question of how you blow and whether you blow down both sides of the instrument or only use half of the instrument's capacity.

Despite my commitment to the orchestra, please do not think that I had in any way deserted Foden's. Far from it. Not only was I still as busy with the band but I had also taken on a handful of smaller local bands as professional conductor, and from which I unashamedly poached likely talent to strengthen the band at Foden's. Congleton provided no less than four of Foden's successful team of the thirties: Charles Cook, whose father was the Congleton bandmaster, Jack Cotteril on the horn, Bill Pedley, cornet, and Harry Stanway who was featured in Foden's concerts as a boy cornetist and a rising star. A fifth player invited to join us was Desmond Thomas, from Ammanford, South Wales, a band which I conducted at the National Eisteddfod – one of the first Sassenachs to win this famous Welsh competition. He accepted the invitation and became my deputy. Thus, in the later years of the twenties, was Foden's gradually brought to the strength which it relied on to see it through the most successful ten years ever to be enjoyed by any band before or since.

Apart from the fertile ground of Congleton, I was also conducting Knutsford, my first professional job, Leek British Legion and Burbage near Buxton. I often wonder, when I look back on those days, how on earth I managed to fit everything in and not fall flat on my back. The simple answer is that I didn't, and if I did not exactly fall flat on my back, it was only due to the timely intervention of Fred and Mr Halliwell who insisted that I take an enforced break. To this end, unlikely as it may seem, I was sent packing to Abram Colliery (later known by the more famous name of Bickershaw Colliery). After a month of reluctant silence I was allowed to play with the Abram Band. It was a few years later, and just before the pits were nationalized, that I was invited back as conductor.

In those days of private pit ownership, the coalfield was owned by a gentleman – and I use the word advisedly – named Colonel Hart. Just in case you were brought up on a surfeit of Victorian melodrama where the pit-owner was the villain of the piece, let me tell you about Colonel Hart. Every morning he donned his boots and went down the shaft to see how things were going. He knew every man by name, and knew their lives intimately. An employee's wife who had given birth would look forward confidently to a bouquet of flowers from the boss – often it was the only grand bouquet any of them were to receive all their lives. When nationalization freed the pits from these 'fortunate land-owners' and Colonel Hart lost contact with his family of workers, he found that the very reason for existence had gone and he ended his life, tragically, under the wheels of a train. Not all employers were so paternalistic in those hard times but, at their best, the mill-owners, land-owners and engineering overlords, such as the Foden family, were much more tangible employers than the large international or state-owned companies can ever hope to be. There was a contact there. Not always good, it is true, but at least the boss was a figure who appeared most days, not just a name which appears in the news when there is industrial unrest. Small wonder that the modern shop-steward holds such sway when he is the only approachable figure of authority.

The sad story of Colonel Hart was a long time after my stay at Abram. I only knew it as a friendly and recuperative place from which I returned with new vigour

A Welsh miner playing 'Land of my Fathers' to celebrate the Nationalisation of the coal mines in January 1947. Right: practice time at the pit.

to the self-imposed hard work of my various activities, mainly in the family atmosphere of Foden's. And what a family it was, too. Not only were there the Mortimers, but the Webbs – Arthur Webb and brother Frank who modestly signed himself in a visitor's book as 'King of the Euphs' and, later on, Arthur junior. Then there were the Moores – Joe and his son, Reg, and the Stathams – two brothers, Albert and Ted. Elder statesman of the band was an E flat bass player, Tip Hylton, who spoke in the broadest of Cheshire accents. His never-to-be-forgotten proud boast was that his band, Foden's, had won 'Three fusses at three contesses in concussion' which, roughly translated for the benefit of the English speaking reader, means 'Three firsts at three contests in succession'.

In October 1980 I was delighted to be with two other members of that band: Hubert Shergold, who was ninety-one and who had played the flugel horn, and Edgar Spurr, a mere seventy-eight, who had played the E flat bass. The occasion for this reunion was the celebration of Fred Mortimer's centenary. My sole remaining brother, Rex, was of course also there and conducted the modern Foden's band. It was a memorable occasion, not least for the sight of Hubert, a normally modest man, raising his hands in salute to the audience, rather like a heavyweight champion. It was, alas, to be my last memory of him as he died soon afterwards. On that day he was 'Hubert the Great'. How fitting that he should end his long association with Foden's on such an exciting note.

They were a wonderful group of men, those Foden's players. Judges and audiences used to remark on how well we all played together, but surely the secret of that, apart from the musical training, was the spirit of the band. We all knew and respected one another. Discipline, after the first few months, was not a thing imposed by Fred or anyone else. It was a thing from within the heart of the band – a bond and a feeling of individual responsibility. No band, whatever its history, can accomplish much, and certainly not prolonged success, without it.

At my father's centenary concert I again met Edgar Spurr and Hubert Shergold (seated). Hubert in his earlier days can be seen on page 19, second from the right on the top row.

The economic climate of the country was drab and jobs were not easily come by or held, but the band held fast. In loyalty it was second only to the family. To some it *was* the family. How can that be adequately explained today? Standards have changed and allegiance has a subtly different meaning. There are more demands on players today which distract them from the band, and a sense of belonging is less important than it was. Bands will continue, of course, and playing standards will possibly improve all the time – individual standards at any rate – but how fortunate to have lived in that era and to have been with that band, which I still feel was the best and most consistent there ever was. An opinion voiced by hundreds of musicians and bandsmen who were lucky enough to have heard them at the time. The facts will bear me out.

We are always being reminded by our elders and betters that the seasons were much more clearly defined in their day than they are now. That is possibly true. Summers were certainly more reliable and many was the time we sweltered in an open field some Saturday or Sunday afternoon, providing a musical accompaniment to somebody's garden party or fête. Winter, equally, was sharper. But a bandsman's seasons were even *more* sharply contrasted.

Spring was a time for preparation and a minor claw-sharpening contest or two. Summer was the season of concerts, tours, one-nighters and whole week engagements. All around the coast the summer evenings rang to the sound of brass from the bandstand. Military and brass bands followed one another with clock-setting regularity into all those seaside and inland spa towns. A promenade without a band was only a seaside walk. Before the average family even knew of the existence of Benidorm or the Costa del Fortune, they would pack their cases every year and come flocking out of the industrial towns into Worthing, Eastbourne, Torquay, Scarborough and all the rest, and it was accepted that part of their week or fortnight's entertainment was a band. Not to be able to listen to the band was like a stick of rock without the lettering.

Not all brass bands undertook these engagements, but at Foden's we were fortunate in having an understanding and helpful management who appreciated the importance of having the name of Foden's emblazoned on hoardings around the country. Mind you, names like Foden's and Black Dyke have a ring about them which looks and sounds good on hoardings. Not all the bands were so fortunate: Crossfield's Soap Works Band, for instance, loses some of the magic in the printing. Each of these summer venues has a story of its own and each evokes a unique memory.

Worthing, where we very nearly lost a brand new set of E flat basses in a fire. These gleaming monsters had been sitting in the band room all week, still with their labels on. On the Saturday night, in order to make a hasty getaway (the next venue always seemed to be the other end of the country, and that weekend we travelled to Dunfermline in Scotland) they had been placed in the band coach ready for the off. Just as well, because the band room caught fire that night.

Southport was a sort of Mecca for the bands in those days, because it was always

One of the best loved bandstands in the south of England was Eastbourne. The old bandstand was replaced by the new one (below), vastly more comfortable for audience and performer alike.

associated with William Rimmer. Even after the great man died, many a player who would normally count himself as a pragmatist still half expected to see him taking his customary afternoon constitutional in the direction of the Lord Street bandstand. Somehow we seemed to play all the better for his presence, real or imaginary.

Westcliff was high in the popularity polls of both bandsmen and audiences. The place was regularly packed to the limit a good half an hour before the performance was due to begin. It was said, although I never found enough bars rest to count them, that the stage and arena were garlanded with two thousand light bulbs. I suppose that it was somebody's full time occupation to go round replacing the duds – a job somewhat akin to painting the Forth Bridge. It was not just the bulbs and the packed houses, though, which stand out in the memory. It was here that we were to be party to a wonderful example of what we might call the 'Peaked-cap' mentality – the over-enthusiastic application of a little authority. We had been going to Westcliff-on-Sea for season after season and had rather taken for granted the presence of the resident stage-manager, an affable fellow who went out of his way to be helpful and who had been there since before living memory. And then, one year, he was not to be seen. Whether he had retired or been demoted to deck-chair superintendent we never knew but, oh! how we missed him. His place was taken by an ex-naval Petty Officer. This one had obviously heard all about those dreadful civilian chappies and was determined to bring his own brand of Naval discipline to Westcliff. It was just our misfortune that his first week happened to coincide with our visit. As brass bands went, Foden's was one of the smartest. Perhaps we lacked the sparkle and polish of the Guards or the Marines, but at least we tried to look our best. Tunics were buttoned right to the top, trousers neatly pressed, and black shoes immaculately shone. Fred, in fact, was one of the best turned out conductors you could possibly wish to meet, with his long frock-coat and sash topped by a cap which, unlike this particular son, he wore at a faultless degree of straightness. (I have to admit that my own cap was invariably at a slightly rakish angle – just natural vanity I suppose – but I can pick myself out on faded photographs merely by the angle of my cap.)

Our new stage manager had watched our performance on the first night and come to some interesting conclusions. We were sloppy. We were un-military and he was going to put a stop to it. Good Lord, one man had actually been seen sitting with his knees more than two inches apart! First thing next morning he was down at the Council depot commandeering some high stools – a sort of cross between a bar stool and a parrot's perch. By the evening they were in position and we were faced with a fait accompli. Despite our muted protests we scaled the upholstered heights to start the programme, which, it must be confessed, went perfectly well – until the National Anthem! Up till then the band had plenty of time to mount and dismount when it was required for a solo, and anyway they only had to do it one at a time. On the roll of the drums for the Anthem, however, we were expected to be on our feet pretty smartly. If you have ever tried to descend from a perch with an E flat bass in your grasp and keep your dignity and composure all at the same time, you will have some idea of the difficulty encountered by the men. It only took one with shorter legs than the others to stumble, and the whole lot collapsed like a house of cards. A bass shoved a trombonist, who in turn knocked a euphonium player, who responded by sending his music stand flying; a mute travelled across the platform and amidst all this din the drummer was still rolling away like mad waiting for Fred to bring in the rest of the band. The only one not to show even a trace of amusement was the stage manager scowling away in the wings. I hadn't laughed so much since ... oh, at least the week before when we were at Dunfermline.

It was at Dunfermline that we ran headlong into a musical disaster. As band sergeant, one of my more tedious duties was to set the music on the stands and make sure that we all, including Fred, had the pieces in the right order. It was, from a morale point of view, important that we as Champion Band made a good impression on the Scots, who would be delighted to be given the opportunity to feel superior to the Auld Enemy. For the price of a penny it was possible to purchase the entire week's programme, a facility of which the Scottish band-masters for miles around would gladly avail themselves. Armed with this vital information they could pick and choose which items they wanted to hear and come and go as they felt fit.

The overture went well, followed by an equally successful selection. Then disaster struck! According to my music stand we were due to play 'Aisha' – an intermezzo. When Fred counted it in it appeared that one of two things could be wrong: either he was suffering from a brainstorm and was intending to take it at the pace of a gallop, or he had the wrong piece in front of him. The second of these two conjectures proved conclusively to be right when I heard, from the euphoniums and trombones, a counter-melody which could only have come from *The Arcadians*. By the look on Fred's startled face, this was no nearer to agreeing with what was on his stand than 'Aisha' would have been. I never did find out what it was that I had put on his running order, but I have a sneaking suspicion that it might have been the 'Ride of the Valkyries'. After a bar or three of disconcerting cacophony he cut us short and tried to start again, but the results were no better. In a dramatic stage whisper, heard clearly all the way to the Cairngorms, Fred asked me, 'What the Hell are we supposed to be playing?' 'Aisha,' I croaked back, and immediately he counted us in once again, this time in intermezzo tempo, and everything would then have been well had not the other side of the band, realizing that *The Arcadians* was wrong, convened a hasty meeting and come to the unanimous decision that what they should have had was *Tales from the Vienna Woods*. The effect was, if anything, slightly worse than before. Fred allowed himself the luxury of a blasphemy or two, by which time the word had got around that 'Aisha' was the correct piece. In the end 'Aisha' and common sense prevailed and the rest of the first half followed an uneventful course.

The interval had then to be faced when the local bandmasters would follow the usual habit of special visitors and come round the back to say hello. With as much

Isobel Baillie and Gladys Ripley on either side of Malcolm Sargent at the recording of the Messiah in 1947.

panache as he could muster, Fred coolly asked them if they had enjoyed the first half.

'Aye,' came the reply, accompanied by much chin-rubbing and apparent consideration, 'You've a guid band, but I dinna care for these novelty numbers ye play.'

And so those wonderful summers went on, but always at the back of every bandsman's mind was the autumn. This was, and is, the season of the major contests. The British Open at Belle Vue, Manchester, and The National in London at Crystal Palace. It seemed strange that the band which could accomplish the all too rare hat-trick at one contest should consistently finish down the list at the other. The Foden family were so concerned about this fact that they even went to the lengths of having the engineering department take a look at the problem. One bright spark, having gone to the trouble of building models of both halls, pronounced that in his opinion Foden's sound suited the acoustics of Belle Vue but not those of the Crystal Palace. He even went so far as to suggest that our unique sound hit the ceiling and, by the time it had reached the judge's box, had become distorted. Ingenious, but wrong! The real reason was, at the same time, both more simple and more complicated.

We were becoming more and more orchestrally minded, and the works which suited this style were not at that time being selected for the Crystal Palace contest, or if they were, as with Holst's *Moorside Suite*, the judges then at Crystal Palace were not sufficiently up with the developments of brass writing to appreciate what the music should sound like. It is, of course, the cry of every bandsman who has not won that the judges were either wrong, stupid, cloth-eared or plain bent, and I fall into this trap with trepidation, but as they are all gone to the great bandstand in the sky and I am still here I feel reasonably free to indulge in the brass player's lament that it was not we, but they who could be wrong.

The fourth season in the bandsman's calendar is Christmas; *Messiah* time, and for me the *Messiah* is special. As an up-and-coming young soloist in those days I fitted in quite a few Messiahs around the northern towns, as did solo singers. Ladies like the splendid Dames Isobel Baillie and Eva Turner organized their Novembers and Decembers around a demanding programme of northern choral societies' presentations of the *Messiah*. These days we tend to think of the great Huddersfield Choral Society and the Glasgow Orpheus Choir, but in those less hurried days every northern town worthy of the name boasted its own production. Soloists engaged from London for the occasion found them a very lucrative income. Fortunately the work requires a trumpet soloist as well as the four main singers, and I joined in the round with great delight. I suppose that each separate town and each presentation should remain firmly in my memory; to each society it was, of course, their big night of the year, but human nature being what it is and whatever other wild claims I may make, I do not pretend to be other than mortal and after the first dozen or so, one tends to be blurred with another. But my deep affection for the work has never faltered, no matter how many times I played it – the test of great music.

That affection didn't stop me from becoming blasé about it and, although I always carried the music with me, I came to a point where I seldom referred to it. Fred warned me that one day I would come unstuck. How nice, for once, to be able to say he was wrong. It was quite the reverse, in fact, as it was only my intimate knowledge of the piece which saved a potential disaster. No, disaster is too strong a word. Let's say mishap.

It was my first Christmas with the Hallé and I was merely the third trumpet. When *Messiahs* were being handed out, they were not likely to come my way, especially if the town involved was Huddersfield or Bradford, where they took their *Messiah* very seriously indeed. It so happened that this particular year there was a 'flu epidemic and the Hallé, including the principal trumpet, was due to appear at Bolton. The 'flu aimed its dart very carefully and laid low not only the principal trumpet, but his number two as well. Sir Hamilton Harty, though concerned, felt he could entrust me with the job (I had played it for my audition, remember). Fred, almost as a matter of course, came with me. He wasn't going to miss seeing his son play the solo with the Hallé Orchestra. On arrival in Bolton, we were greeted with the news that the 'flu had claimed yet another victim, this time it was Joseph Farrington, a famous bass of his day who had been engaged to sing the bass arias. Bolton was scoured for a bass who knew the part and who could take over at such short notice. Just in time a church soloist was found who had sung the part only a few nights before. He was rushed to the hall in an indecent haste in time to be hurled on the platform before he even had a chance to get nervous. It was only later in the programme that his nerves got the better of him. Just in time for his aria: 'The Trumpet shall Sound', in fact. Well, the trumpet sounded, but the bass remained silent. I played the introduction again, in time honoured fashion, just to give him a second run at it. Silence. There was only one thing for it. I played his melody as well, hoping that he would join in as soon as he felt confident. This appeared to do the trick as, eventually, he found his voice just in time to sing ' ... and the dead shall be raised incorrrrrUPtible'. Poor chap, I imagine he turned cold for years afterwards every time he remembered the incident. It occurred to me afterwards that perhaps he would have been happier singing those other immortal lines, 'Their sound is gone Out'.

'There,' said Fred afterwards, 'I knew you'd come unstuck one of these days!' The injustice of that remark scarred me for life. Despite my nervousness, it was a fairly good performance, and Sir Hamilton, thank goodness, was very charitable. On the way back to Manchester he asked me into his (first class) compartment where, having expressed his pleasure at my evening's work, offered me the post of principal trumpet for the coming season. Naturally I was delighted, but never being one to leave well alone I tried to make conditions.

'If I don't make a success on principal, would you put me back on third trumpet? I don't want to be out of the orchestra altogether.'

'That,' he remarked coldly, 'Is a reflection on my judgement.' I was dismissed from the compartment. Or, more accurately, I retreated from the compartment and the sight of his reddening neck and fixed stare. I did not take the job, however.

After two days at home, kicking myself for being so stupid, my guardian angel resolved the matter for me. A letter dropped on to the door mat, inviting me to join the Liverpool Philharmonic ... as principal trumpet. Gladly I accepted. The post was ideal for me. The Liverpool Phil only played one concert a fortnight, as opposed to the two concerts a week at the Hallé, thus giving me an opportunity to familiarize myself with the classical repertoire at a less hectic pace. Also, unlike the Hallé, the Liverpool Philharmonic had no permanent conductor and engaged a different guest for each concert. To my surprise, I received a letter from Sir Hamilton congratulating me on my appointment and informing me that the first guest conductor for the new season was to be – himself! To celebrate the reunion, he told me that he had selected as one of the works Handel's Concerto for Trumpet and Organ. Although this was not a work I had ever performed, I embraced the opportunity to prove myself as a principal, and a year later confidently took my place back at the Hallé – in the post Sir Hamilton had invited me to fill and which I had refused. Nevertheless, I shall always believe that I took the right decision. My year's delay was nothing but beneficial.

Music is a strange master, and if asked what I considered to be my most important achievement in eighty years, I would like to be known as the man who brought the merits of brass bands to the notice of eminent players and orchestral conductors of my day. Not just brought them to their notice, but involved them in a way hitherto unheard of. It is something I strove towards for the next thirty or more years. But back to the beginnings of my campaign ...

The season with the Liverpool Philharmonic taught me more than just how to play the Handel Trumpet and Organ Concerto, it taught me a great deal about music and conductors, particularly about the much quoted and much fictionalized Sir Thomas Beecham.

If my encounters with Harty taught me to tread warily, then Beecham demanded a positively tiptoe approach. Much has been said, a great deal of it secondhand knowledge, about the cutting edge of Beecham's wit, which has tended to obscure the fact that the man was a genius. Technically there have been better conductors, those whose beat was much more easily followed. A musician playing for the first time under him could have an extremely difficult time following what was going on. There were occasions, even, when he did not conduct at all and was content to stand back and admire the view, but that was only when the music was going well, when the sight of the maestro carving great slices of air would have been merely a distraction; there were other times when he would indulge in what we came to know as 'stirring it' ... a descriptive phrase. Once his interpretation was being carried out he saw no need to impose himself further on the orchestra. That is not to say that he was not a showman – his final bars were as dramatic as anybody's – but it was in the quieter passages that one felt instinctively that his influence was there even if he was simply standing on the rostrum with his eyes closed and his hands gently folded. A lesson for any player with 'stick-itch' – that curious disease which afflicts most musicians from time to time. It might be more accurate to say that he directed the performance, rather than merely conducted. My very first concert for him was very nearly my last. Whether it was because he was unaccustomed to seeing such a young man in the principal's chair, or whether I was that bad I shall never know, but I had the distinct impression that I was being singled out as the unwilling butt of his displeasure. My reaction to this treatment was to sink further and further into my protective shell and say nothing even in reply to a direct question. I had, after all, been used to being the big fish in the little pond, and now that I was in the large sea of the orchestral world it came as a shock to be singled out for rough treatment. Fred was capable of belligerence on the odd occasion, but this was a sustained attack which I felt was not only unwarranted but unacceptable. Seeing my reluctance even to answer Beecham's provocative questioning, my colleagues urged me to say something and not make matters worse.

'Tell him,' I said, 'that if he doesn't leave me alone, I shall not be here tonight.'

Beecham's long-range hearing, which would have been the envy of Jodrell Bank, picked this up immediately. 'Well,' he crooned, 'Out of the mouths ... Play it your own way. It's too late to get anyone else for tonight.'

'Play it your own way. It's too late to get anyone else for tonight.'

Such an inauspicious beginning should have put paid to any hope of working together amicably in the future. Not so. After the concert, which went extraordinarily well, we became the best of friends and when the first trumpet position in the newly-formed BBC Northern Orchestra had to be filled, he asked for 'The young man from Liverpool. He's very awkward, but a good player.' His foibles and wit became a treat to look forward to, rather than something to dread –

90

as long as they were aimed at someone else, that is. My second encounter with him
was the one which laid the foundation of our lifelong respect for one another.
During a tea-break, instead of lining up for my cracked cup of strong, sweet and
dark brown fluid, I stayed behind on the platform to rehearse privately a sticky solo
passage in the symphony we were preparing. It was not actually the notes which
were troubling me, but fitting them all in to his confusing (to a newcomer) beat. To

my horror Sir Thomas, seeing me still sitting there, advanced majestically up the steps towards me, asked me what it was that was giving me trouble, and I tried, as tactfully as possible, to tell him. Taking the music from me he proceeded to sing the passage in his peculiarly unmusical and strident voice – quite frankly, no help at all. His next remarks, though, were ones which I shall never forget and with which this book started: 'You must keep your eye on me, and I shall keep my eye on you. You have something which is very important: you temporarily live the part.'

That was his secret. He conducted from *inside* the music, and it became magic. He lived it. To him the notes were the framework, the basics which had to be right, but the music was inside the frame. Did you ever hear a soloist playing a popular song, be it modern or old like 'Sweet Lass of Richmond Hill', which had all the impact of a damp sponge? Ever wondered why it is, when every note is played perfectly with not so much as a split or a slight wavering of intonation, that it means nothing? It is because he is just playing the notes without thought to their meaning. It could be even simpler than that: it could be that he just does not know, and has not seen fit to find out, the meaning of the words. With orchestral music you generally do not have the advantage of words to help you, so the music has to come from a more obscure source. For want of a better word, I shall call it the spirit. Yes, that will do nicely. It is the spirit of the music, or the ability to discern it, which separates the musician from the player.

The subject of Sir Thomas Beecham cannot be left without one or two personal anecdotes.

To the unfortunate librarian who incurred Beecham's mild wrath:

'What's your name?'

'Ball, Sir Thomas.'

'Ball, eh? How very singular.'

Beecham at rehearsal:

'This is wrong, woodwinds!'

Second oboe: 'Sorry, Sir Thomas, I was a bar out.'

'What's a bar amongst so many friends ... but you will, I hope keep in touch with me from time to time throughout the symphony?'

The last word should go to Harty, who replied to a question on Sir Thomas: 'The man's a genius, blast him!'

I returned to the Hallé much better equipped to do the job both in terms of confidence and ability, thereby vindicating my decision of the previous year.

My career has been like one of those drawstring bags: when the bag is opened out flat you can put one article on one side and another on the other side. As long as the bag stays flat they will remain separate. In my bag of music I have placed the band, the orchestras, conducting and administration. They have all retained their individual identities and got along side by side. Except every now and again, when somebody came along and pulled the drawstring, and there they were, all mixed happily together, usually to the benefit of them all.

In 1930 Sir Edward Elgar, at the height of his career, wrote a piece for brass bands called *The Severn Suite*, the preparation and playing of which marked the beginning of Foden's greatest years. Sir Edward Elgar was at that time president of the Hallé, and thus came about the first pull of the drawstring. If I have given the impression that the orchestral life had supplanted my work with Foden's, it is an error which should be quickly dispelled. Throughout these years I led a sort of double life, and somehow the demands of both band and orchestra were equally satisfied, even if at times my life seemed to be one continuous dash between the two.

1929 had been a blank year for Foden's. Having completed a hat-trick of wins at the British Open we were automatically disqualified from entering that year. We had enjoyed our annual non-success at Crystal Palace, which left us 'potless' – a strange feeling for the men of Foden's. But better things were on the way.

The test-piece for 1930 at Crystal Palace was Elgar's *The Severn Suite*. Naturally Harty was interested to hear the piece, and eagerly fell in with my suggestion that he should come down to Sandbach to sit in on a rehearsal. It was not entirely without misgivings that I introduced Harty to Father, who for the first time was in complete artistic charge of Foden's. Fred had seen Harty conduct on many occasions, as he always tried to come along when I was performing, whether it was a band or an orchestra, but Fred was not overawed by reputations and although he was proud to have Sir Hamilton attend one of his rehearsals he certainly had no intention of bowing and scraping to any man (a breed to be found in profusion on the eastern side of the Pennines). I was not sure if it was pride or dread which occupied my mind when I introduced the two men in the bandroom that summer evening.

Without any further fuss, Sir Hamilton was seated and we played right through *The Severn Suite*. I seem to remember that we played at our very best that night; no doubt the important visitor impressed the men. At the end of the piece Sir Hamilton, surprised, I think, by the quality of musicianship displayed, went to congratulate Fred. He, setting a match to his customary pipe, cut short the praise and went straight to the heart of the matter.

'Now, Sir Hamilton,' he said, puffing thoughtfully. 'Before you go I want your opinion on this bar here. Elgar has written an A flat and I think he's wrong. Every time I hear it, I'm sure it should be a natural. What do you think?', and he thrust the score at Sir Hamilton.

Harty perused the offending bar.

'I'm sure Sir Edward is right. An A flat,' he said with an air of finality which would stop any of his Hallé players in their tracks, but which singularly failed to impress Fred.

'I don't know,' he said, 'It doesn't sound right to me.'

At this point I was wondering if there might be a convenient hole into which I could disappear. The rest of the band were warming to the possibility of a good clash, and enjoying my obvious discomfort. You see, back in Manchester, Harty's word was the law. If the sun was blazing, and he insisted that it was raining, you put up your umbrella. And here was Father arguing the toss over an A flat, while Harty's neck grew a darker shade of puce – always a sign to show discretion rather than valour. Even I had learnt that much. Undeterred, Fred started the piece all over again with special emphasis on the offending bar.

In the silence which ensued, Harty walked across to Fred and said, 'You were quite right. Definitely an A natural.'

On leaving the bandroom and bidding us good-night, he added, 'I feel bound to say that I cannot see your band being beaten on this piece.'

Like Fred, he too had a habit of being right.

The fact that Sir Edward Elgar was President of the Hallé gave Foden's a slight advantage over their rivals when it came to playing *The Severn Suite*. Through his frequent visits I had come to know the man and his music fairly well. Another gentle knight of the baton, he was not above telling a story against himself. I warmed to him greatly one day at the end of a rather dull rehearsal of his work 'The Dream of Gerontius'. The fact that it was a tedious rehearsal was the fault of the orchestra and not of Sir Edward. Finally he gave up the struggle, and laying down his baton said,

'Gentlemen, you play this music as if you didn't like it. Let me tell you a story. At its second performance in this hall I was guest of honour and sat in that box next to the Lord Mayor of Manchester. Unfortunately he arrived late so there was no time to introduce us to one another. Half-way through the first section he leaned over to me and said, "Very dull music, this." So as not to embarrass him I murmured agreement. At the interval, before he could realize his mistake, I made my apologies. "Excuse me, Lord Mayor, I'm afraid I have to go." "That's all right, old chap," he said, "I wish to God I could come with you." Now, gentlemen – let's try again.'

The Severn Suite was the beginning of the most successful decade to be enjoyed by any band, eclipsing even the achievements of the great Black Dyke. It was also the decade in which I would enjoy the best of all musical worlds, combining orchestral playing and band playing with recording and celebrity concerts. And, of course, conducting.

Foden's had by now developed an individual style of performance, a style which did not come overnight, but which took two or three years to perfect. The years around the turn of the century are often referred to as the Golden Years, but to me the real golden age was in the thirties – those years in which band music came of age and was taken seriously by composers normally associated with the orchestral repertoire. The 'beer 'n baccy' image was finally being laid to rest, with no undue regret from the players, and a greater awareness of musical subtlety was being brought in by the younger players and embraced, for the most part, by the older bandsmen.

94

In 1910 Edwin Foden gave five shillings to each of the old people of Elworth to celebrate winning the National. His son E. R. Foden promised to double it if they won again, which they did in 1930 – the winning band is shown above. He promised £1 next time they won, which was paid in 1932, after which he lost his nerve, which was just as well: we won six times in the next seven years.

Fred, let us be quite clear about it, was ever in the vanguard of this new movement, although he would never recognize it as such. To him it was a natural development and fruition of all that he had learned in a lifetime of banding, and the fact that his band won the National Contest seven times between 1930 and 1938 bears out the point. We failed to win only in 1931. (The other year when Foden's name does not appear as winners, 1935, was the year we had to sit it out, having completed a hat-trick.) In all those years the musical test-piece was a substantial work, usually of descriptive nature, at which Fred was the undoubted master.

It never occurred to me, for instance, that he took an over-serious and studious stance when the test-piece 'Kenilworth' was announced in 1936. Arthur Bliss had written this work as an impression of Kenilworth Castle, a stately ruin. Before we had even tried the music through, I accompanied Fred on a pilgrimage to see the pile of stone which had inspired the piece. This was followed by several visits to the cinema to see a film of H. G. Wells', *Things to Come*, the musical score for which was composed by Bliss, and by the time we got down to serious rehearsal we knew the composer's moods almost as well as he did himself. Such meticulous preparation had its reward when we won the contest which set us on the road to our

Father and three sons after winning in 1936, the beginning of our second hat-trick.

second National hat-trick in succession – a run of success which took a second world war to halt.

But 1936 was remarkable for more than that.

Almost as soon as the dust had settled from our triumphant return to Sandbach we were off again, this time to South Africa. We had been invited to tour that wonderful but sad country to share in their Empire Exhibition year, and so sailed off in damp autumn weather to a climate which was the envy of all those we had left behind.

How much banding in this country owes to the sympathy and goodwill of industrialists can never be measured, but it is to the eternal credit of the Foden's management that they were willing to release the band for five weeks to fill this prestigious engagement. True, we carried the name of Foden across the world with us, but the men's absence must have had some disruptive effect on production. How much greater still, then, was the help given to Besses and Black Dyke back in 1906 when they undertook world tours which necessitated their absence not for weeks, but for months? Probably we shall never know, but what we do know is that those immense tours did more to spread the gospel of banding than did anything until the advent of radio. Perhaps I never fully appreciated this fact until many

Fred travelled first class when we sailed on the
Caernarvon Castle (above) to South Africa in
1936. Below: Alex relaxing in the South African
sunshine. We came back on the Edinburgh Castle,
seen right in Madeira harbour, where we were
plagued by sellers of souvenirs all made in
Birmingham!

years later on an 'in transit' trip to Singapore. Although there was no evidence of brass bands as such, I was intrigued to come across a shop tucked neatly away down a side-alley which proudly bore the sign of Besson's, the brass instrument makers, advertising the Harry Mortimer mouthpiece!

As the Isle of Wight disappeared in the distance I breathed a silent thank you to the directors of Foden's for making the South African trip possible. We had even been provided with a new set of red and gold uniforms for the occasion. As Cheshire's brass band ambassadors, nobody would be able to say we had been less than the best.

The journey was very nearly marred for us before it had properly begun: only two or three days out to sea, the message was telegraphed to the ship that the Crystal Palace had burnt down. It was like losing a home. Could any building, we wondered, ever take the place of that wonderful hot-house? 1923 and Luton's success; 'Severn Suite', 'Downland Suite', 'Prometheus Unbound', 'Comedy Overture' – all these memories came flooding into my mind as I leaned over the rail and watched the wake of our ship stretching out to the horizon. There would never be another Crystal Palace. Would the National itself survive? Melancholy thoughts with which to start a great voyage.

To be honest, I do not think that any future home of the National ever managed to live up to the atmosphere of Upper Norwood. Alexandra Palace was its immediate successor, and that, too, has recently been destroyed by fire. The Albert Hall may be in a more fashionable part of London, but strange though it may seem to a bandsman these days, the Albert Hall is small compared to the Crystal Palace, and the scale of the contest is small to one who remembers those years before it was lost.

Our initial impression of South Africa was a disappointing one. Not the country or the climate, certainly, but the size of the audiences. Even the charismatic Henry Wood had not managed to fill a concert hall there, so we should have been warned. The concerts were very good, and the ardent few who attended were most enthusiastic in their appreciation. It was my first experience of an overseas tour and my first realization that, in any country, the one audience you can always count on would be the Salvation Army members; in later years I found this to be true of Canada, Australia, New Zealand – even Scandinavia. Even at contests, although their own guiding principles make no provision for contesting, they always make up a large proportion of any audience, and this was certainly the case in South Africa.

If the attendances were disappointing, then the venues were quite the reverse. All of us who were there will never forget a bandstand at Johannesburg which was constructed especially for the visit. It was quite the most magnificent location we had ever seen. The bandstand and the audience were separated by a lake some twenty-five yards in width, which had been made as part of the architect's over all design. Sound, especially on the warm evening air, has a magical quality when

98

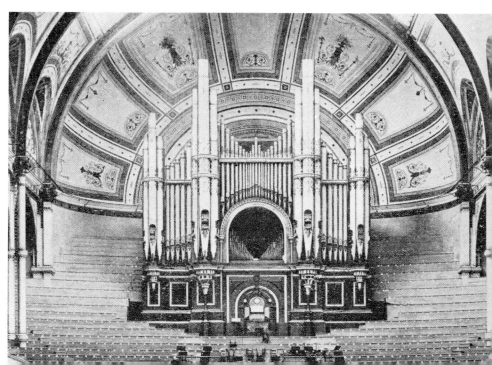

The burning of Crystal Palace marked the end of an era. The National in 1937 and 1938 was held in Alexandra Palace, the auditorium of which is shown right, recently also destroyed by fire.

amplified by water, and it was pure delight to hear the gentle echo floating across to the open-air audience. The only snag was that it was some six thousand feet above sea level which tended to make us, unacclimatized as we were, gulp for breath. Legato numbers like 'Jeannie with the light Brown Hair', with its long phrases, were something of a struggle.

As part of the tour we were invited to inspect a gold mine, something of a novelty to a group of men from Cheshire where salt is the main commodity. For our benefit the authorities engaged the services of a local African band, whose instruments consisted of empty oil-drum casks and other useful items. The tuning of these makeshift instruments was not all it might have been, and the range of notes they could produce was even more limited. Their number one hit at the time was 'I want to be Happy' from *No, No, Nanette*, which went something like this:

I want to be happy, but I can't be happy, till I make you happy too!

The National Anthem was, if anything, slightly less correct:

God save our gracious King, Long live our noble King, God save the King.

Be that as it may, it was all performed with great sincerity and enthusiasm, for which one could forgive anything.

As we stood and listened to the band, and later did a tour of inspection of the mine, I experienced a growing sense of awareness that I was being shadowed. At every turn there was one of these bandsmen who never took his eyes off me. Not so much unnerving as uncanny. I had been brought up on the jingoisms of the Boer War and I had a feeling that something was not right. Towards the end of our visit and after I had been trying to avoid his gaze he asked an African official if he might speak to me. The message was relayed and I agreed willingly, though not without some apprehension. I need not have worried. This gentle soul, who could speak no English, took from the pocket of his tattered shirt an old publicity picture of me extolling the virtues of a particular brand of cornet. I thought that perhaps he wanted me to sign it, but no. Next he produced an ancient brown note which he placed on the picture. It gradually became apparent that he wanted me to take the money back to England and buy him a cornet, or, more accurately, this particular cornet. (The advertising men did not know what they started when they printed those pictures.) The incredible thing was that he had managed to scrape that money together out of his salary of a few shillings a month. Before we left Africa I made several enquiries, but it appeared that I stood more chance of smuggling gold out of that mine than I had of getting a cornet in from England. Even had I sent it I was warned that the chances of it arriving at its destination were remote. The problem was solved eventually through our good friends of the Salvation Army. I spoke to the nearest corps and, as far as I know, they secured him his longed-for cornet. The mild acceptance of fate came naturally to that African. In recent years such subservience has been replaced by bitterness, which is the tragedy of South Africa.

The trip back to England was full of interest. Eating our Christmas turkey in 100^0 may come naturally to an Australian, but it did not seem right to a British brass band, I can assure you, and if it seemed strange to us, what did our fellow voyagers make of it? On board were a Russian ballet company who amused us by their constant practice every day, and an all girl band from the Midlands who travelled under the name of Don Rico's Band. Many a harmonic friendship was struck up on that return trip and we were often short of a player or two when we wanted a practice. Strange that so many of our chaps who showed no previous interest in teaching were to be found below decks, explaining the intricacies of triple-tonguing to eager members of the Don Rico Band.

After a flurry of farewell embraces and promises to keep in touch – promises often sincerely meant, but seldom kept – we all disembarked at Southampton and went on home to Sandbach. Already the thought was uppermost in our minds that the next important engagement, after a brief respite with our various families, was a Royal Command to appear at Windsor Castle where we were to entertain the Royal Household.

Now there was an occasion to remember!

After we had been playing for most of the afternoon, Fred, resplendent in his frock-coat and white gloves, was presented to the Queen and the young Princess Elizabeth. The Princess (now Her Majesty the Queen) asked Fred about the big bass instruments and Fred, ever one to educate a possible future recruit, unselfconsciously guided her through the ranks of amazed bandsmen, explaining each instrument as they came to it. We were all mentally conjuring up a picture of our next engagement which, the way Fred was going, might well be the Tower. But our Fred had a gift for these occasions. The very fact that he was doing exactly what came naturally to him made it all right. Protocol did not matter and everybody was delighted.

If we may jump a year or two, this story has a sequel. I forget the reason, but the King and Queen were to make a Royal visit to Crewe. Perhaps they felt that a town

By Royal Command at Windsor

which owes most of its fame to the fact that everybody, at some time or another, changes trains there, deserved a little more recognition. They were to meet all the local dignitaries on, of all places, the football pitch and the band was engaged to play suitable music. As we were not on the list of hands-to-shake you can imagine our surprise when we saw the Royal party picking its way across the centre spot and bearing down on us. Just as they got within earshot the Queen, now our dear Queen Mother, exclaimed triumphantly to the King, 'There you are dear; I told you. It's that nice Mr Mortimer.'

The notes sparkled from our instruments as never before. Even Fred allowed himself a broad beam of delight.

The Royal Command at Windsor Castle was not the only thing on my mind when I got back to Sandbach after returning from South Africa. Sifting through the backlog of post I was intrigued to come across an invitation to exploratory talks with Sir Richard Fairey, the head of Fairey Aviation. A bandsman lives a sometimes cloistered life, and the name Fairey meant little to me: I vaguely thought that they might have been involved in the manufacture of fairy cycles, and was even more intrigued to see the business card of the man who had written the invitation.

FRANK SMITH
Trumpet and Sax.

Trumpet and Sax? What sort of a brass band man was this? (As it turned out, a very good one. After valuable service to Fairey's he decided to make a fresh start in New Zealand, where he became one of that country's most successful band trainers.) Sir Richard Fairey, I was to learn, had been a famous Flying Corps pilot,

'That nice Mr Mortimer.'

and his engineering works were turning out some of the best light aircraft in the country. A band had been formed a year before which now needed some extra guidance to set it on the right road, and some charitable fellow, presumably Frank Smith, had suggested me. I had been having some modest success with several second section bands and felt ready for a new challenge, so the circumstances were made to measure for all concerned.

The interview went something like this:

'Now Mr Mortimer, we've got a band here. I know nothing about it, but the men tell me you're the chap they want to take the band on. If we can agree terms, would you like to come?'

'Yes, I would.'

'Right. You can start. If you're a success, I hope you will stay with us. If you're not, you'll get the sack.'

'I accept those terms.'

The deal was done with the minimum of fuss. Assuming that he flew aircraft in much the same way, I was left feeling sorry for any enemy who got within his sights. No wonder we won the war in the air. Forty-three years later I am still more or less with the Fairey band, so I am forced to the far from reluctant conclusion that I was a success.

My bow was, by this time, so full of strings that it is a miracle that I was able to twang it with any hope of success at all, but hard work of the right kind rarely did anybody any harm and in the next two decades I was to take even more.

Just for the record, here is a recap of my activities in those mid-thirties.

My first allegiance was still to the Foden Band, as leader, soloist and occasional conductor. Then there was the Hallé – two concerts a week and a new innovation – Monday Morning Municipal concerts organized by the indefatigable Sir Robert Mayer, who celebrated his hundredth birthday while this book was in preparation. These concerts, mainly for the benefit of schoolchildren, attracted vast audiences and provided a unique musical education for schools all around the Manchester area. They also provided a useful piece of education for me: I had become very friendly with a harpist from the Hallé named Charles Collier, who had been with the orchestra for years and knew every piece in the repertoire. He made it his job to tip me off every Monday morning about the following Thursday's concert. Any pieces which he felt I might not know (and they were many), he would give me prior warning so that I had a chance to look them up in the library beforehand. This led to another little extra on my list of activities. Charles and I took to performing recitals together – something of a unique combination, trumpet and harp – but even though the combination worked wonderfully well we never quite reached the stage where we would do a 'spot' in the Hallé concerts.

Charles was an extraordinary-looking man, not unlike Rachmaninov in appearance, with a head far too big for the frail body, but his personality far outweighed any physical shortcomings.

'Good morning, you old sod,' was the greeting reserved for his friends.

(Luckily he was a man almost without enemies, which is just as well for I hate to think what appellation they might have attracted.) Our repertoire was a mixture of songs and suitable classics, like 'How beautiful they are' (*The Fairy Song*), and even included the ultimate test for a trumpeter, 'Killarney'. I refer to it as the ultimate test because it was always Fred's contention that if a brass player could play 'Killarney' and not sound as though he were (a) drunk to the point of sentimentality or (b) busking outside the Odeon, he could consider himself an artist. A bit of a generalization, perhaps, but there is some truth there somewhere.

Next on my list of activities was the popular Celebrity Concert circuit. This would take me, mainly at week-ends, on journeys all over England, Scotland and Wales where I would appear with one other artist and the local municipal orchestra. I suppose there were not all that many of us doing the circuit because you kept coming up against the same fellow artists throughout the season. It was a bit like a band of strolling players who only performed on Sunday nights. I was always pleased to see Isobel Baillie on the same bill. Dear Isobel, I feel sure she won't mind me telling the story of the night we were both met at Cardiff station by the concert secretary who was, by nature, a choir and brass band man. He came straight up to me and shook hands, completely ignoring Isobel. When I could get the odd word in, I politely pointed out that the lady standing with me was Miss Isobel Baillie.

'Oh, I'm sorry,' he said, 'I didn't recognize you. You look so much younger in your photographs.' She took it well, and gave them a splendid concert that night. Afterwards she came to my room. 'Tell me, if you don't think it rude to ask,' she said, 'How much do you get for these concerts?'

I told her. Seven guineas plus the railway fare.

'Do you realise,' she said, 'that most of those people out there tonight came to see you?'

'Oh, do you think so?'

'Certainly,' she said. 'You must come with me to my agents as soon as you are in London next.'

So I did. I was taken to see Emmie Bass at the famous Ibbs and Tillett Concert Agency, and from that day I was never allowed to work for less than a magnificent twenty pounds a concert – *plus* railway fare.

Then, of course, there was Dame Eva Turner, the only lady singer I ever knew who could, without artificial aid, not only make herself heard above the sound of five massed bands, but positively drown them. She was a dear woman, though, and whenever we were playing an open-air concert in Hyde Park would often arrive, pushing her invalid father in his wheelchair.

There were so many others: Robert Easton, Dennis Noble, a splendid, handsome baritone, Gwen Catley, Margaret Eaves, Kathleen Ferrier, Gladys Ripley, Walter Midgeley, Frank Titterton, Norman Allin, Anne Ziegler, Webster

Booth, Heddle Nash (who addressed Sir Malcolm Sargent, 'Look here, Sergeant Malcolm') and many more. It was an incredible musical decade. I had the best of all musical worlds and will never cease to be thankful that I was able to enjoy them all. Not that there was any time left over to be miserable.

All through this changing era the industry which was making the greatest strides was probably the recording business: it may come as something of a nasty shock to younger readers that the stars of the record sales in those days of 'pre-pop' were opera singers (Gigli was undoubtedly one of the recording companies' greatest assets), instrumentalists, dance bands and brass bands. I found myself making records with orchestras and bands as well as the duets with Charles Collier and – possibly the best trumpet player of them all – Jack Mackintosh. 'Mac and Mort' was a tune I wrote for this combination – it seemed a good title at the time.

Let me tell you about Jack. He died recently, but his memory is as fresh as ever. He was the first of the professionals. His first job, like mine, was in a pit orchestra for the silent films; and like me he also went to St Hilda's for a spell as number two for the famous Arthur Laycock. He was a brilliant player with a technique and a tone which defied belief. In the first contest after the war St Hilda's were, against the odds, beaten by the lesser known Harton Colliery who, fired by their success, were on Jack's doorstep the following morning with a lucrative offer. It was an easy decision for Jack to make and, besides, it meant that he could continue his other professional activities at Sunderland Empire. In 1927 he was featured as the soloist in the Festival Concert at the National at the Crystal Palace, and was heard by a representative of EMI who immediately signed him to record twelve solo discs a year. It was during this period that we were paired and made some interesting recordings, most of which have disappeared but two of which, 'Mac and Mort' and Swallow Serenade' have been de-scratched and are on the double album published at the same time as this book.

Fifty years ago, in 1930, Jack was signed as a founder member of the new BBC Symphony Orchestra by Dr (now Sir) Adrian Boult, a position he enjoyed but which tended to restrict his naturally free style. His latter years were spent teaching at Kneller Hall, the Royal Military School of Music near Twickenham rugby football ground.

The public's appetite for records grew daily. Not, perhaps, a good thing when you consider that sheet music sales, conversely, declined. It meant that the musical public were slowly becoming conditioned to listening to others instead of trying it for themselves, which, in the long term, could not enhance the development of music. Dance band records were the biggest sellers: anything that Jack Hylton or Harry Roy cared to commit to wax was eagerly snapped up by a buying public who could not, apparently, keep their feet still. Nevertheless, when a letter arrived from the Jack Hylton office inviting me to join his orchestra, I cannot pretend that I was not tempted. Discussing the situation with Fred, we came to the conclusion that dance bands would not last and that there was little future in joining one. The

106

'Mac and Mort'

sentiment may have been right, but the reasoning was surely unsound. Still, it was quite a compliment to be invited. An ex-contest rival of mine since a boy had given the medium a try with some success. His name was Ted Heath.

Whilst no one would wish to get bogged down in a morass of data concerning which band won what and where, it is an inescapable fact that no book can ever be written about bands without reference to contest results. The contest is the life-blood of banding, and it is impossible to foresee a future without these annual bouts of hostility. True, the result is not the big press story which it was in the thirties, when the *Daily Herald*, that long-dead champion of brass bands, would fill a whole page with pictures of the winners marching in splendour through their home town. Those days are gone, but the contests still hold the same magic and power within the ranks of bandsmen.

The prestige which goes with winning one of the major contests remains undiminished in the eyes of the combatants, and if there is any doubt of that, a visit to Belle Vue or the Albert Hall will convince even the most hardened unbeliever. The atmosphere when the results are being announced (in reverse order), will bear ample testimony to this fact. 'Miss World' was never so agonising.

The contest is the yardstick. Only the best can claim to appear regularly in the winner's list – the elusive hat-trick has been won by very few bands: Fairey's, Foden's, Black Dyke, Brighouse, Besses – it is no accident that these are the best known bands. The contest is the bed-rock of the movement, and the gateway to all the peripheral advantages. If the press no longer sees a result as hot news, it in no way diminishes the pride with which a bandsman will refer to his band as the Champions, and that is very healthy. But is it the right arena for a professional musician? I had my doubts in the late thirties, and even my most trusted friends were uneasy. The question of professionalism is still unresolved, but for me, at the age of thirty-six, it seemed a good time to call a halt. It was at this ripe old age that I decided that I had had enough of *playing* in contests. I was, too, beginning to find that success has its own limitations.

As a matter of fact it proved to be a well-timed decision. It was 1938 at the National, held at the Alexandra Palace: Foden's had just won for the seventh time since 1930 with a record mark – 199 out of 200. Intrigued by this strange score, Fred tackled the judges afterwards at the celebration dinner. How come we had lost one point? It turned out to be my fault – apparently I had missed a semi-quaver in some florid passage and it was gratefully pounced upon as cause to deduct a mark from a score which would have set a difficult precedent. (Just as well I didn't miss a minim – we might have come last!) Sir William Morris of Morris Motor Works chided Fred over the dinner table that the Foden's men obviously spent no time at all in the factory, and every minute in the band-room. Fred, never a respecter of great personages, replied that, 'My lads will take on yours any time, either working or playing, and beat 'em!'

There may have been some justification in William Morris' remarks, though, for Foden's certainly went out of their way to give the band every opportunity to get it right. Even so, a fair day's work was demanded of the men. Mind you, our summer touring was never seriously curtailed by thoughts of factory production, which was not always the case with the Morris men.

A famous Morris band secretary called Tommy Morcombe managed, unwittingly, to put the situation in a nutshell. His band had been offered two weeks engagement at Eastbourne, a prestigious date, and Tommy, bursting at the seams with pride went to the factory manager's office to get formal permission. Permission which he had not dreamed would be denied. The manager, unfortunately, did not share Tommy's enthusiasm, and flatly rejected the idea, reminding the disappointed bandsman that the absence of the band for two whole weeks could have an undesirable effect on production.

The undress rehearsal: the final polish in the Foden works yard before the National in 1938.

'I don't know,' said the despairing Mr Morcombe, 'All you people here think about is making bloody motor cars...'

To Tommy, and many more like him, industry is merely an unfortunate interruption to music, and only exists to provide bands with a rehearsal room and a name.

My decision to stop playing in contests was not because of any of these limitations. I was, after all, independent of the Foden factory, being able to earn a relatively comfortable living in music. Conducting was becoming an increasingly absorbing interest, and I was being offered better and better bands. While I was still playing solo for Foden's I could hardly reappear with a baton in front of a rival band, and 'stick-itch' was beginning to take a tighter grip on my ambitions. I had plenty of playing, after all, in concerts, both with the orchestra and the band, as well as recording, so something had to go. I am afraid it was contest playing.

It turned out to be a good time to make my exit, as this was to be the last National Contest until 1945, although I was not to know that at the time. The war put an end to all that and, in an odd way, drew a line across my career. For contesting purposes I was no longer a Foden's man, although I was to return later as their conductor. If

Hebden Bridge had been my nursery and Luton my apprenticeship, certainly Foden's had been my university, where I had been able to bring to my craft all that Fred, William Halliwell and William Rimmer could pass on to me.

Before we leave the subject of my contest playing career, though, there are two stories concerning Foden's which sum up all the fun of those pre-war years.

One of everybody's favourite venues was Scarborough at Festival time. Scarborough was to the North what Eastbourne was to the South – a sort of thinking man's Blackpool, though I am sure that neither town will relish the comparison. Almost unique among bandstands is the one in Peasholm Park, Scarborough. Not content with being an ordinary bandstand, this one was built on an island in the middle of a lake. To reach it we had to be ferried across in threes and fours, leaving the bandmaster, Fred, to be rowed over in solitary state. It was an idyllic spot, but one which had a major disadvantage – a singular lack of sanitary arrangements. Not a fact which worried us over much, as we all made sure we were good and comfortable before we started playing, but it was a situation fraught with danger, as I was to find to my cost.

Walking along the promenade earlier in the evening I had met, quite by chance, some cronies from the Hallé. The inevitable 'quick one' was suggested, which became a quick two, and then one for the road, by which time I had to make a hasty exit to join my fellow bandsmen. Having allowed myself ample time for the necessities of life, I was duly ferried across the lake.

Our national beverage has some strange characteristics, not the least of which is that, once having found the correct route through the bodily system, it has a preference for several re-runs – each time, apparently, more urgent than the last. By the end of the overture I was feeling distinctly uncomfortable, and by the coda of the second item, my legs were resolutely crossed. The next item was my solo – probably something singularly appropriate, like 'The Trumpet Voluntary'. It was not, however, the 'voluntary' which worried me as much as the *in*voluntary! Apart from an unusually tentative top note at the end I managed to get through, but there was no doubt that the situation could not go any further unresolved. After a cautious bow or two I sauntered as casually as possible to the back of the stand where, once out of view of the audience, I made a headlong dash for the boat, much to the surprise of the dozing ferryman. He soon grasped the urgency of the situation, however, and rowed me back to the shore with all the haste of a paraplegic tortoise, or so it seemed at the time. Mustering all the dignity I could summon up, I disembarked in full view of an audience of two thousand or so and made my heavy way to the changing rooms and blessed relief. Some two or three minutes later, and lighter of step, I sauntered as casually as possible back to the boat. Was it my imagination or did some wag start a ripple of muted applause?

To cover such unforeseen circumstances, Fred had a golden rule which I learned quite early in life: if you must leave the stand, and it happens to us all at some time or another, always reappear clutching a piece of music. You may not fool many of them, but at least some of the audience will think, charitably, that your mission was a missing score.

That was the unintentional farce of the night, which all but overshadowed the real highlight of the concert. It was our practice, on festive occasions, to enter into the spirit of the thing and introduce a little novelty. In Scarborough this took the shape of a large gentleman, immaculately dressed in white tie and tails, introduced as our singer. He would then launch into a horrendous version of 'The Road to Mandalay' or 'Come into the Garden Maud' in a voice which conjured up a picture of a yak suffering from a particularly nasty attack of hernia. After a few bars he would get sharper and sharper until he was singing a good tone higher than the accompaniment, at which point two of us would rise from our seats and, with a well choreographed move, hurl him headlong into the lake!

They don't do concerts like that any more!

Even in those less sophisticated days, though, it was possible to take audience participation a shade too far ... What passed as innocent fun in seaside towns was not always a good idea in Tunbridge Wells, the cucumber sandwich and spa water capital of the South. We, naturally, tailored our programme to the type of audience, but not every band was so considerate.

We had, as regular visitors, come to know the Entertainment Manager quite well, and he would often seek Fred's advice on a new band, just to make sure that it would be suitable entertainment for his customers. One such band was a South American outfit from Birmingham which went under the name of Don Pedro and his Mexican Band. Unfortunately, by the time he asked Fred's advice on the subject, he had already signed the contract and Don Pedro was due to appear the following week. I hasten to point out that this band was in no way connected to Don Rico's band of young ladies whom we encountered on the voyage back from South Africa, although stemming from roughly the same era. We did not want to alarm the Entertainments Manager too much, but we tried to warn him, tactfully, that this Don Pedro would need a firm eye kept on him.

The next time we played Tunbridge Wells he was there to meet us with the story.

'That blasted Don Pedro chap – you know, the one who followed you in last year – well, I don't know. First thing was we had someone here waiting for him with a bill because he still owed for those fancy costumes they wear. We had to pay that off before they could start the week. We shouldn't have bothered. When they got on the bandstand it was worse.

'First number, some chap conducting away right as rain, when all of a sudden Don Pedro comes from the back of the audience, pulls out a gun, shoots the conductor, then takes over himself with some Mexican tune, all whooping and carrying on. My audiences had never seen anything like it! While they're playing, they're chewing tobacco and spitting over the side of the stand – [pretending of course]. I ask you – in Tunbridge Wells!

'Well, we had to pay them off by Wednesday. They'd emptied the place!'

It was obviously a painful memory which would haunt the poor man for the rest of his career. But we had tried to warn him.

With such memories ringing in my years, the Foden's era ended. I can think of no other band at the time which would have given me the opportunities I had enjoyed in those thirteen years. I had been able to straddle the musical fence which divides the orchestras from the bands in a way which was, at the time, unique. I had also been set on course towards conducting some of the finest bands in Britain, and had been privileged to work under Fred at his very peak. In the coming years I was to take yet another of the many side-roads my life has offered me. There was an ominous rumble of war on the winds from Europe, and few of us could know with certainty which way those winds would blow.

Fodens, ever ready to support the band, cast a radiator cap in the form of Fred Mortimer, used on their range of Bandmaster wagons.

4 Why do the Nations...

The BBC had come a long way since Savoy Hill, where I played with Foden's as long ago as 1926. From being a curiosity eagerly received by a few enthusiasts with a scientific bent and a set of cat's whiskers, it had become a national institution, as British as the Changing of the Guard, or roast beef, and more influential than either. The proud banner of the BBC, 'Nation shall speak peace unto Nation', was to be put to a practical test by the end of the thirties. Speaking peace was not to be enough, and broadcasting took on the role of the national conscience and morale booster.

The ten years leading up to the Second World War swept away many of these false premises, although some of the old anomalies still remained, like the announcers wearing impeccable dinner attire to read the news to an unseeing microphone. During the war this practice faded away, although for all broadcasts which the public attended (such as our 'Saturday Bandstand' shows), announcer, producer and artistes were expected to appear in dinner suits – and in the days of clothing coupons, if one did not own such niceties the BBC was prepared to pay a hiring fee to Moss Bros. for the loan of the appropriate suit. Looking back, it had a charming unsophistication about it, as did the majority of broadcasting. Thank goodness the idea of 'giving the public what it wants' – that reprehensible excuse for unimaginative but, above all, cheap programming – had not gained a foothold. A sharp contrast can be drawn between those formal days and recent developments in the presentation of 'Friday Night is Music Night', where the orchestra now sits in full public view dressed in denim or sweaters, shirtsleeves, sandals – a motley collection which would not disgrace the rails of an Oxfam Shop. Strangely, though, the guest brass or military bands are expected to wear full uniform. However, in those days, the BBC was well aware that quality should be high on the list of priorities. If some of the output was comparatively naïve, it was not through lack of imagination on the part of the controllers and planners in their offices along the corridors of Broadcasting House.

It is an interesting comparison that what took the time of one man and two secretaries in 1942 now takes at least six people to do less efficiently – or is that just the jaundiced view of one who has done his stint? I like to think not. Take music, for example; any kind of music. Until my future title of Brass and Military Bands

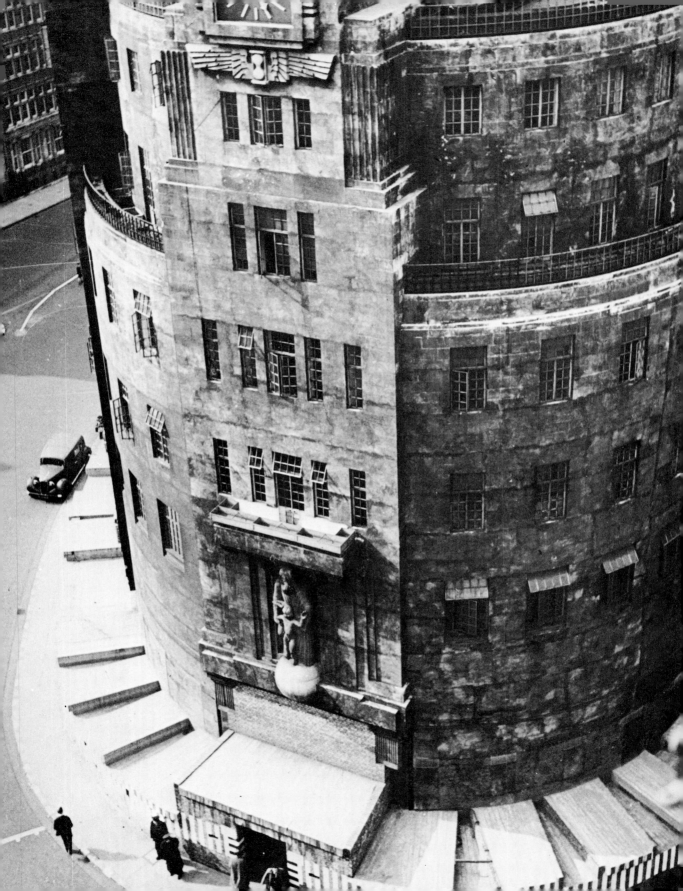

Supervisor was conjured up, all brass and military music output was under the basic care of two men and an overlord. But *what* two men! Arthur Bliss (later Sir) and Dr Denis Wright, worked under that great gentleman Adrian Boult. True, they were aided and abetted by the respective Directors of Music of the various BBC Regions in provincial cities, who out of courtesy were consulted about bands playing in their Regions. But the over-all control was centred in London, and these were not faceless administration men but highly skilled and revered musicians. Music, for them, was not a commodity to be packaged and foisted on a gullible public as a national panacea, or as an alternative to thought or conversation. They were concerned that listeners should have the best. If any prophet could have told them that the radio, or at least the two popular BBC stations, would be used as a shop counter for the record industry or, worse, as a Speakers Corner for politicians, they would probably not have believed him.

If the public is presented with poor quality all the time, it soon begins to accept it as the norm. The public, the great consumer, basically wants what it gets, but that is not necessarily the same as saying that it gets what it deserves. Those three men – Boult, Bliss and Wright – and many others in the Music Department, in Features and Drama, and even in the Gramophone Department, took their jobs very seriously indeed, and a programme was the outcome of a great deal of thought, not a haphazard guess at how to fill up time at the least cost. (In this respect, of course, performers' fees have risen astronomically since those early days, when it was regarded as an honour to broadcast, whatever the fee offered.) Today, virtually all new concepts and interesting ideas are relegated to the minority Radio 3. It is a saddening reflection. Sound broadcasting had a rare quality in those days which we shall probably never hear again – and, what is more, it was fun as well!

Having stuck to my avowed intention of retiring from playing in contests, and concentrating instead on conducting and orchestral playing, it is easy to see that when the BBC offered me not only a post but a whole department, I was more than a little excited and, of course, flattered. I was known to Arthur Bliss and Denis Wright – both of whom had joined the BBC in 1937 – as a young(ish) man who understood bands and band music, who had served more than ten years in the Hallé, and who was enthusiastic about the newer trends in writing (the avant garde of that time) and could present them to a public whose appreciation was growing, due to the thoughtful work which Bliss and Denis Wright, among others, were putting into their broadcasts.

Arthur Bliss is probably a better known name to non-bandsmen. A man of great charm and a composer of imagination, he was later knighted and became Master of the Queen's Musick, an ancient and honourable title. His writing was known not only to listeners at orchestral concerts, but to a vast audience through his film scores (another exciting new medium) and to bandsmen for his test-piece of 1936, 'Kenilworth'. Dr Denis Wright had made his mark in the band world earlier. A Bedfordshire schoolmaster, he gained instant recognition in 1927 when he

My first day at the BBC – I take over from Denis Wright. Opposite: Henry Wood transcribed the timpani part of the 1812 Overture in his own fair hand, to be used at the Jubilee Concert, 1944.

submitted a test-piece called 'The White Rider' for the National Contest – the outcome of a competition sponsored by John Henry Iles through the *British Bandsman*. His next major contribution was the Belle Vue test-piece 'Princess Nada' (1933), and it was not until 1945 that another Denis Wright original score was used as a test-piece at a major contest – the appropriately named 'Overture for an Epic Occasion'. He was also responsible for the first Cornet Concerto ever to be written for that instrument – he very kindly dedicated this to me, and I gave its first performance with the BBC Military Band in Glasgow in 1941. But it was perhaps as an arranger that Denis left his greatest legacy. As William Rimmer in an earlier age was responsible for the vast majority of band arrangements, so, too, was Denis in his era. His output was vast, and few concerts were complete without at least one Denis Wright arrangement. Indeed, the great massed brass concert at the Royal Albert Hall in 1944, to celebrate Henry Wood's Jubilee, was almost entirely his work, including the brilliant arrangement of the overture *1812* which we still use extensively. Denis was tireless and at the same time meticulous in everything he

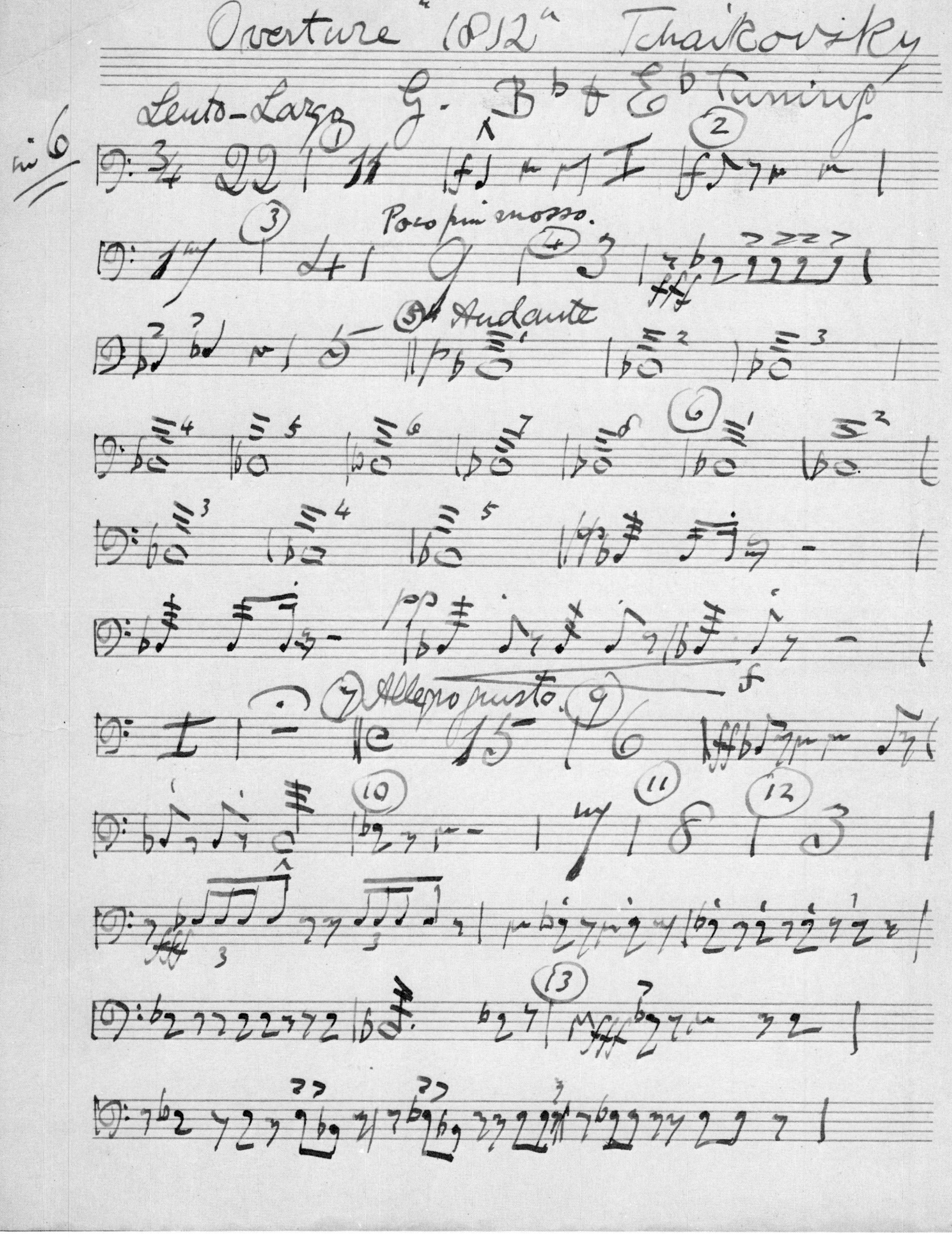
Overture "1812" Tchaikovsky
Lento-Largo
G- B♭ & E♭ Tuning
Poco piu mosso.
Andante
Allegro giusto.

did, and when I joined the Corporation he was given the task of looking after all overseas music, a responsible job in time of war.

My change of occupation, however, was not quite as sudden as I have made it sound. When war was first declared I was still a player with the Hallé and Liverpool Philharmonic orchestras, and of an age to be called up. Many of my contemporaries had forestalled the buff envelope and joined a Guards Band, and I was about to follow in their footsteps. The Scots Guards were at that time conducted by Lieutenant Sam Rhodes, who came from Rochdale and as a young cornet player had his roots in brass bands. They were in need of one or two new members and the appropriate enquiries were made. I duly received my warrant to travel to London in order to sign on the dotted line, but at the eleventh hour one or two of my former colleagues sent me a telegram – brief, but clear – 'For God's sake *don't* join this Army!' As none of us could know just how long the war would last, it seemed only common sense not to involve myself in an open-ended contract with His Majesty's Forces – remember how long Father had been away in the last European tiff. Further, marching had never been one of my stronger points, so I changed my mind and substituted a factory job turning out tanks for the war effort for the prospect of a bearskin. It is surprising that Sam Rhodes ever forgave me for this renegade behaviour, but in later years we were the best of friends and I came to know him well.

The factory at Foden's had changed from making motor lorries to the more important tank production, and for convenience it could hardly be surpassed. There was, of course, still the band, of which I was even then an active member, and it was at home. I was put in charge of Stores and Material Control, which involved co-ordinating all the vast quantities of parts which go into the making of a tank. 'Give us the tools and we will finish the job!' was the battle cry on the industrial front in 1940, and if anything was required urgently, it was my job to seek it out – at least on the Home Front! At the outset I knew nothing about the workings of these monsters, but I quickly learned, and above all I was an energetic and tenacious seeker-out of spare parts often hard to come by. Although I was able to enjoy the responsibility of war work, it still allowed a little time to participate in the CEMA (the highbrow ENSA) concerts which often took place in the evenings, and sometimes even at midnight in the factories, during the meal breaks of the night-shift. Foden's Band was also kept busy in what spare time the players had, so although playing took perhaps a slightly lesser part of my life, I still managed to 'keep my lip in'. And in addition to the civilian bands which I conducted, the Crewe Air Training Corps Band filled in any extra time (as their bandmaster I was given the rank of Pilot Officer).

After two years of this war work I received from the BBC the invitation to discuss the future of brass and military band broadcasts. Denis Wright had been largely responsible for these, along with other music programmes, but the idea was to create a new post of Brass and Military Bands Supervisor, covering the whole of

118

Great Britain and Northern Ireland, and, at a later date, all military bands stationed in BAOR. So I was summoned to the BBC Music Factory – as opposed to the Tank Factory – for exploratory talks (their phrase, not mine). Held before a panel of musicians from all sections, including Light Music, few of whom had much time for bands anyway, this meeting was something of a joke and I took the next train back to Cheshire wondering why I had gone in the first place. Briefly, what we had discussed was that I should be offered the new position as BMBS (Brass and Military Bands Supervisor) at a salary roughly the equivalent of half my current earnings gained from the factory and playing and conducting appointments with the several bands now already under my care – bands which included Foden's, Faireys and Brighouse and Rastrick. Despite the extra glittering carrot of first class rail fares everywhere, I felt I had to decline the offer. Not that my primary concern was financial; the real stumbling block was that in order to take the job I had to be prepared to give up all my connections with bands. Now there's a strange paradox: chosen because I was well acquainted with the subject, I must renounce all the practical first-hand knowledge in order to become an administrator! Rather akin to appointing a minister for Agriculture and Fisheries who was a vegetarian! Not for me!

Before I was recalled for a second interview, a different board this time, Arthur Bliss had told the panel of my experience in the band world, an advocacy I had neither sought nor expected, but a welcome and, indeed, gratifying one. I later learned that in a moment of misguided rhetoric he had compared the original proposal with the idea of appointing Moiseiwitsch to the post of Head of Piano Recitals providing that he gave up playing the piano. I also had the support of Denis Wright, and of his namesake Kenneth Wright (no relation) who was one of the oldest-serving members in the Music Department. Between them, they steered their masters towards a typical British compromise. An elastic agreement was reached whereby I would continue my band interests so long as I was aware that the elastic could, and would, be shortened if it was deemed that I was stretching it too far. Honour was satisfied in all quarters, and it was announced to the press that the new appointment was to be made. The popular papers were delighted at the news. Democracy had come to the BBC!

But first my release from Foden's had to be arranged. Nobody could have said that I was an essential cog in the wheel at the factory (I had been grooming my deputy quietly for a month or two). Nevertheless the Ministry of Labour permits had to go through and this seemed to take an unnecessarily long time. So life went on much as usual, with the Belle Vue September Contest of 1942 almost upon us. I remember the test-piece that year so well: to accommodate bands who perhaps had less time than usual for rehearsal, there was a choice of 'Lorenzo' or 'Pageantry' – both of them favourites of mine and connected with Foden's in my days as leader. But in 1942 it was as conductor of the Fairey Aviation Band that I was competing, and chose the more modern of the two works as I felt that it suited their brilliant style of playing. The contest took place on 5 September 1942 – and Fairey's and 'Pageantry' won the day. On Monday, 7 September, with this latest feather in my cap I set off for London and the BBC, a very different journey south from that undertaken thirty years before from Hebden Bridge to Luton, but an equally important one.

Even in wartime, trains occasionally ran late, and that morning my train was held up. On arrival at Portland Place I was escorted through a maze of corridors (so well-known to all BBC employees), given my BBC badge and identity card (essential, then, to gain admittance to any BBC building) and finally taken to my new office at Number 35, Marylebone High Street. This is now the home of *Radio Times*, but in 1942 it housed all those Music Staff who had not been dispersed at the beginning of the war to Bedford, Bristol or Glasgow. So here was my office – but I use the term loosely, since actually it was a screened-off area with a hat-peg and a desk, at which I sat down to sort out what I was supposed to be doing. The awful conclusion which gradually dawned upon me was that I had very little to do at all. One or two programmes were already planned and merely had to be supervised, but there seemed to be virtually no scope for new programmes. The air-time allotted was, to say the least, limited, and most of what there was had already been earmarked for an anomaly called the BBC Military Band. This was not, in fact, a military band in anything but style. Under the direction of B. ('Bandie') Walton O'Donnell, and later his brother P.S.G. ('Porkie') O'Donnell, it played what we would now call 'symphonic wind band music', and its library of special arrangements was colossal. The players were up to symphony orchestra standard, and included among their ranks such names as Gilbert Vinter (a brilliant bassoon player before taking to the baton and composer's pen), and Philip Catelinet on euphonium. At the beginning of the war this combination had been packed off to Glasgow, where it languished until it was eventually disbanded on the grounds of economy, about eighteen months after my arrival. Although musically it was a pity to see the demise of this great band, its end was inevitable. The standard of the Service Bands had risen dramatically with the influx of many young orchestral players who had rushed to join them at the outbreak of the war. Men like Dennis Brain, Harry Dilley, Geoffrey Gilbert and many more had raised the musical standards in the ranks to a point where the Service Bands could be relied on to present a highly professional performance – we had never before been so spoiled for choice.

Despite all this talent at my disposal, I still had only four or five programmes a week, which left a miserably low number of broadcasts to distribute between brass and military bands. Great things had been expected of me, and this was no way for a new broom to sweep. My life to date had always been a busy one, and I could not see my future sitting at a desk killing time. What we needed was action, and that meant pressing hard for more programme time if I was to keep faith with the bands. Fortunately, there were two arguments in my favour: first that the British

Left: P. S. G. O'Donnell – a great friend and adviser on military music. Right: Gilbert Vinter, player, bandmaster and, most important, composer of brass band music.

public should be encouraged in its daily life by being able to hear stirring music of a military nature, and second that a brass band was a comparatively cheap means of entertainment.

My new secretary shared my concern. Strangely, Margaret had come from the same part of the world which had produced the Mortimers – the West Riding of Yorkshire – and had, unknown to me, been a keen supporter of the Hallé from her mid-teens. Her interest in music had led her to apply for a secretarial post in the BBC, where she hoped that her musical interest and knowledge would be put to good use. She was scaling the promotional ladder when a metaphorical rung slipped and she landed in my department. I was to learn later that the thought of brass bands horrified her, but it was, after all, music of a kind, and maybe a jumping-off place for better things. However, for the moment she set to work with a will and enthusiasm which led me to believe that, like many others, she had come under the spell of brass. Perhaps, on the other hand, it was just natural professionalism. I still am not sure, and she still has not 'jumped off' – we have been happily together now for forty years, during which time she has been secretary, organizer, pillar of strength, constant companion and ideal musician's wife (the last of these being, undoubtedly, one of life's more difficult roles).

So what did we do in our open-plan broom cupboard to improve the lot of the British bands? What every right-minded BBC production office does in similar circumstances. We wrote memos – hundreds of them. To the Programme Controllers, to Arthur Bliss, even to the Director General. All of which were a complete waste of paper, at first. Then Margaret came up with an idea which we thought would be bound to impress even the hardest-hearted demi-gods in Portland Place.

It was an enormous, multicoloured chart, which showed every band of consequence and a bright row of gaudy 'chimney-pots' to correspond with the

121

number of times that each band had broadcast in the last year. Not unnaturally, the BBC Military Band had the tallest chimneys and, going down the scale, some of the lesser bands – and even very famous Salvation Army bands, who also came under my wing – hardly appeared at all. Not that it proved a great deal, but it certainly looked impressive, like a Lego skyline. This was accompanied by a graph which also set out to prove that our plea for more programme time was not an unwarranted one. In desperation I waylaid the always sympathetic Arthur Bliss as he passed my office, and confronted him with the information that I had no work to do, that I was wasting my time, and unless I could have more than the meagre few programmes a week which was my current ration, I would have to resign. So much for all the aspirations and hopes with which I had arrived only a few weeks before! The most reasonable of men, he agreed that I had a valid point and together we made an appointment to see the Programme Controller at the Big House.

Armed only with an iron nerve, a coloured chart and a sure knowledge of the justice of my mission, we entered this gentleman's office and put our case as forcibly as possible. We must have argued quite eloquently because, almost to our surprise, he asked how many slots a week I thought necessary to present a balanced output. When I suggested that ten was the least number, and should probably be more, he merely went a little pale, but promised he would see what could be done. Good as his word, my allocation started to rise. It hardly stopped rising, as a matter of fact. I spent twenty-two years in the job and the average output rose to about sixteen shows a week – the majority of them 'live'. Dare it be said that such a thing would be unthinkable these days – although, in fairness, with the gradual disappearance of so many of our Line Regimental Bands on the grounds of economy, it would not be so easy to fill these slots in such quantity.

Not a bully by nature, though some of my former bandsmen might dispute the point, I became the *enfant terrible* of the department, and for years defended with tooth and claw any threat of incursion on what became my territory. It became an unwritten rule that if a programme was to be taken out of the schedules for any reason, it would be better to poach some other producer's river. On one occasion the Sports Department wanted to run live commentary on one of the top sports events of the week during a Saturday lunchtime. Somebody actually considered sports commentaries more important than 'Listen to the Band!', the star spot of the band week. They were soon disabused of this heresy – although I must add that nowadays, forty years later, I am a dedicated watcher of most TV sport.

The immediate task was to fill the newly won time. The top Service Bands, of course, were fairly readily available, and I was helped enormously throughout my sojourn in the BBC by the friendship of so many Military Directors of Music. When I started my job, many friends in the Army, Marines and Air Force whom I had met regularly on seaside peacetime bandstands had graduated from the Line Regiments to the Brigade of Guards and Staff Bands. Conductors such as Owen Geary, who had been Bandmaster of the Border Regiment, and was installed at

Woolwich with the Royal Artillery; Sam Rhodes with the Scots, Fred Harris with the Grenadiers, Tommy Chandler with the Welsh, 'Jay' Windram with the Coldstream, and George Willcocks with the Irish Guards. F. J. Ricketts ('Kenneth Alford' of Colonel Bogey fame) was still in charge of the Royal Marines at Plymouth, where we had often met when Foden's played on the Hoe in happier days. The third of the O'Donnell brothers – R.P. – was Director of Music of the Royal Air Force, and it was he, I think, who started the habit of addressing me as H.M. He would send in a list of programme items, attached to a letter which started 'Dear H.M.' and ended 'Yours ever – R.P.' All these, and many more, were characters in their own right, and as such were valued friends on whom I came to rely for programmes required at short notice. They were the backbone of our broadcast output from London, and in spite of an initial feeling in some quarters that a brass band man should not have been put in charge of military band output, they always respected my musical judgment and soon realized that we were all in the broadcasting business for the benefit of band music in general.

The top-grade brass bands were also well known to me. Bands had always been auditioned and graded and now we set about the job with a new purpose. There were four grades of band as far as broadcasting went: A, B, C and Z – the last of these being the fate of any band not up to the other three. Grade A bands naturally got a good proportion of the work, with Grade B its own regular share. Grade C might, at a push, be invited to perform an item or two, with careful choice of programme. But Grade Z were invited to try again in a year's time. To a proud local committee the label of Z (actually a mythical grade, as nobody was really labelled so unkindly) was an anathema and something to be avoided at all costs. Sometimes the methods used to avoid this shame were little short of sharp practice, and at other times naïvely unsophisticated.

On a tour of Welsh bands, for example. Mansel Thomas and I set off, one dark night, on a round trip through the Valleys. He was the Director of Music for Welsh Radio and it was our task to find the best representatives for his region. At our first port of call, we were courteously greeted and sat down to listen. Definitely grade Z, with the exception of corner men or section leaders. Over a thick cup of tea the bad news was broken as gently as possible, and we were on our way to the next bandroom. This one was of similar standard to the last, including the corner men, who bore an uncanny resemblance to the previous ones. Another cup of strong tea and another encouraging word to the bandmaster, and on again to the third audition, where the band were in the C grade with the corner men once more doing a grand job and, surprise, looking exactly like the same ones again. Yet another cup of tea from yet another cracked cup, but this time accompanied by better news. Having made good time, we thought we would wait awhile and watch the band pack up. It was immediately noticeable that the corner men were in a greater hurry than their colleagues so, with all the charm I could muster, I called them over.

'If, like us, you're thinking of going on to our next band at Ystalyfera, perhaps we can offer you a lift. You must be tired out after all this rushing about.'

Other bands may have tried the same ploy, but not with me.

On another of these auditions, this time in Scotland, the City of Edinburgh Band were on my list to be heard, and although the band itself was not of a very high standard it was clear that they had an outstanding conductor – a small man of flair, who also played the cornet very well, but a stranger to me. Appreciating his talent, I enquired what he was doing conducting a band of this calibre, to which he replied in a broad Scottish accent, 'Can you find me a better job?' I was able to tell him that I could, and forthwith recommended him to the Cory Band in South Wales. This man, in fact, was Walter Hargreaves, christened by my father 'Taffy McTavish' after his sojourn in Wales, who proceeded to make a name for himself there, and later as Cornet Professor at the Royal Marines School of Music at Deal.

Another of the first auditions I undertook in 1942 at the beginning of my days at the BBC was in Bournemouth, where the Royal Canadian Air Force Band was stationed. Under the direction of Martin Boundy – originally a euphonium player and organist, with roots in the north-east of England – this was a fine band which made many friends in England during its years in Europe. A large proportion of the brass players were drawn from the Salvation Army, whose bands flourish in Canada. In the reverse direction, many of our younger brass players from Britain emigrated after the war to play with some of these Canadian Service and Salvation Army bands, and thus add to the rather few band fanatics in that country. One such band buff was a young bomber pilot called Murray Peden, a brave and much decorated RCAF airman who spent part of his service career in Britain. In his brilliantly written book *A Thousand Shall Fall* he tells of the thrill of wandering to the Hyde Park bandstand one free day, and actually hearing Foden's band – until then a legend to him – playing there. Towards the end of his book, on packing his bag to return to Canada, he mentions that among his luggage was a much-prized record of Foden's which he had managed to acquire while here. Murray is *still* mad about British bands, and though now an eminent QC, is still an avid collector of tapes and records of our bands. He is only one of thousands of such enthusiasts scattered around the world – and, to me, a very special one.

Wartime broadcasting had all its own unique problems. The main studios then, as now, were at Maida Vale, occupying an enormous area in the midst of grand red-brick Victorian terraces. Of relatively functional design, having originally been conceived as a skating rink, the studios themselves are all underground and are reached by long, bleak corridors lined with giant air ducts. Ideal, you might think, in an air raid. But not so. Although the studios are below ground, there is little between them and the sky except a corrugated roof which would have trouble keeping out a hail storm. There was no chance of protection against a German bomb. If you were unfortunate enough to be broadcasting during an air raid, you had to be prepared to abandon instruments and run for it like the rest of London. All eyes, even the seasoned campaigners', were on a mesmerizing set of lights on

Murray Peden has been a lifelong ambassador for brass bands and their music in Canada. Here I try his hat on a visit he made to England.

the wall of every studio. If the blue came on, get nervous; if the red followed, run like hell. It hardly made for relaxed playing, as may be easily imagined. Although some of the steelier ones refused to be panicked, most of us never really became too sanguine about our prospects for survival.

Certainly Foden's band never took the bombs lightly. They, and I, had been on the receiving end of a nasty experience in the summer of 1944. After the first fears about daylight raids had subsided – a period during which all park entertainment had been stopped – the authorities decided that it was safe enough to re-open the Hyde Park bandstand, and Foden's were invited to perform there for a week. Having been through a few unpleasant experiences, I warned them that it would not be much fun, Hyde Park being right in the middle of the battle area. At that time there were anti-aircraft guns actually positioned in the Park. Dismissing my fears as being fussy, the band voted to go. Let me tell you about Hyde Park Bandstand. In the middle of fashionable London it may have been; a prestige engagement it may have been (it was the biggest of the Royal Parks in London); salubrious it was not. The amenities at the bandstand were far from luxurious. An area *under the stage* was all that was provided for the band, both for changing and all the other offices to which flesh is heir. Bent almost double under the low roof, one was able to perceive by the light of the single electric bulb a row of nails on the wall for coats, and a clanking bucket in the corner for all other purposes. It was no place for the squeamish in hot weather; and when Foden's started their engagement it was hot.

The one that got away – Hyde Park bandstand, uncomfortable, insanitary, but much loved.

Stretched out on the grass soaking up the sun, the fearless men of Foden's were positively crowing.

'Where's all the bombs, then?', 'Don't know what all the fuss is about,' etc ...

That night all hell broke loose. It was not easy to say whether there was more danger from Hitler or from our own defence batteries, firing almost across the chimneypots in an attempt to bring down the fearsome doodle-bugs. If they were lucky enough to hit one, further explosion and devastation followed as the thing disintegrated. The noise was indescribable, and the worst I had encountered. Father, that seasoned old trouper, had decided to stay for the week with an old Italian friend, Oscar Grasso, who kept a small hotel in Hammersmith. He remained stoicly in his room throughout the barrage, until all the windows suddenly shattered and his bedroom door landed on top of his bed. First thing next morning at least three of the men remembered pressing engagements at home, or thought their place was with their families, and hastily packed their bags. Nor did it boost their morale much when they saw that they had been in shelter number thirteen all night, that being the only one empty when they ran for cover. I was able to replace them at such short notice with some bandsmen I knew serving with the RAF Bomber Command Band, stationed conveniently at High Wycombe, through the good offices of their conductor, George Malcolm (now a world famous harpsichordist), who very kindly arranged their duties to fit in with ours – and so we continued the week's engagement.

Next day the raids started earlier – a grim warning. By the third day the Germans were into a phase of daylight raids and look-out men were posted all round the bandstand perimeter. I would like to state, here and now, that it is not easy to conduct or play beautiful music with one ear cocked for the sound of a doodle-bug engine, one hand searching for the strap of your gas mask, placed conveniently on the floor, and one eye wandering aloft if the said flying-bomb engine were to cut out – the signal that it was about to descend, one knew not where. And it is even harder to conduct whilst gradually beginning to cower under a music stand. Not easy at all.

Despite our fears we finished the week intact, and the Hyde Park bandstand still occupies the same place and is still unharmed. It has probably suffered more from recent vandalism than it ever did during the war, which according to many a hardened campaigner and connoisseur of bandstands is a pity. It may have better hygiene facilities or, perhaps, only a newer bucket nowadays, but the Luftwaffe missed a golden opportunity when they spared it. Just one little bomb would have done it – when it was unoccupied, of course, and minus the audience which still congregated in the deck chairs surrounding it, in spite of the hazards of war. I am sure some of them used the deck chairs for a blissful snooze – perhaps after having been on duty somewhere all night – but we always played to a certain number of people who continued to turn up daily, maybe feeling safer in the open air.

Back at the studios there was another peril, more insidious than the bombs, for which at least there was a warning.

The new menace was a chap who called himself Lord Haw-Haw. A nasty piece of work, he had the unfortunate knack of broadcasting from Germany on BBC wavelengths, interrupting broadcasts with his propaganda messages, and while he was on duty there could be no relaxation. Any pause in the proceedings and he was in, telling British listeners what fools they were and what a nice fellow this Mr Hitler was, and not to believe all they read in the papers. All our battleships had been sunk, convoys destroyed, and the British people were being led to destruction. And worse, Mr Churchill's cigars were paid for with money which should have been buying milk for babies! To counteract this, we were given strict instructions to leave no gaps in programmes. As soon as the music stopped, the announcer had to jump straight in with his next introduction. Likewise, as soon as the piece was announced, the band had to be ready to play the first bar at once. No room for subtle pauses. Any more than two seconds and His Lordship was off on his maniacal banter which, though risible, did not make for enjoyment of programmes. The BBC, after all, was noted for truth. Listeners found it upsetting to hear treason and heresy coming from their wireless sets. This rapid-fire announce, play, announce, play, announce, play had devastating effects on some otherwise cool-as-a-cucumber BBC announcers. I remember the poor chap who, in his haste, announced the same piece twice. The first time the band were ready and played. The second time was met with a stunned silence, followed by a loudly-whispered, 'We've just done that one,' followed in turn by the sound of rustling papers and another announcement. Luckily Lord Haw-Haw was off duty at the time.

As just about all programmes were live in those days – prerecording was a long way off as a general practice – such hair-raising moments were not infrequent. This electric atmosphere, though not without its frustrations, added a tremendous excitement and spontaneity to broadcasting. We could never be sure what would happen next. Perhaps for this reason even our so-called leisure time was spent in the company of fellow-broadcasters and producers, many of whom camped-out in their offices when air raids made it difficult or impossible to get to their suburban homes. We were also scheduled for fire-watching, or Home Guard duty on a regular basis (Denis Wright even started a BBC Home Guard Band, composed of enthusiastic, but not very proficient, members of staff!). The BBC canteen, The Stag and The Gluepot (otherwise known as The George), and the conveniently situated Marie Lloyd Club, which opened its doors when the pubs closed theirs, were always full of musicians, poets, actors and eminent producers and writers, taking time off from programmes which often went out in the middle of the night. I wonder how many still remember a journalist on the *Daily Express* known as George Stagge. Being a musician he was able to mix freely with BBC staff in both The George and The Stag – hence the pseudonym George Stagge. Without our realizing it, he was thus able to gain intimate knowledge of the workings of the BBC for his column. We often wondered how such information managed to be so accurate, until it eventually dawned upon us that George Stagge was, in fact, the well known jazz musician and broadcaster Spike Hughes, one of our drinking companions! Wordsmiths such as Dylan Thomas, Louis McNeice and A. G. Street were then on the BBC payroll. Producer Francis (Jack) Dillon; composer Constant Lambert – whose early 'Rio Grande' I had played in the Hallé – and the young Elizabeth Lutyens (then, as now, something of an avant garde musician) were among a host of similar celebrated people in the artistic world who congregated to chat – over a pint, of course – in those heady days.

Never quite sure which Service Band would be available – the War Office naturally did not consult me before a unit was packed off abroad – we came to rely heavily on the excellent Guards Bands stationed in London. There was usually one or the other available, until one sunny Sunday morning in the summer of 1944 when a flying-bomb cruelly fell directly on the Guards Chapel at Wellington

Barracks. The Chapel was packed with Army personnel, including the Coldstream Guards Band. It was a regular duty for one of the five Brigade of Guards Bands to play for morning service on a Sunday, and as a limited number of the general public was also allowed to attend, I occasionally went down there on a Sunday to listen to the hymns, so beautifully played in that most impressive setting. Mercifully that Sunday morning I was elsewhere. The Scots Guards Band, assembled on the Parade Ground outside the Chapel, took the blast of the bomb and some were slightly injured. The Chapel itself was devastated. Our dear old friend, Major 'Jay' Causley Windram, and several bandsmen were killed instantly. Casualty figures for this catastrophe were never released, but so far as we were concerned it was a great tragedy to lose one of our most-used military bands. Happily the Coldstream soon re-formed, this time under the conductorship of another Director of Music who thus became a life-long friend and brass band enthusiast, now Lieutenant Colonel Douglas Pope.

Among all these tragic and sometimes comic happenings our regular programmes took the air, always on time and only rarely with any kind of hitch. 'Music While You Work' was broadcast three times a day to most factories in the country, and we supplied band programmes each week for three of these sessions. This, at the time, not only filled a much-needed gap in what was often a very boring factory day- or night-shift, but it was also a marvellous morale booster. Twenty-nine and a half minutes' continuous music was a hard blow, even though some of the music included had of necessity to be of an extremely light nature, the workers being encouraged to sing to all the tunes which they knew. Whether it was good for the national effort or not, it certainly built up a link between shop floor workers all over the country, and if by any chance that factory also had a band of its own, so much the better.

There were many times when we found ourselves making programmes in the middle of the night, both for overseas consumption and for night-shift workers, and these sometimes presented us with a new problem. It was not enough to be forever on the alert for air raids or for Lord Haw-Haw's interruptions; burning he midnight oil as well was to invite mistakes. I offer as an excuse that I was tired and – as I was often conducting, playing and announcing, as well as planning programmes – over-worked, when the following incident happened. Travelling from the North with my old friend Wilfred Pickles late one night on our way to Nottingham for a night broadcast, we got to sharing an unaccustomed luxury – a bottle of Scotch. It was a cold 'neet' and, as usual, there was no heating in the train and not very much light, either, in those blacked-out days, so the bottle came as a welcome source of comfort. I am not saying that we overdid it – I am sure we did not – but I regret to report that it was on that broadcast that I boldly announced to the night-shifts from Lands End to John o'Groats, 'And now for one of Bitten's Brest Brass Bands – the Ransome and Worles Marks Band!'

Having been working extremely hard for so long, I was delighted to be invited to take the Fairey Band one weekend to a far-off haven in the north of Scotland called Machrahanish, a Fleet Air Arm Station way up past the Kyles of Bute. It was here that injured or fatigued pilots and air crews were sent for recuperation, and it was a heavenly place, especially after being in London. The unpolluted silver sands stretched, apparently, for miles, fading into the blue hills in the distance. What a wonderful change it must have been from peering down a gun-sight or wrestling with reluctant aircraft. It should be pointed out that Fairey's were asked to go on this trip, which was something of a perk, because not only were they concerned with the aircraft industry, as manufacturers of sea-planes, but they were also among the most successful bands in the country. To be fair, the players were at an advantage in that they were in a reserved occupation, the aeroplane manufacturing industry, and so were able to stay together. Although the National Band Festival had come to a temporary halt (its natural home, the Crystal Palace, having been burnt down and its second venue, the Alexandra Palace, being in BBC occupation), the British Open Championship at Belle Vue was still an annual event, and Fairey's won this no less than seven times between 1941 and 1950. ENSA, the troops' entertainment organization, were quick to see that the men of Fairey's could perform other tasks equally as important to the war effort as plane making, and used us whenever possible. Machrahanish was the first of many ENSA engagements.

The journey seemed interminable. Train to Glasgow, then a coach, and finally a ferry. No wonder the airmen needed a rest; we were exhausted just getting there. And besides, I had done a rather foolish thing on the train. To while away the hours on the journey north we played cards. I was never, even at school, the world's greatest athlete, but I never thought that even I could sustain an injury playing cards. Railway rolling stock in those days was not up to inter-city standards, in fact it was decidedly tatty. At least this one was. I was standing up while the train entered a station, about to play an ace when, without warning, there was an almighty lurch. Sailing gracelessly backwards, my coccyx (or tail, if you prefer) connected sickeningly with an un-upholstered arm-rest. It was the sort of accident which looks hilarious to the spectator, but which leaves the recipient helpless with pain and loss of dignity. As the journey progressed the initial sharp agony gave way to a nagging, numbing pain, and all I longed for was to arrive at our destination. Eventually we were at Machrahanish, where the first ritual to be observed was the daily rum ration. There was no mistaking the genuine warmth of our welcome which was cemented with an extra ration, presumably to make up for the long journey. Any sailor who has seen more than fifteen years' service will tell you that there is nothing with which to compare the genuine navy rum. Its original purpose was as a cheap form of central heating, but to a civilian not used to such delicacies it is a lethal dose. It even, temporarily, made me forget the pain in my rear.

Unfortunately man cannot live by rum alone and next day the pain grew worse, which was a great pity because it was spoiling what was obviously going to be a

130

marvellous week for the band. After two more days, during which I grew more and more uncomfortable, I had to give up the unequal struggle and was flown from Machrahanish to Speke Hospital where I suffered the further indignity of having to lie face downwards, my trousers hanging neatly on the end of the bed, while teams of doctors and nurses paraded round me occasionally prodding and poking, and asking damn silly questions like, 'Does that hurt?' after a particularly vicious jab from something which felt like a cold jemmy. They never did make up their minds what was wrong but, to be safe, issued me with a salmon pink rubber cushion with a hole in the middle, rather like an inflatable giant polo mint, which I was instructed to take with me everywhere until the pain wore off, which, of course, after a week or two it did.

The war ground on and on. The first war had taught the older members of the community not to be over-optimistic about the chances of an early settlement. One by one the provincial cities took their grim turn to be devastated: Manchester, Liverpool, Bristol, Coventry and, of course, London a perpetual target. In all these cities the BBC had studios, all of which bore the burden of informing and encouraging the beleaguered population. Although my particular responsibility was brass and military music (more military than brass for much of the time), I, like my colleagues in all the other departments, came to admire the efforts of the Light Entertainment offices.

Comedy always appears to thrive under the worst conditions, and out of the nightmare of bombing and homelessness grew those wonderful programmes like Tommy Handley's 'ITMA' – a format which was to set the pattern and the standard of comedy for many years to come. Who is to say whether radio and, later, television comedy would have developed the way in which it did, had it not been for the rapid-fire lunacy of Handley or the charming absurdity of Jack Train? Like the sport of boxing, comedy thrives best on hard times. It is one of the better qualities of our race that we can usually laugh in the face of adversity, and the BBC were quick to exploit this trait to their everlasting credit. It seems extraordinary now to think that radio comedy, in a time of enormous hardship, could unite the country in an ability to laugh at such unlaughable things as ration books and income tax, but this is what they did.

Every single department added something to the war effort. If the news bulletin was depressing, follow it with a laugh. Follow the laugh with some stirring band music and you had a population which fully believed that its country could pull through anything. And, of course, they were right. Not for British and Commonwealth audiences the persistent tub-thumping of military and political leaders – the BBC had its own unique style. It sometimes seemed incredible that a programme ever took to the air at all, and many times it must have been touch and go, and I daresay that some of the output would, by today's standards, seem amateur and even naïve. The point is that a service was provided day after day, night after night, and always an underlying integrity and an awareness of the importance of truth was at the very heart of every broadcast. They were difficult days, but they were days to look back on with great pride. To have been a part of them was to be a witness to the birth of broadcasting standards. That radio was to become the impoverished relation of television and would find itself scavenging for crumbs left over from its master's table is a saddening reflection, and an injustice. No mass entertainment medium ever exercised the minds of its followers as did radio.

Apart from sending me, with the Fairey Band, to such exotic places as Machrahanish, the troops entertainment office known as ENSA also sent Foden's over to Europe towards the end of the war, when movement became possible. I was still a playing member of that illustrious band for many years to come, and the BBC were generous in allowing me time to join my former colleagues. Arrangements tended to be a little haphazard on these tours and there was more than one occasion when we arrived at a unit, only to find that they were expecting somebody else. The most memorable of these was our arrival at a unit who had prepared themselves eagerly for a recital by Isobel Baillie (dear Bella, our paths never ceased to cross and re-cross). Isobel was, at the same time, at the camp which was expecting Foden's. On comparing notes afterwards it appeared that both of our concerts had gone well, despite the inauspicious start. But, then, they would, wouldn't they? Both Foden's and Bella could be relied on to give only of their best, and the entertainment-hungry troops knew their good fortune. What only the keenest brass bandsman among those troops might have noticed, though, was that Foden's had one rather unusual member of the band.

In the early thirties, Frank Wright, the champion cornet player of Australasia – a distinction of which he was justly proud – came to England and very quickly became a prominent figure in our brass band circles. Like his unrelated namesake, Denis Wright, he is best remembered for his arrangements – he arranged the National test-piece no less than ten times between 1952 and 1971, and his arrangement of Berlioz' 'Le Carnival Romain' was used at the British Open Championship as recently as 1979. 'The Rainbow' was probably his greatest achievement, but that was yet to come. When Frank heard that Foden's were to go overseas on an ENSA tour he begged to go with us to sit in on second cornet. How could we refuse? There is still the programme which bears testimony to his presence.

Over the next twenty-five years or so, Frank and I were to meet and work together many a time. Firstly when I was involved in broadcasting his music, and later in his capacity as Director of Parks Music to the (then) London County Council, a post at which he excelled. The London parks are all the richer for Frank's years in command, and the excellent Kenwood House bandstand stands as a lasting tribute to him. A similar testament is the bandstand in Embankment Gardens, where music from Mozart to Lennon and McCartney competes with the incessant rumble of the overhead trains and the intermittent announcements from

132

Frank Wright, a many-talented Australian.

Charing Cross Station informing commuters that 'the train standing on platform five is for ...'.

Another important area where the lives of Frank Wright and Harry Mortimer crossed was the Annual Boys' Brigade Festivals in London. For various reasons – mainly financial – Boys' Brigade Bands are not as popular as they once were. Perhaps a uniform (any uniform) does not have the appeal it used to have, but, whatever the reason, there is less willingness to join such junior para-military organizations these days. In 1883, when the Boys' Brigade was founded by a military man named Alexander Smith, there was a need for such a thing and, like Baden-Powell's Scouts later on, boys were eager to join. The lack of other, more easily attained diversions obviously had a great influence on their choice. Bands very quickly became a part of the Boys' Brigade tradition, though the first one was made up entirely of flutes – sixteen of them. Brass was to come later. Although there are still some Boys' Brigade flute bands in existence, it is the more strident tone of the bugle and the beat of the side drum which most of us think of as the hallmark of the Boys' Brigade – almost as inseparable from the image as the black and white pill-box hat.

Two World Wars did wonders for recruitment. Every boy wanted to be in a uniform, and most of them wanted to be in a band. By 1948 there were enough bands of a high standard in London alone to merit a great festival which was to be held at Central Hall, Westminster. Frank Wright and I were honoured to be asked to direct the event, which was to become an annual one, later moving to the Albert Hall. It is an occasion to which I have returned many times to conduct the massed bands and – until 1970, when he died – Frank was always there as well.

Youth banding is a thing with which I have always been proud to be connected – perhaps a hangover from the early Luton days – but more and more it is an uphill struggle to keep an independent band going. Until recently it was only the education authorities and the Salvation Army who could meet the escalating costs of instruments and equipment. Consider that the Boys' Brigade of Aberdeen, in 1892, collected the sum of twelve pounds which enabled them to buy a set of instruments. Perhaps not the best instruments, but adequate to form the band. Four years later it cost £38 to replace the bugles which had been lost in a fire (the sum took another four years to collect). At the time of writing it would cost £20,000 to equip a brass band. Not surprising, therefore, that young bands find it hard to continue without some form of sponsorship.

Before we leave the subject of Boys' Brigade it would be appropriate to pay a small tribute to the late George Scarfe. Whilst Frank and I caught all the publicity at the Annual Festival, it should be said that George, the most loyal and industrious servant any organization could wish to have, gave his time and talent all year round. His own band at Enfield was consistently at the top of the Boys' Brigade charts, but he never tired of going to brigades all round the area to help and guide. His wise counsel was ceaselessly sought and never withheld.

By the Spring of 1944 Sir Henry Wood was celebrating his Golden Jubilee year and as a tribute to the fine wartime work done by brass and military bands, he invited me to organize a massed band concert at the Albert Hall. Sir Henry had always been a champion of brass players and had featured a cornet player in his very first Prom. in 1895, and had regularly included brass quartets and soloists ever since. Jack Mackintosh was just one of the many who had been honoured in this way. Like many other famous conductors since, the challenge of conducting a massed band concert was one he could not refuse.

We tried to make the bands, as far as possible, representative of all the regions and so Black Dyke, City of Coventry, Luton, Enfield and, of course, Foden's and Fairey's, were invited to add their individual talents to the grand occasion. It has not, I hope, gone unnoticed by the astute reader that all of these bands represented aspects of my past career. All of them? Enfield? Apart from being a very good band at the time, Enfield had another special qualification. For such an important occasion I had to have bands and conductors whom I knew would prepare for the big night in a sympathetic way. It would be no good having six different interpretations turning up on the day, all struggling for supremacy. I had to know that I could rely on them to bring a concerted effort to the Albert Hall. The conductor at Enfield was none other than Ted Carter, my contemporary from Luton – the same Ted Carter who threw his flugel horn under a passing train. Fred was responsible for Foden's, of course, and I had more than a passing interest in the others.

As I was still officially a playing member of the Foden Band I was appointed leader for the day. Most of the men had no experience of working with any of the sometimes temperamental Knights of the Baton, so I went to great lengths to impress upon them the need for utmost concentration and discipline. Sir Henry Wood was not a man to take lightly.

The first rehearsal of the day was taken by the gentle Sir Adrian Boult, who went through the programme in his own unhurried and quiet way, so that any qualms the men might have felt were soon dissipated by the easy charm of his authority. Indeed, one or two voiced the opinion that I must have been trying to scare them, when Sir Henry, appearing from his seat in the darkness of the Albert Hall, mounted the rostrum. Suddenly the air was charged with a new pulse. A hush descended. Sir Henry fixed us with an appraising look. In a slow, deliberate move he raised his baton and appeared to grow with it in stature. One crisp command:

Sir Henry Wood, the artist.

'Every eye!', and down came the baton on the first note of the introduction to Act 3 of *Lohengrin*. In the sound of that chord every man knew, as never before, why he was a bandsman. We were all a part of a total living being – each a single atom. Fuse the atoms and you have a mountain, a cathedral or any other thing of rare beauty. It was a sound never forgotten by we privileged few. The concert that night was the success we all knew it would be.

The bulk of the arrangements were by my BBC colleague, Denis Wright, whose influence was so vital in my employment by the Corporation in the first place. It was appropriate that he should have had such an important role in this, till then the highlight of my broadcasting career.

Another happy coincidence was the inclusion of Sir Hamilton Harty's arrangement of Handel's *Water Music*. He, of course, was the first of the great orchestral conductors I had managed to involve in brass band music back in the *Severn Suite* days of 1930.

Reginald Pond's excellent biography of Sir Henry Wood quotes a letter to Sir Henry from one John K. Young, a regular correspondent from Scotland who was listening to the broadcast that night.

He wrote, 'Brass bands are not a form of music that appeals to me as a rule, but yesterday's performance was magnificent. The smoothness of tone and absolute unanimity you got were very remarkable.'

Thank you, sir.

Sir Henry Wood, sadly, died a few months after the concert, which was to be one of his last public appearances. It is with supreme gratitude that the brass band world should remember what he did for us that day. My own career, certainly, took on a new meaning from then onwards. The success of that venture led me to plan and to agitate for massed bands at every conceivable occasion and we were to have many more such satisfying experiences. What I had always felt had been proved to be true, that however good an individual band it could never hope to reach the heights of three or four all playing together. The idea was beginning to formulate in my mind that there was a scope and a public for a permanent massed band who would give concerts, broadcasts and, even in those days of 78 rpm, make records. What else should they be called but 'Men o' Brass'? Filing the idea away under 'Things to be done when peace breaks out', I returned to the routine, if that is the right word, of filling several hours a week with broadcast music.

5 The people who walked in darkness

Suddenly it was all over. The crowds were gathering outside Buckingham Palace to sing, cheer and dance for the news of the signing of the peace in Europe.

And where was I? Somewhere near Brussels! The BBC had granted me leave to go to Europe with Foden's band, on the condition that I should return immediately if peace looked imminent, and providing me with papers which would speed me on my way in such a crisis. It is worth noting that the band were afforded officers' privileges in all but rank. This meant that we had a comparatively generous ration of drinks, cigarettes and chocolate – but no money. Luckily the good people of Brussels had money but no luxuries, so a roaring, but illegal, trade went on organized mainly by the hotel waiters. They would arrange for our wares to be displayed, and the local dealers (including boys of no more than ten years old) would take what they wanted in exchange for hard currency. Strangely, the only commodity nobody bought was one of those typically spartan wartime products known as National Chocolate, which many will remember from its pale blue wrapper. This was frowned on by those citizens of Europe whose palates were not impaired by four and a half years of deprivation. However, I shall draw a veil over that subject in case some over-zealous Military Policeman should see fit to prosecute us for misappropriation of government property even now, thirty-five years later.

My chief concern on VE day was to get back home and to my office, where I was expected to be at the helm of some of the musical aspects of the celebrations. Armed with my papers from the BBC I contacted the Colonel in charge of such matters. Not easy to do, as it turned out, because he was in the middle of a round of golf with the prettiest caddy(ess) you could ever wish to see, and was not in the slightest bit interested in my problems. He had a point, mind you, she had a wonderful putting action!

Foolishly I tried to insist he helped me back to Blighty, for which I escaped being put on a charge only by a hair's breadth. As luck would have it, though, I was pointed in the direction of Air Transport Command stationed near Brussels, where a corporal and I immediately recognized each other as brass bandsmen – we are wonderful at sticking together in a crisis. 'OK,' he said, 'You're with the Redcaps and Officers.' And I was. In no time I was rushing down the Western Avenue between Northolt and the BBC, where I immediately set about the task of organizing the biggest band ever. It comprised the Artillery, the Brigade of Guards, the Royal Marines, the RAF and the Household Cavalry – twenty-five from each – 250 players and the organ! The only time a bigger military massed band was formed for a broadcast, in my experience, was to celebrate the birth of Prince Charles. That, too, was crammed into the bulging Number One studio at Maida Vale.

The excitement of those weeks over, we could all settle down once more to an ordered existence. In fact, nothing was to be the same ever again; not broadcasting, which was to flower in the next few years, and certainly not the National Contest. John Henry Iles, who had fathered the contest back in 1900 and had been its driving force ever since, was never to be quite the same dominant factor – not surprising after nearly half a century of hard work.

The National Championships had not taken place for the whole of the war years,

138

*The massed military bands conducted in Maida Vale Studio by R. P. O'Donnell. The bands'
Directors of Music stand in front of the 250 players.*

but Belle Vue had continued as usual, still under the aegis of John Henry Iles. Both
May and September contests continued, plus a new Marching contest, started in
1942. In September 1944 with the end of the war in sight, a grand patriotic display
entitled March to Freedom was staged at Belle Vue, featuring ten massed bands
and a vast choir, with John Henry in his element as director of this mammoth
gathering. Frank Parker of Belle Vue was responsible for its organization but, most
importantly, the whole affair was sponsored for the first time by a newspaper, the
Daily Herald.

Having made contact with the *Herald*, who were most impressed by the public's response, John Henry pressed his cause and suggested to them that they might be interested in taking an active part in the National Festival as soon as wartime restrictions made it possible to organize it again in London. Eventually, a meeting was arranged to discuss all the ramifications of an event of this kind. The two Palaces – Crystal and Alexandra – were no longer available, and there was no other Hall of comparable proportions. John Henry had memories of his first 'Absent-minded Beggar' concert in 1900 in the magnificent setting of the Royal Albert Hall, which mercifully had survived the blitz on London.

At this important meeting, John Henry invited Father and me to join him – perhaps to see fair play for the bands – and the two representatives from the *Herald* were Jerome Chester and Edward P. Genn, 'special events' organizers for Odhams Press, which controlled the *Daily Herald*. First, their willingness to take over the running of the National and all its financial burdens was established; secondly, John Henry would remain as the figurehead, to present the prizes and, above all, to retain his beloved place on the rostrum fora small part of the massed bands finale – to have removed this privilege from John Henry would have been to deprive him of his annual pride and joy. So far, everyone was in agreement.

Next came ideas for a new concept in the running of the Contest. It was obvious that the normal practice of having seven sections would not now be a practicality – in fact, the Albert Hall could not cope with more than the Championship section. But the most far-reaching amendment to the rules was that Finals Day would, in fact, be just that. The bands taking part would no longer appear by invitation, but would qualify in their own areas for the privilege of the trip to London. To achieve this, the country was split into eight regions – Yorkshire, the North-East, the North-West, the Midlands, London, the West, Scotland and Wales. These area contests would embrace four sections – Championship, Second, Third and Fourth – the top two bands from each qualifying for their respective finals. Despite changes of ownership and procedure over the years since 1945, this system has remained substantially the same, although a qualification exists for the benefit of the stronger areas, where there are many top bands, so that an adjudicator may recommend that an extra band may go through, if the standard merits it.

And so the National was back in business. John Henry was able to utilize his connection with Belle Vue to stage the Finals of the three lower sections there, and in October 1945 the Royal Albert Hall saw the first National Championship Final since 1938.

With the untiring help and know-how of the former Secretary of the National Band Festival, Frances Bantin, things went well. Frances had worked with, and for, John Henry Iles for twenty-five years, all her adult life. I remembered her as a pig-tailed office girl in John Henry's eyrie-like office at the top of 210 Strand in London. Bands were her life, and fortunately her husband, Frank, realized this – he was so often introduced to bandsmen as 'Miss Bantin's husband', but took this

All the competing bands playing under the baton of John Henry Iles whilst awaiting the results of the first National Final after the war. The judges are in-carcerated in the white box at bottom right.

and a considerable loss of home-life in a good-humoured way. With the two *Daily Herald* principals, Jerry Chester and Teddy Genn, in control, the changes went smoothly. Teddy Genn – an experienced organizer of pageants and with theatrical production behind him – was an easy person to work with: an amiable character, with a fund of anecdotes which he could produce on almost any subject connected with show business, he was full of enthusiasm for the job in hand, and relished the planning of the evening concert. Yet he was a lonely man in many ways, and it was a sad day when he was found dead in his office. In his short period of control I suggested to him that the concert would be enhanced by the engagement of an orchestral conductor of renown for the evening concert which followed the contest. We had tried this successfully at Belle Vue in 1943–5 when, under the auspices of the BBC, Sir Adrian Boult, Sir Malcolm Sargent and Sir John Barbirolli had conducted massed bands concerts with great success and to much public and press acclaim. Sir Adrian Boult was, therefore, the first of a long line of such eminent conductors at the Royal Albert Hall, and was followed by Sir Malcolm Sargent.

The *Daily Herald*'s interest in the National continued until that paper ceased publication in 1964, when the Festival was handed over to a sister paper, *The People*. Edward Vaughan Morris with his two lieutenants, Messrs Nixon and Williamson, continued to organize the competitions after Jerome Chester left the scene, and over the years various changes took place.

On a personal note, although we did not always agree, I have nothing but praise for the way in which Vaughan Morris tightened the rules concerning registrations (one player – one band), platform discipline and in general added more prestige and dignity to the whole structure than even his worthy predecessors. I had already aired my views on the borrowed player question many years before – now something was done about it. The National Registry was started in John Henry's time, and run by the National Brass Band Club from 1952. It grew into such a responsibility that it became obvious it could not be handled on a part-time basis by the Club's hard-working representative, Sam Griffin, so it was very soon handed to the *Daily Herald*, and retained by them and their successors, *The People*, until being passed to Belle Vue where it still remains.

The following year, on his retirement from the staff of Odhams Press, Vaughan Morris was invited to continue to organize the National, and when *The People* also pulled out of the enterprise it was Vaughan Morris who completed an arrangement with them whereby he was to continue administering and organizing the National. Some people described him as a dictator – an organizer he certainly was – and the National went on as usual under his auspices, for which we should be grateful. When he retired in 1971, Vaughan Morris handed over the National to the new owners of the *British Bandsman* – Geoffrey Brand and Raymond Dutfield – and so it returned once again to its original home at 210 Strand, this time under the title of Band Promotions. Peter Wilson came from Scotland to become the new organizing secretary, a post he filled with much distinction and success. But it was to be a

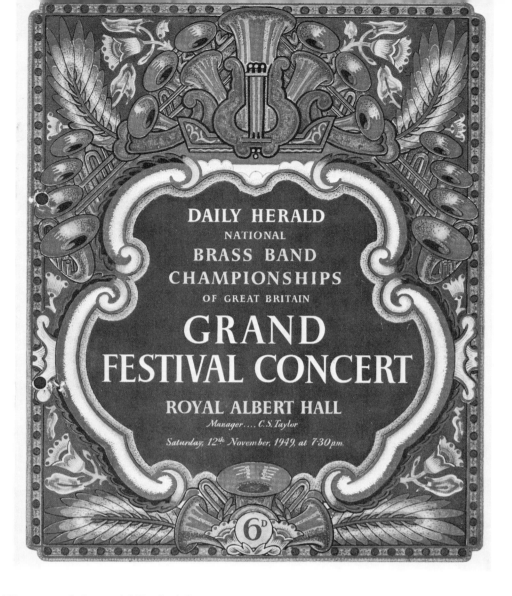

The cover of the special Festival Concert programme, 1949, when the Queen (then Princess Elizabeth) presented the prizes to the winners of the National.

short-lived arrangement. The lease on the world-famous office at 210 Strand was running out, and Geoffrey and Raymond decided that the time had come to hand over their responsibilities. They were both busy people, and running a weekly newspaper, a publishing company and the Regional Qualifying Contests and National Finals was a time-consuming business. Geoffrey decided to retain R. Smith and Company, who still continue to publish music for bands, but the *British Bandsman* and the National were to go.

In 1975 I was a prospective buyer, with the sole intention of handing over the Festival to the bands themselves. I really had hopes that the Federation of Bands might gather *all* the Associations to their bosom, but alas, this is still not a reality, and my hopes for the complete unity of the brass band world are something of a pipe-dream. Fate decreed that my offer be not accepted, and the ownership passed to Robert D. Alexander who had started a paper called *The Brass Band Review* and who, also, had his brass band roots in the Salvation Army. The *British Bandsman* continued in parallel with the National for two more years, with Peter Wilson still organizing the Festival. When the *Bandsman* was purchased by Rosehill Instruments in 1977, Peter Wilson became its new Editor, and Robert Alexander took over complete control of the National.

And here, regrettably, comes a sad, but not unexpected end to this particular saga. Despite £20,000 sponsorship from The Bank of America, plus something like another £10,000 at least from Butlins, who for the past seven years had sponsored the Youth Championships which were now part of the National Finals, there came a problem of cash flow (a modern phrase to describe what we have all had for years). The prizes had recently risen to such unbelievable heights as £2,000 for the first prize. As there had been packed houses at the Contests and Festival Concert, and a considerable number of bandsmen assembling on the following day for the European Contests, all with top-price tickets of up to £8.50, there was great bewilderment when financial chaos hit the brass band movement. Even in these more sophisticated days, bandsmen do not think 'big money'. However, the famous instrument firm of Boosey and Hawkes have rescued the sinking ship, and under their sponsorship we can look to the future with more confidence than has been the case for some time.

Opposite *A glittering golden fantasy, the priceless 'thousand guinea' trophy awarded to the winners of the National Brass Band Championship. It is now the property of the Greater London Council.*

Overleaf *There is nothing sacred about the positions of the players in a brass band, but they usually play in the configuration shown here. At the back are the basses or tubas, two E flat and two B flat, the B flat basses lying at either end of the group. On the left side are the cornets: closest to the conductor are the four first cornets (some bands have five); behind them and nearest the camera, is, first, the E flat soprano cornet, a slightly smaller instrument; next to this is the repiano cornet, the same as the B flat cornet but playing a different part; beyond, the three second and third cornets (some bands have a total of five). In the centre towards the rear are the three E flat tenor horns, and in front of them is the single B flat flugel horn, which is the link between the cornet and tenor horn families – it is, in fact, played with its bell facing outwards, like the cornets, and not with the bell upwards, like the tenor horns. In the foreground on the right are the two B flat euphoniums, and behind them the two baritones. In the rear, on the right, are three trombones, two tenor and one bass. Percussion instruments are not shown in this picture, although used by all bands for concert work, and in recent years at contests. The latter has only become accepted in the last six or seven years, and an increasing number of different percussion instruments added to modern scores for brass bands. In fact, this is now becoming a feature with certain composers.*

The above instrumentation is that accepted by British bands; many overseas bands are considerably larger (sometimes twice the above number) and some use orchestral-type French horns to replace, or in addition to, the E flat tenor horns.

144

CRYSTAL PALACE TRVSTEES
CHALLENGE PRIZE
NATIONAL BAND FESTIVAL

6 Listen to the band

Tin hats and ARP Wardens may have disappeared, but there was still much to remind us of the war. Almost as soon as the celebrations had died down the grim problems took on their real proportions. Problems from which this poor old country of ours still suffers today.

In 1945 the scars and the rubble were round every corner. Nowhere could it be escaped, except, perhaps, in some rural corner miles away from the nearest city. Rationing was to remain for several years, but at least the average diet would become a little more imaginative than it had been. A whole new generation was starting school for the first time – five-year-olds who had never seen a grapefruit or a banana, and who thought that eggs were a yellow powder from a tin. Thousands of returning servicemen suddenly found themselves in a strange new world which bore little or no relationship to the one they had left five years earlier. Never before had civilians taken so much of the brunt of war. There was an air of disillusionment. The Brave New World had missed the boat again!

Radio, as the most influential of the media, had an enormous responsibility thrust upon its shoulders. It must inform, entertain, uplift, guide and comfort a great new public. Is it my prejudice because I was there and part of those days, or is it, possibly, the natural conceit of the older generation in thinking that the past was always better? I think not. The British Broadcasting Corporation rose to the occasion magnificently. No fuss. No overstaffing. Just a concern for the well-being of the nation and an acute awareness of the importance of its own contribution.

Perhaps you would not agree that producing light music is work of national importance, and maybe you would be right, but, at the time, the departments at the BBC took their jobs very seriously and each did his very best to improve his output and then improve it again. You might think that my department's total weekly ration of air time would be on the decrease, now that the war was over and the public no longer needed to hear the military bands as proof positive that the 'boys' were still doing their bit. But not so. Since I had joined the Corporation the number of programmes alloted to the Brass and Military Band Department had been steadily growing. From a mere four or five in 1942 I had succeeded in securing a regular nine or ten, and it was only just beginning. Was I an early manifestation of a disease later to be diagnosed as 'workaholism' or was I simply power mad?

Neither, I think.

Despite my love of orchestral music and my delight in being a member of the Hallé for so long, I had, and still have, a fundamental belief in brass bands and their music. It is truly the music of the people. The modern bandsman is probably a far better musician than his ancestors, due partly to a better education and partly to a wider and more complex repertoire, but the basic premise remains unaltered: brass music is more accessible to the musician of average gift. It has a simple appeal which goes straight to the heart of the matter. I have already tried to explain the effect that the sound of the Henry Wood concert had on me. It is an emotion that only brass can stir. Not just for me, but for thousands of people, some of whom would not consider themselves to be musicians in any sense of the word. A gut reaction, to use an ugly but apt phrase. The average brass player only recognizes this as an abstract notion. He plays his cornet, euphonium, trombone, horn or bass simply because he wants to. It gives him a necessary outlet for his musicality.

The Salvation Army, on the other hand, uses brass for a different purpose. First there was the drum, the use of which was not primarily to keep the marchers in step, but was thought of more as a portable church bell, the difference being that while the bell invites people to worship on Sunday mornings, the drum says, 'We're coming to fetch you, like it or not!'

Brass became a necessary appendage to the drum almost by chance. Just over a hundred years ago Charles Fry, a new convert to Salvationism, and his three sons attended a meeting in Salisbury, taking with them their brass instruments. In an attempt to calm the enraged crowd gathering round the preacher, one James Dowdle, the Fry family struck up a tune and the effect was an instant calm. It was noted that the music held the attention of the crowd and helped the preacher to get his message across. General Booth, founder of the Salvation Army and ever one to keep his sights firmly fixed on his object was, at first, doubtful about the value of brass bands and issued strict instructions as to their use:

> They are to work for the good of the Corps and for the salvation of souls, and nothing else. We are not going to stick them up on the platform, nor march them through the streets for them to perform and be admired. They are to go there and blow what they are told and what the Commanding Officer thinks will be best for the good of the Corps and the salvation of souls, and if they won't blow for this object, let them stop their playing. We want nobody like that amongst us. The man must blow his cornet and shut his eyes, and believe while he plays that he is blowing salvation into somebody and doing something that will be some good.

If the style is somewhat repetitious, the sentiment is clear and unequivocal. These rules still exist, and although many of the top Salvation Army bands could give

146

Newcastle Temple Band 1897: the blowers of Salvation.

some of our best brass bands a run for their money in a contest, that situation will never arise. That is not to say, however, that an element of competition does not occasionally enter into the great Salvation Army Festivals. Having had the honour to be invited to 'take the chair' at many of these festivals, I can vouch for the fact that a healthy, but friendly, rivalry exists amongst the top few bands who jealously guard their reputations.

It had become a tradition, during the days of National Service, for Salvation Army bandsmen to join a Guards Regiment, and for those who received their call-up during the war it was the first choice for hundreds of the men to exchange their peaked caps for a bearskin. Demobilization brought them back into their chosen army where they returned as better and more skilled musicians, and so it was that the Salvation Army could boast more accomplished bands than ever before, bands which deserved a wider exposure to the public by means of radio. If their own edict of 'not being stuck up on a platform for entertainment' was not sufficiently inhibiting, there was another, apparently even more insurmountable hurdle in the way.

When I put forward the suggestion that the Salvation Army should have its own programme, along the lines of the highly successful 'Listen to the Band', I met a barrage of objections, best summed up by the attitude, 'Oh no! If they insist on

147

playing soul-saving music, then they must come under the religious department, not Light Music.' (An early example of a demarcation dispute.) My argument that to a proportion of the public the Salvation Army and brass were synonymous, fell on deaf ears. Obviously a compromise was called for which meant that both sides had to shift from their ideals in some small way. The BBC heads feared that the Salvation Army bands would want to fill a programme with hymns and had to be convinced that they had progressed, musically, far beyond that. True, all Salvation Army Music has to be passed by their own publishing department before its performance is permitted, and the overriding consideration of that department is to ensure that any new music has some sacred element, although this did not preclude the performance of, say, Schubert's 'Unfinished Symphony' or Handel's 'Largo'. Who is to say that the spiritual well-being which good music can endow is not sacred?

When in doubt, go to the top. As a nine-carat Salvationist myself (I was a twenty-two carat model until I started smoking, when I dropped to eighteen carats – a palate finely tuned to benefits of our national beverage demoted me further to nine carats), I was well acquainted with the hierarchy of the Salvation Army, and went to see Commissioner Bill Allen who had, at one time, been a member of John Philip Sousa's band. A man with such a pedigree took his music very seriously and was keen to see a radio series for his Army bands. I was invited to lunch at Salvation Army Headquarters, where I was greeted by the Commissioner. His idea of a BBC producer's life must have been one of endless business lunches interrupted only occasionally by the odd stint in the office, as his first words were,

'Ah, Harry, how nice to see you. Now, about lunch. I imagine you like a drop of wine with yours. I'm afraid I couldn't do much about that, but, as a special dispensation, I've managed to rustle up some sherry trifle!' Despite the intoxicating effects of that lethal concoction, we were able to stay clear-headed enough to reach some conclusions which would solve the problem.

It was not long before 'Lift up the Banner' took to the air – a programme which proved as popular as I had always known it would. Musically it contained many fine performances of potted classics – albeit with a subtle title change – and, of course, hymns as well. And why not? A brass band plays hymns better than any other musical instrument or group of instruments. The church organ, after all, is a comparatively modern innovation. Those good folk of the country parishes in the early Victorian days fought long and hard against the introduction of the organ, preferring their old way of using the church 'quire' – a group of instrumentalists who left their fields once a week, put on their best boots and sawed away at fiddle, cello and viols in the gallery on Sundays. The direct ancestors of the Salvation Army musician, perhaps? Not only hymns and adaptations of classics were performed, but some new, often exciting works commissioned by the Army who, in their by now world-wide organization, had many fine musicians and composers.

None more so than my dear friend, Eric Ball. Eric had risen through the ranks of

148

Eric Ball, an impeccable musician.

the Salvation Army from bandsman to conductor of the International Staff Band. An impeccable musician, his own personal crusade was to convince the world of the spiritual value of music – any good music. I have seen him hold an audience spellbound on a trip to Canada which he shared with Geoffrey Brand and me, plus Black Dyke, CWS Manchester, The Fairey Band and GUS Footwear, where he took this subject as a basis for his seminar. The setting for that occasion was a vast auditorium seating five thousand, at the Skylon Tower, with Niagara Falls as a backdrop. Eric's seminars are always a treat but in that inspired setting he surpassed himself. If he needed any renewal of faith in his belief in the value of beauty, surely that wonder of the world must have provided it.

As he was conductor of the International Staff Band I got to know Eric very well, and came to appreciate his fine intellect and ready wit. For personal reasons he decided to leave the Salvation Army in 1946, and it was with some regret that I realized that the wonderful flow of compositions which had come from him and found their way into the Salvation Army repertoire would cease. Such a man, however, was not to be wasted and when Brighouse and Rastrick, a band with whom I had been closely associated over the years, asked my opinion about a new conductor, I was able to recommend Eric wholeheartedly. The suggestion was met with surprise in many quarters. After all, here was a man who had made a respected name in the Salvation Army. There had, over the years, been many defections to 'outside' bands, as we are known by the Salvationists, but never before, or possibly since, had a man of Eric's reputation taken on such a well-known contesting band.

Eric took the job and quickly established himself as the best choice that Brighouse could have made. His immediate repayment to me for suggesting him was to beat one of my bands into second place at the National in 1946. To

149

compound the felony, the test-piece was none other than 'Oliver Cromwell' – the same piece with which Luton Red Cross had won the National all those years ago. Although my bands were to win the National in the following three years, the sweetest revenge came in 1950 at Belle Vue. By now Eric had moved to CWS Manchester, and the test-piece for that year was his own composition 'Resurgam'. Whilst I won the contest with the Fairey Band, Eric only managed fourth place. The first to offer his sincere congratulations, he did something which confirmed, if such confirmation was needed, my opinion that he was the most noble of friends and the least conceited of musicians, avowing that I understood the piece better than he did, and found more depth in it than he had imagined. I still believe it is his best composition, and have always been proud to be associated with it. No matter how many times I conduct it, it never fails to move me. An experience of mind and soul every time.

At the top of the S.A. tree there is the International Staff Band and some excellent Corps Bands, such as Cambridge Heath, Chalk Farm, Enfield (now Tottenham) and Coventry. In Australia there is the Melbourne Band, and so on. Every country has its own top bands, some with their individual characteristics – like Sweden, where I was invited to visit as a guest of the Army. An amazing sight there were the guitar-playing songsters – a group of lovelies who would put the average chorus line to shame. Sitting there watching them open-mouthed I was reminded of one Salvation Army man, who shall remain nameless. He and I were

Doing an 'open air', Leicester.

watching the antics of a lady conductor in a contest. As this was in the days of mini-skirts and she was being particularly animated, whipping her band into a frenzy of sound, my companion leaned across to me and whispered, 'What a pity I was saved so young!'

Less applauded than these top bands, but perhaps better known to thousands of town-dwellers all over the world, are the everyday Corps Bands. Men and women who go out in all weathers and to all areas taking their message, doing what is known as an 'open-air'. They all play an important role in the musical development of children all over the world, where, long before peripatetic teachers were employed in schools, they were 'catching them young' and giving youngsters a thorough grounding in music. Without these Army members we would not have many of our finest brass players, including such exalted names as Don Lusher and many orchestral players. But I am sure that they would not like to be thought of as simply a music school. The 'open-air' has a fundamental role in the philosophy of the Salvation Army. It is not, however, without its lighter side, and I particularly enjoyed the (true) story of the small corps in the Midlands who went out, one Sunday morning, to a street corner which had not been visited for some time.

151

Hymn number one was 'Wash me in the blood of the Lamb, and I shall be whiter than Snow'. As curtains were parted and front doors opened by the local residents, curious to see what was going on, it became increasingly obvious that the whole street was populated by immigrants from the West Indies, Pakistan and India ... cut verses 3, 4 and 5 and get on with the next hymn!

Before leaving the subject of the Salvation Army let me quote a greater authority than I, John Philip Sousa, the American March King:

> Music, even in its most primitive forms, seems to have an influence on some portion of mankind. The Salvation Army, for instance, has depended on banjos, accordians, guitars, tambourines ... anything that was musical to spread the Gospel. From this have grown many fine bands. I was recently honoured by having a request from that great woman, Evangeline Booth, to write a Salvation Army march. Of course, I gladly complied ... If you want to know one of the very good reasons why the world needs bands, just ask one of the Salvation Army warriors who for years have marched, carrying the message of the Cross, through the back alleys of life ... Let him tell of the armies of men who have turned toward a better life by first hearing the sounds of a Salvation Army Band. The next time you hear a Salvation Army Band, no matter how humble, take off your hat!

The new regime for the National having been satisfactorily sorted out in London, I was able once more, with the BBC's blessing, to undertake an ENSA tour with the Fairey Band. It was while we were away in France on this tour that the new test-piece was announced, and copies of the score sent to us. As befitted the first new-style National to be held at the great Albert Hall and the first to be held since the war, the piece was called 'Overture for an Epic Occasion' and written by Denis Wright.

The Fairey Band and I had won the British Open at Belle Vue in 1941, '42 and '44 (we were second in '43) and, although we could not know it at the time, were to win in 1945 as well. We were quite determined to do equally well in London. Being on a concert tour is a great help to a band, especially if that tour is overseas. In total secrecy, away from prying ears you can include the forthcoming test-piece in your repertoire straight away, and polish as you go along. The important thing is the experience which comes from playing the piece before a real audience. Practice is obviously important, but five minutes performance is worth hours of patient band-room slog. You may learn the technical merits of a piece in practice sessions, but an audience somehow helps you to get the feel of what you are playing.

Every performance included 'Overture for an Epic Occasion' and each unit we played it for helped us to gain a deeper understanding of what the piece was all about. By the time we arrived back in England, shortly before the contest, we could have played it in our sleep, and I daresay a few of the band did just that.

Hard work usually pays off and this was no exception. We won, of course, and

The Fairey band of 1941, winners of the British Open. On my right, behind the shield, is Elgar Clayton, now Director of the Rotorua Band, New Zealand. On my left, Frank Smith, 'Trumpet and Sax', formerly of Timaru Band, New Zealand.

Jack Writtle's cartoon, which made me proud at the time, earned me much criticism for my habit of conducting in shirtsleeves. I have since remonstrated with all others who do the same!

having also won Belle Vue with Kenneth Wright's 'Pride of Race' we completed a neat, patriotic double.

I was to get to know Europe fairly intimately in the following few years, and our acquaintanceship has hardly abated ever since. There was now a substantial Army of Occupation in Germany, and one of my most pleasurable tasks in the mid-forties was to take a BBC unit over there to record what was known as the Line Bands. Regiments like the Gloucesters and the Worcesters, to name but two, had fine bands which were worth recording. It was also a good exercise in morale, as those regiments which took turns to occupy the Rhine Lands (known as BAOR) must, at times, have felt cut off, being in a strange land amidst a people with whom we had only recently been at war. For the most part we simply had to record the bands and return with the discs (not tapes) so that the music could be broadcast on the Empire Service, a world-wide network which enabled the BBC to reach such far off places as Australia and Canada. Occasionally we made 'live' programmes from Germany, but that held no terrors for the engineers. We had been producing live shows all through the war. In fact, the recording facility was a luxury. In some ways it is regrettable that quality recording was a later development, as there were some programmes, and not just the musical ones, which will never again be heard. Where we have recorded material available it is a valuable source of history. Sadly some of the best material was live and lost for ever.

Whilst 'Saturday Bandstand' continued to be the highlight of the week for brass bands, there now followed a spate of military programmes which fed the listener's apparently insatiable appetite for wartime reminiscing. It is never easy to see why so many people enjoy talking about wartime experiences. I suppose one answer is that, for many, it was an undreamt-of adventure – an exciting interval in an otherwise uneventful life. Most ex-soldiers would agree that they enjoyed greater comradeship in those five years or so than ever before or since. There is no doubt that the deprivations of war bring people closer, and neighbours become friends. Whatever the answer it will take many more years yet before a whole section of society ceases to think of their lives as being pre and post war. In the meantime television programme makers (most of whom, I imagine, have no recollection of war at all) continue to rake over the ashes of the past with a morbid curiosity. I daresay they are right and the world should never be allowed to forget. Certainly in 1946 nobody wanted to forget and the next ten years or so brought some military band series which acquired all the merits of longevity usually associated with 'Mrs Dale's Diary' or 'The Archers'.

The students of the Royal Military School of Music at Twickenham, known as Kneller Hall, and their Director of Music, Meredith (Taffy) Roberts, became as much the backbone of my military band broadcasts as the Guards had been earlier. 'Music of the Regiments' started as a thirteen-programme series, proved itself popular and continued in bouts of thirteen for many years. The idea was basically simple: every regiment had a story to tell, and music was part of that story (this was in the days before War Office economies robbed many regiments of their identities). With the aid of a military expert we had a wonderful cottage industry going in my office. Scripts were discussed, prepared and written, music was researched and the scores sent off to Kneller Hall. It was a fascinating series to work on, and usually so much material to choose from. The Line Bands had, without a doubt, the widest and most diverse music libraries in the British Army, and their stories were legion. Strangely the Guards were much more limited in their scope, their stories were as good, sometimes even better, with memories of

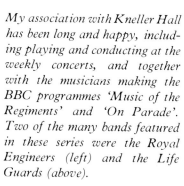

My association with Kneller Hall has been long and happy, including playing and conducting at the weekly concerts, and together with the musicians making the BBC programmes 'Music of the Regiments' and 'On Parade'. Two of the many bands featured in these series were the Royal Engineers (left) and the Life Guards (above).

Each year the students of Kneller Hall compete for the Fred Mortimer trophy for the best brass band march composition.

157

glorious deeds in their ancient and recent history, but somehow there was not the wealth of music to illustrate them. The Lancers, on the other hand, had one extraordinary piece of music which was their sole property – a Spanish chant given to them by a convent to which they had rendered valuable service. I cannot recall what that service was now, but it must have been exceptionally good! Every now and again we would receive a postal broadside from a peppery Colonel or retired Brigadier when we had got some detail not quite right but, by and large, we managed to please even the strictest martinet – no easy matter – and the mistakes grew fewer as the series grew older. The students of Kneller Hall performed the music for every programme (sometimes recording two in one day), a great comfort for me and a wonderful experience for them.

In presenting military programmes there is always the risk of the wrath of an expert, and anyone who rose above the rank of lance-corporal considers himself a military scholar. But the experts were not always right. The 'On Parade' series was a case in point.

Down in the large Maida Vale studio Number One, we set out to recreate the atmosphere of the barracks square. The sound-effects men had a marvellous time imitating the sounds of dozens of stamping and marching size elevens, rifle slapping, and even the odd horse noises in the background. For the vocal effects we hired the genuine article – a retired RSM. With the studio band comfortably seated and everybody on stand-by, the light would go on and away they went in the imaginations of thousands of listeners including, no doubt, a few proud mums who fondly imagined that they could hear their young Cyril marching away with the best of them. The studio band joined in the spirit of the thing and, on the order 'Present Arms' would enthusiastically slap their trombone or trumpet. Here was the British Army at its best! Or so they thought. If only they could have seen those studio chair marchers smartly clicking their heels on the command 'Atten.....shun!'

It all got too much for a Colonel from Brigade Headquarters. Listening to the programme one day, it suddenly occurred to him that he had no recollection of ever signing a form giving the BBC permission to come and record in his barracks. A bristling letter was duly delivered by special messenger to the Director General's office expressing fierce indignation at this flagrant breach of trust etc., etc. It was only when he was put through to the studio by 'phone that he fully believed the explanation, whereupon he had the grace to apologise for jumping to the wrong conclusion and confessed himself an admirer of the programme. Several points to the effects department, I think!

As the 1944 Henry Wood Jubilee Concert had been a watershed in my professional life, convincing me that the way ahead was to use massed bands, an opportunity now presented itself to strike the first major blow for my belief.

The 1944 concert had used traditional concert scores, some of which, it must be said, would be described by Thomas Beecham as 'lollipops'. Now there was talk of a new work with music by Thomas Wood and words by Christopher Hassall, better known for his lyrics for several of Ivor Novello's operettas. The work, *The Rainbow,* told in music the story of the retreat from Dunkirk, and its performance demanded three bands and a large choir and soloists. The arrangement was by Frank Wright – an arrangement which, even by his standards, was outstanding. The first performance of *The Rainbow* was conducted by Adrian Boult, and broadcast. It was on the whole received better by musicians than by the general public, which was only to be expected. The second performance was conducted by Frank himself. The third, and as far as I know, last performance was one which I had the pleasure of conducting. It was an all-Welsh occasion, with the massed bands of Cory's, Parc and Dare and Gwaen-cae-Gurwen, complemented by the famous Treorchy Male Voice Choir in the Brangwyn Hall, Swansea. The difficulty of the work and the cost involved would seem to forbid its frequent use, but I heartily wish that an occasion would arise which would merit its revival. Good music should not lie neglected for too long.

It should be mentioned that my own playing career was far from stagnating all this time. It could never do that while there were still such wonderful weekly radio productions as – dare I mention the title? – 'Tea and Trumpets'. They don't think up titles like that any more! This regular tea-time Home Service programme was a strange hybrid and possibly typical of its age, featuring as it did a combination of talents as diverse as could be imagined. There were three of us – Dr George Thalben Ball, the highly respected City Temple organist, Johnny Claes and his Clay Pigeons, who played jazz, and me playing everything from Killarney to Haydn. The strange thing was that it worked!

Thomas Wood, composer of 'The Rainbow',
which was conducted by Adrian Boult (right).

7 Friday night is travelling night

My Morri Eight

I suppose it was asking for trouble.

Whilst keeping my concert work going and, at the same time, looking after an increasingly busy department at the BBC, I was also spending a good deal of my time conducting up to five top bands. The ritual was to leave my desk in London at about four o'clock on Fridays, and set off on a punishing round of conducting which took me firstly to Kettering, to Munn and Feltons, where the resident conductor was Stanley Boddington, without question one of the finest band trainers of this century (in fact, my father was once heard to refer to him as 'the best bandmaster in Britain' – and that was praise indeed from Fred). Then on to Cheshire, around the Pennines, and back home again – often five rehearsals in the space of that Friday evening, Saturday and occasionally Sunday morning. Black Dyke was usually the last port of call, where the veteran conductor Arthur O. Pearce had been the bandmaster for many years, and ruled with an iron hand.

160

Queensbury necessitated a drive along a narrow and lonely road across the Pennines in those pre-M62 days. Had the roads been as busy as they are now, there is no doubt the whole trip would have been inconceivable, but on the other hand, had they not been so quiet and, at times, desolate, I doubt if I would have come such a cropper. A breakdown was the most dreaded mishap which I could have imagined. It never seriously occurred to me that worse things might happen.

On a particularly cold and frosty winter's night, crossing the Pennines with only the dim headlights of my Morris Eight to show me the way, I was suddenly confronted with a sheep whilst negotiating the twisty Nont Sarahs moorlands road. I could not have been going very fast – a Morris Eight was not built for Brooklands – but an instinctive foot on the brake produced disastrous results.

Some while later I awoke to the sound of the car horn blaring out a message to the darkness, and a few puzzled sheep. When I recovered what senses I was born with, I realized that I was sitting on the horn button. Why, I wondered, was I sitting upside down in a car on a lonely moor in the middle of a chilly night? And what was this nagging pain in my back? What on earth was I doing peering through a pile of assorted upholstery into a steamed-up rear window? A shift in position stopped the blaring horn and I was left with the even more disquieting sound of the tic-tic-tic from the petrol pump. Shaking some sense into my head I recovered sufficiently to reach down between my knees to turn off the ignition. Then the silence – the deepest silence I had ever known – surrounded me.

Slowly the events of the last few seconds before I took my enforced nap began to unfold in my mind. A short deliberation convinced me that I was certainly alive, and this was not the pearly gates and most certainly not the fiery furnace. What is more, if I wanted to stay alive I had better do something about it. As I could not unwind the window, the sensible thing seemed to be to smash my way out of it so, grabbing the starting handle which had somehow found its way into a corner behind my left ear, I tried to bludgeon a hole through the side window. All to no avail, as there was not enough room to take a good enough swing, and anyway I seemed to lack the strength to make a good job of it. It was about this time that I once more dozed off, a pattern which was to repeat itself over and over all night.

Daylight found me still in much the same position and, surprisingly, not too uncomfortable, but my first serious look out of the window froze me with horror. I had been aware for some hours that the car was on its back like a helpless beetle but, what I could not have known – and just as well – was that I was overhanging a sheer drop of some two hundred and fifty feet or so on the side from which I had endeavoured, only a few hours ago in the dark, to force my way out. Had I succeeded I would most certainly have ended up in the cold burn at the bottom of the hill. It was still dawn, with a chill in the air made worse by the fact that I was in no position to exercise my aching limbs for the blood to do its job of warming me up. Not surprisingly, I felt very lonely indeed. Even the early sheep who had arrived to see what was going on soon became bored and went off in search of breakfast. It was quieter than Loredo High Street on gunfight day, and all I could do was wait and hope.

Eventually, of course, I was spotted and a tractor was summoned to the rescue, and, with much manhandling, put the car back on its wheels. The amazing end to the story is that my faithful little Morris Eight, far from refusing to see me any further, leapt back to life with only the most cursory shake of its little sparking plugs, and the journey was continued.

It was only the previous year that I had taken on the Morris Motor Works Band. Was this, perhaps, a good omen? It was a sad day when I parted with that little car, but I could hardly refuse Sir William Morris himself when he begged to have it back as a prime example of his engineering. As a compensation I was given a Morris Ten instead, which was a step up in the world. Morris's engineering was obviously better than mine, for the pain in my back was to continue to nag me for years. Even now I am never quite sure if I have lumbago or am still feeling the effects of that accident.

Somewhere along the course of all that bandroom touring I gained the nickname of 'The Pope'. Perhaps I was feeling a little terse one night at a Fairey Band rehearsal, but I was having a slight difference of opinion with one or two of the bandsmen over some minute point of interpretation. As the conductor must always be right or, at any rate, allowed to be wrong with impunity, I settled the discussion with the words, 'There's only one Pope in Rome'. Not, perhaps, the most intellectual of arguments, but one which made the point at the time. Anyway, the name stuck. Only recently I entered the bar at a large hotel in Manchester where I was staying, to be greeted by the words, 'How's the Pope tonight, then?' There, sitting in the corner, enjoying a quiet moment, was Violet Carson (Ena Sharples), with whom I had worked so many years ago in the early days of broadcasting from Manchester.

The use of that gently mocking name reminded me of an incident in Holland. In the last thirty years the band movement has grown faster in Holland than in almost any other part of the world, and in those post-war years the Dutch people were eager to bring our bands over, where they would be treated to the sort of hospitality for which that race is so rightly famous. There are few audiences in the world who will listen with more concentration than the Dutch. From the platform you can almost feel the absorption. In a country noted for its good manners and reserve it can come as a shock to be treated to a wildly enthusiastic standing ovation. If they like you, you are left in no doubt about it. And flowers ... even in those days of rebuilding a nation which took some of the worst which both the Axis and Allied bombs could hurl at it, there was never an apparent shortage of flowers. At one such concert given by the Fairey Band at the famous Concertgebouw in The Hague, we ended an exciting evening with the almost inevitable *1812* Overture, with bells, cannon – the lot. Liberation is what that piece of music is all about, and the Dutch took it to heart. Before the last chord had died the hall was erupting.

The audience was on its feet cheering and applauding so wildly that we thought, for a moment, we had just performed the real liberation. A delightful young lady arrived on the stage bearing a large floral garland which, accompanied by a kiss, she placed on my shoulders. Flushed with delight, I was taking the umpteenth bow when, still in a bending position, I saw out of the corner of my eye a strapping young policeman advancing towards me with the biggest, heaviest laurel wreath you have ever seen. Before I could regain an upright position and brace myself for the green millstone, it was on me and I was being smartly saluted. With an effort of will-power I straightened up and tried to look as though this sort of thing happened all the time. The band, enjoying every minute of this slap-stick scene, were, to a man, sympathetic. 'How does the Pope feel now, then?' was one of the milder remarks which wafted down to the footlights.

Contests and festivals sprang up in Holland faster than tulip bulbs and, to my delight, I was to return again and again with one or other of my British bands. A grand annual event was the Festival in Hillegom which was attended by bands from all over France, Belgium and, of course, Holland. The first time we ventured into this new arena we wondered what we had done. It was like Fred's encounter with the French back in the Luton days – the Continental bands were as much as eighty-five strong compared to our meagre twenty-seven. We were naturally worried that we might sound just a little thin by comparison, but in the end it made little difference as continental brass was only in its infancy, and I think it would not be unfair to say that our contest-hardened men were able to produce a more vibrant sound despite their lack of numbers.

There was one rather impressive feature of these contests which was food for thought. The age-old question of judging – whether a judge should see the band, how to make valid comparisons between bands which perform early and those which take the later places in the draw – was given a new perspective. In Holland they had their own system which, although still not perfect, at least added another line of thought to the problem. At the end of each performance the judges, who were able to see and be seen, passed the marks to an official and they were immediately flashed on an illuminated screen for all to see. The main drawback was that a band whose marks were shown to be low knew that there was nothing to be gained from waiting and so drifted off. It left the end of the contest as something of an anticlimax. If, on the other hand, your band had done well and you still held the top mark when there were only a handful of performances yet to come, the tension was well-nigh unbearable. Especially if you had a 'plane to catch.

Even more grand than the Hillegom Festival was Kerkrade Festival, a twenty-one day event. The first time I attended one of these I took not one, but two bands – Brighouse & Rastrick and the Fairey Band. The normally quiet town was bulging with bandsmen speaking a grand mixture of languages and all having to be billeted somewhere nearby. It fell to our lot to be boarded at the local convent – not, you might think, the ideal accommodation for fifty bandsmen whose main interest was not in the local bulb-growing sights. The first evening's events finished about eleven o'clock and the lads, understandably, felt that they had earned a drink to finish the day off. I have no idea what time the last of the revellers returned to their sombre billets, but after two disturbed nights I was summoned to the Mother Superior's room where she icily enquired as to whether I was in charge of the bands. Despite my denials she decided that I was as likely a candidate as any other and entrusted me with her message.

'Tell them,' she said, 'That this night, at twelve o'clock, the doors are closed!'

I did. They were. A couple of dozen British Bandsmen had to resort to scaling the walls well into the night!

The BBC, my masters, were understandably anxious that I should not spend all my time flying like a hyperactive homing pigeon between the Pennines and the Netherlands, so it is with regret that I admit to a little cheating on occasion. One particularly tempting invitation came to Fairey's to visit, yet again, the hospitable people of Holland and the players were keen to accept. As the office was running smoothly under the watchful eye of Margaret I felt it reasonable to disappear for a day or two, leaving a telephone number where I could be contacted in case of emergency, and off I went. Just as things were going smoothly, sure enough some superior decided to call a meeting and my presence was required back in London. Unfortunately the appropriate airport was away on the other side of Holland, and the only way round the problem was a mad taxi dash. Luckily we had already performed and were awaiting the results, but there was nothing else for it – they would have to await the outcome without my calming influence.

In common with sixty million other Englishmen, my Dutch conversation is not all it should be. This deficiency does not usually matter as most Dutchmen speak a fair smattering of English, and one almost invariably manages to scrape by. Except with taxi drivers. Why is it that taxi drivers in every country want to hold a 'meaningful' conversation? In New York the garrulous driver is a tourist attraction, whilst in Greece he is an ambassador. In London he is silent as a KGB agent, but in Holland he wants you to share the pleasure he feels in driving the mythical 'Tommy' – or, at least, he did in those days. Tommy has dropped a point or two in his estimation since then. This one insisted on trying out his RAF inspired English, to which I could make no sensible reply as it was totally incomprehensible to me. I tried a few dazzling gambits, like 'Automobile – Goot!' and 'Delft – Goot!' but to no avail. He simply shrugged his shoulders and carried on with his own stream of happy banter. Finally we both gave up the unequal struggle and lapsed into a mutual silence. I sank into my back seat and left him free to concentrate on avoiding the oncoming traffic. This pact continued without further interruption until, just as we were approaching Amsterdam, we passed a gas-works. Fired with new inspiration he suddenly became animated once more and, with a self-satisfied grin turned to me and pronounced 'Shtink'. You cannot follow a speech of that magnitude so we both lapsed once more into silence all the way to the airport.

Another dash across London brought me back to my office with time to spare and nobody even suspected that I had left my desk. The experience cost me all of £22, which seemed like a lot of money in those days, but think of the plus side. Not only did I learn that the band won the contest, but I had gained an invaluable lesson in the art of conversation.

During one of these first trips to Holland I was standing on a bridge over one of the canals in Amsterdam, when I was approached by a tall, typically blond Dutchman who said to me in a friendly way 'You are MOR-TIMER? I am Molenaar – I know Eric Ball!' This was almost the extent of his English, but his vocabulary and his (then) small music business grew immensely over the years. His tiny music shop, selling only a couple of brass band marches among all the hymn tunes and military band music, expanded with the popularity of brass in Holland and the neighbouring countries until, when Piet Molenaar died only a few years ago, he left behind a flourishing publishing business and a mammoth printing factory, probably one of the biggest producers of brass band publications in the whole of Europe, and certainly in the Benelux countries.

Piet was always full of enthusiasm for everything he did, and it was he who organized many tours by British bands, not only to the big cities of Holland, but to some of the smaller places where brass bands were only just beginning to take the interest of music-lovers. One of these tours included a moving visit to the War Cemetary at Arnhem. The Salvation Army – the Staff Band in Amsterdam, and some smaller Corps bands – were among the few truly brass bands in Holland at that time, but with the rapid increase in their popularity, the VARA Broadcasting Company in Hilversum ten years ago arranged a band contest in which ten top class Dutch bands take part each year. The event is televised, and it has been the custom for a guest-band from England to be included in the Festival Concert which follows. So far, visitors have been Brighouse & Rastrick, Black Dyke, Besses o'the Barn, and my own Men o'Brass (Foden's, Fairey's and Morris Motors). The man behind this great upsurge is Harry Gaarenstroom, and with the exception of 1980, when a clash of engagements prevented my attendance, I have been present at every one of these excellent and interesting festivals; the improvement in performance standard in ten years has been truly remarkable. In many ways, possibly because their movement is younger and not over-burdened with tradition, bands are better organized in Holland than they are here. They have a strong and active Band Association – an over-all governing body which the British bands lack – and, as in most Continental contests, the jury (as the adjudicators are known) sit in the open, unlike our own screened-off heroes.

Such is the standard of Continental bands these days that the European Contest which follows our own National each year welcomes bands from Switzerland, Belgium, Holland, Norway and Denmark – all countries which I visited in the forties, fifties and sixties with British bands, when interest in brass was only just beginning. In fact, the International Music Festival at Kerkrade (where my bands were once treated to the hospitality of the local convent) now attracts bands from as far away as New Zealand. The more recent development of the European 'Town Twinning' has also added a new dimension to visits by British bands.

Never let anyone say that banding is a parochial affair, or the concern of a few isolated enthusiasts.

Brighouse & Rastrick was the guest band at the VARA brass band festival, in Utrecht, in May 1981, with conductors James Scott and Derek Broadbent, and myself as third man.

166

8 O.B.E.

Sorry to go on about it, but that back injury sustained whilst bouncing about in an upturned car was beginning to be a bit of a problem, causing severe bouts of pain which even a visit to The Gluepot was unable to relieve.

The final crunch came at a concert in Southampton, where I was guest artist with the Bournemouth Symphony Orchestra in a performance of the Haydn Trumpet Concerto. This was in the days when muscular pain was treated by the infallible method of covering the offending limb with a wrapping of Thermogene. I think the idea was to take your mind off the first pain by overpowering it with the cure. In this case the pain had travelled to my leg – something to do with the sciatic nerve, I suppose. Before I went on stage I did as I was told and liberally bound the Thermogene round the aching leg – too liberally I am afraid. I can only think that Haydn was uppermost in my mind at the time because I made the foolish and painful mistake of applying the wrapping too far up the leg! By the time I realized my mistake it was too late and the conductor, George Weldon, awaited my presence on the platform. After a few bars he must have been surprised to see his soloist walking around the stage and occasionally shaking a leg in every tacet bar. The heat of the lights merely served to exacerbate the problem, and by the end of the concerto I was in burning agony and longed only to get to a cold water tap. Whilst it is nearly always gratifying to be called back time and again by a concert audience, this was one occasion when I heartily wished they would all go home and leave me to my sorrows.

It was also the last time I played the trumpet or cornet in public.

A few days later we recorded the work without the aid of Thermogene, and I was admitted to King Edward VII Hospital to see what a little surgery could do for my back. In this, surely the most civilized of hospitals, I was soon tucked up in a warm bed in a room I shared with a marvellous character – a salty Lieutenant Commander from the New Zealand Navy called Bunty Palmer, who recounted his story with great relish. He was literally bombed off his deck, blown into the air and deposited back on deck breaking both hips in the process. He was in hospital for the small job of replacing the damaged hips. Whether it was the bottle of gin he kept in his locker or just plain grit I will never know, but he was walking before I was – and this at a time when hip replacement was almost unheard of, and certainly in an experimental stage.

167

In the same way that toothache magically disappears once the sufferer faces the drill, so there is nothing like the shadow of the surgeon's knife for precipitating a miracle cure. On the morning of the proposed operation the doctor thought that one more check might be in order, so suggested I try bending. It was a straw to a drowning man and I summoned up all the grit I could muster and managed a passable forty-five degrees bend, which brought a swift reprieve. I never did have that operation, but the seventeen weeks spent on my back were enough to send me once more into the world, if not a new man, then certainly a reconditioned one.

It was during this seventeen weeks that the June Honours List was published and Wilfred Pickles and I both received the OBE. Alreet for a couple of Yorkshire lads! Not being able to go to Buckingham Palace to receive the gong, I had the pleasure of a private investiture from my hospital bed. By a happy coincidence the gentleman who arrived to perform the ceremony was Sir Harold Wernher, the husband of Lady Zia Wernher who had been our patron in the Luton Red Cross days.

Now that I had officially hung up my cornet and all the other various trumpets, I had more time to concentrate on the BBC and conducting, and threw myself back into the musical world with a vengeance. My early retirement from playing is the one regret I have at the end of a long career. Forty-eight, after all, is an age when an artist should be at his most powerful. Perhaps I was in too much of a hurry to meet the day when the technique might not be so secure – a day I dreaded. With hindsight it is easy to say that another ten years or so would have done my reputation no harm at all. It certainly was not a case of boredom, as I was being offered some of the best concert work of my life, so perhaps it was, with some conceit, a wish to bow out gracefully while I was still at the top. Nobody was going to remember Harry Mortimer as a player who had gone on too long!

The other consideration was that I was being invited to some exciting places to conduct or to judge and, what with that and a fully satisfying job with the best broadcasting station in the world, life was getting dangerously full. Something had to go and playing was the obvious casualty, as it was the most ephemeral of all the arts. Perhaps the most important of all, though, was that – like all the luckiest of men – I had married my former secretary. Margaret and I had a son, and this new family was to take precedence over a life of tearing about the country, playing here, there and everywhere. And, to be honest, I did not miss the life at all. It was only in later years that I regretted the decision to stop playing.

There was also another giant with which the next forty years were to be inextricably entangled. Sir William Morris was proud of his Morris Motor Works Band, which had been winning the Southern Area Championship regularly for several years, and I was invited to take them on to see what could be done to push them right to the top. It was an excellent set-up, with full co-operation from the management, a canteen concert once a week, good instruments, and Oxford was a lot closer to home than any of my other bands had ever been.

I conduct the BMC band in Geneva on their goodwill tour after the merger of Austin and Morris.

All good things change, though, and Morris was no exception. The first intimation of troubled times ahead came when Morris and Austin amalgamated – an enforced and never easy marriage, although the band did rather well out of it for a while. We were sent on a European tour whose purpose was to cement relations between the two sets of dealers. Until then the Morris and Austin agencies in Europe had been in direct competition, and now, all of a sudden, they were expected to join forces in selling the same product. Ours was a peace-keeping mission and, for the new partnership, we were renamed the BMC Band.

In no time, it seemed, the pattern was to be disrupted again and the company became BLMC, but now there was a new mood in the boardroom. British cars were not enjoying their former prestige, and in the interests of economy (that frightening phrase) cuts had to be made. Lord Stokes took command of the ailing company and we were among the first to feel the cutting edge of the new regime. The band almost disappeared for ever, but some hard lobbying rewarded them with just one concession. We had free use of the bandroom and library, but apart from that had to be entirely self-supporting. The band managed to stay alive and continued as part of the Men o' Brass ensemble, of which they were founder members. These days I am happy to leave the hard work to the bandmaster, Cliff Edmunds, who is currently enjoying his second spell at the job. His first experience was less happy, as the band, for one brief but inglorious year, became unmanageable; a handful of rebellious players wanted to run things their own way and made his life intolerable. After one particularly bitter wrangle four members walked out and that was it for a whole year. No band for Cliff or for me.

Margaret and I celebrate the visit of Sir Arthur Bliss to the Solo and Quartet Championship of Great Britain, founded by Tommy Morcombe, next to Sir Arthur. On the extreme left is Cliff Edmunds.

It was the enthusiasm of Tommy Morcombe which revived the fortunes of the Morris Concert Band, as it became known. To Tommy, a factory without a band was an unthinkable combination, and he devoted all of his energy towards setting the matter to rights. I was once again invited to fill the conductor's post, only this time it was an honorary position, as it still is.

The faithful few were gathered together again with some new recruits to fill the places of the retired or the rebellious, and it was not long before we were back where we started. Tommy's enthusiasm never flagged, and it was he who was to inaugurate one of our most important annual contests, the Oxford Quartet, and later the 'Solo Contest'.

Wednesday nights are still spent dashing up the M40 for the Morris rehearsal. We have had good years and bad years. If we never made the big prizes it was not for want of enthusiasm, but, who knows, perhaps as the fortunes of the mini Metro rise, ours will rise with them. I have enough pride left in this country to hope that both can be achieved.

1953 was a year in which much happened in my life. For some time my dear father had been failing seriously in health and no longer able to take charge regularly of his beloved Foden's, due to a heart condition which affected him in a most peculiar way. He was able to conduct, but the moment any applause came, then an attack came with it so, alas, he had to keep off the public platform. With typical grit he refused to admit how ill he felt sometimes, and tried to carry on as normally as

170

possible. But we later learned that a London specialist, whom he visited a couple of years before, had told the family doctor that he probably had only two years to live – and although we did not realize this then my mother was worried and anxious about him.

In February 1953 I received an invitation to adjudicate the National Championships in New Zealand, and after much thought decided to take some annual leave from the hustle and bustle of my BBC work, to embark on this exciting journey.

This was a period when travel allowances were very limited, and as I was travelling via the United States I realized that some extra cash would be essential. One evening in our local, the Sun in Splendour at the bottom of Portobello Road, I mentioned my forthcoming trip, and one of the regulars there murmured that he could buy me some dollars – say, £100 worth – to cope with the American part of my journey. I entered into this illicit arrangement, and immediately regretted it, having visions of discovery and newspaper headlines, 'BBC man charged with illegal currency transactions'! Frankly, I had cold feet about the whole affair, but in due course my dollars arrived and my drinking-friend gave me a few words of advice as to where to conceal them until my arrival in the States. I was even more alarmed when my knowledgeable pal asked when and at what time my 'plane left,

'What do you think, Mother?' When Sarah came to Cowley to listen to the Oxford Quartet, she had been a critic of brass band music for almost seventy years.

as he would see me through the Customs! It was a relief when BOAC rang on the morning of my scheduled departure to say that my flight had been delayed, and they were re-scheduling my take-off. On arrival at the airport, in some trepidation I went through the usual Customs check, where in those days the first question asked was 'How much money are you taking out of the country?' I had presented my passport, but before I could reply I was horrified to see the Customs officer pick up his internal telephone and murmur, 'Sir, I have Mr Mortimer here.' At this point I broke into a cold sweat, although trying to appear unconcerned. To my surprise and great relief a four-ringed Customs official appeared and greeted me. Yes, it was my friend from the pub! I never knew his surname, as is the way so often in one's local, and perhaps even now it would be tactful not to mention his Christian name.

So at last I was on my way, and after a day in New York flew on to Hawaii, spending a couple of nights there for a short rest. Having left all my innoculations rather late I was not feeling too bright, so decided to relax on the famous Waikiki Beach during the afternoon. Sunning myself in a deck-chair, I noticed the waiter serving an American gentleman who loudly asked for a 'large Scotch on ice, out of a pinch-bottle'. (This is not a commercial, but anyone old enough to remember the days after the war will recall that not only had whisky been in short supply, but the famous Dimple in that unique and distinctive 'pinch-bottle' was almost unobtainable in Britain.) The temptation was too much to resist, and in my rather fragile and tired condition I felt that it would do me a power of good – so ordered one too. (A few more of my dollars gone!) The friendly American immediately said, 'I guess you're from England – come and join me! My wife and family are having a swim.' So we chatted for a while, and I learned that his son was in the American Air Force stationed at Pearl Harbour, and that they were visiting him in Honolulu. When his wife, son and daughter emerged from the water, he enquired 'What is your name, Sir?' in order to introduce me to them. I told him, and explained that I was on my way to New Zealand to adjudicate at a Musical Festival there. Nothing more was said, but these charming people then invited me to their home for a meal, during which soft music was playing on the radiogram in the corner of the room. Suddenly, towards the end of dinner, my own recording of the Haydn Trumpet Concerto came on. Very startled, I looked at them all in amazement, and they laughed, saying, 'We thought it must be you!' We never met again, but for some years kept up a correspondence. If there is a family by the name of Bailey still living in either Honolulu or California (their other home) who remembers this incident, please accept my thanks once again for much kindness and hospitality to a lone traveller.

On arrival in Auckland I was met by New Zealand Band Association officials and driven by road to Wanganui, a delightful country town on the river. These officials stayed at the same hotel, and two supervisors were allocated to look after the adjudicator (myself) at all times. After we had breakfasted together, they

A Union Jack was wrapped around the judging table in my honour at Wanganui, when I was let out of my caravan to judge the marching contest. I was still chaperoned, however, this time by a Boy Scout.

escorted me to the Contest ground, where a caravan was my home for the day, and indeed for many days, as the competitions in New Zealand go on for a whole week. This is a truly national event. The weather was superb, and I suppose the caravan was less stuffy than the traditional adjudicator's box or tent, while still screening him from view. It had the added advantage of being towable into different positions on the field, so that it turned to face the breeze, if any, allowing the sound of the bands – all of whom played in the open air, of course – to come directly at the caravan. My supervision committee had a full-time job.

An unaccustomed luxury enjoyed by judges in New Zealand is the provision of a 'writer', who takes down notes as you speak and so saves you from scratching away all day. My first reaction on being told of this practice was, 'I hope he speaks band language.' My second reaction was not so casual. Instead of the expected earnest young man, it was a rather beautiful young lady who turned up at the caravan next morning, introducing herself as my writer and apparently about to settle in for the week. Now I do not wish to sound prudish, but I had just left a lovely family on the other side of the world and I did not think that I was ready to have my path strewn with such distractions, so, I am afraid, she had to go and it was back to scratching out my own notes.

The only drawback to these week-long festivals is that, until it is all over, there is no chance of fraternizing with old acquaintances or of meeting new ones. You are simply locked away, even to the extent of a wonderful paragraph in the list of

instructions which reads, if I remember correctly, 'If the adjudicator wishes to pay homage to nature he will ring the bell three times and the stewards will escort him.' Is nothing sacred?

New Zealand had become a traditional hunting-ground for ex-Fairey's men (or a Fairey Grotto, if you like) so there were quite a few people I wanted to see. There was Ken Smith, a brilliant cornet player, and his father who was conductor of the New Zealand National Band – which, that same year, came to Belle Vue and carried home the £2000 Gold Challenge Trophy against opposition from our top bands. Then there was Frank Smith (no relation) whom you may remember as 'Frank Smith – Trumpet and Sax' when I was invited to Fairey's in the first place. The tradition of emigrating to New Zealand carried on for a good few years, with such names as Elgar Clayton, Bob Mulholland, Harry Farrington and several more. The place was thronging with them. I also wanted to see for myself one of the Salvation Army's most talented bands, that of the Wellington Citadel, who were the 'home' band of a successful young composer called Dean Goffin. I particularly wanted to hear them as I had long been an admirer of their gramophone records, and because Dean Goffin had written a stirring piece of music which had been used as the test-piece at the 1948 British Open, and which I had enjoyed conducting. No doubt my enjoyment of the music was heightened by the fact that Fairey's had won the contest. This composition, 'Rhapsody in Brass', had the unusual distinction of being written for a test-piece by a Salvation Army composer. Eric Ball's 'Resurgam' was the only other piece to achieve this dual personality.

A contrast in style: on the left is the National Band of New Zealand; above, Brighouse & Rastrick on a Whit Friday march in Saddleworth.

I was not disappointed by what I heard of the band, who were every bit as good as their recordings. Dean Goffin's home was in Wellington and his father was Officer in Charge there. Dean has since become a member of the upper hierarchy of Salvationist musicians, a surprise to no one.

The great feature of the New Zealand Championships is something which has been neglected in this country or, at least, left to the professionals – the marching contest. The only surviving example of this art in England is the Whit Friday March Contest which is still held in a handful of villages in Yorkshire and Lancashire, but in New Zealand it is taken very seriously. Marching patterns are worked out meticulously and rehearsed by an ex-army sergeant major type, who treats the whole affair like a national crisis. For those who live in the immediate vicinity of the contest area it is a common occurrence to be woken from a deep sleep at six-thirty in the morning by a rasping, '... by the right ... Quiiiiick – M'ch!' The results of all this drill are well worth the effort as it is a splendid sight worthy of the Guards or the Marines. The quality of the music is not neglected either, so the day's contest is a pleasure to both sight and ear. Such is the New Zealand bandsman's enthusiasm for this week's festival that many travel two thousand miles from South Island and camp out for a week in order not to miss anything.

Undoubtedly, though, the pride of New Zealand is its National Band of fifty players. Despite having to make great sacrifices to be a member – its tours are often months long – it is the ambition of every young New Zealand bandsman to pass the audition and be offered a place. Their deportment and discipline is always

175

Trumpet trio. In this picture taken in the late forties, I am standing between Ken Smith, the New Zealander now at the Sydney Conservatoire, and Bram Gay, now Orchestral Director of Covent Garden.

splendid, and their programmes always full of life and humour, and superbly played.

One thing marred that first, exciting visit to New Zealand. Ill though he was, Father had been determined to come to London to see me off. Although we both tried to hide it I do not think that either of us expected to meet again. Dear Fred, I wished so much that he could have come with me – to go to New Zealand was one of his unfulfilled ambitions. Having been a football fan since the Luton Band used to play at Kenilworth Road ground, and despite his illness, he did a strange thing after he left the airport: he went to Queens Park Rangers football ground for the afternoon match, leaving Mother with Margaret and our son Martin to the more peaceful pleasures of Kensington Gardens.

From every place I visited on that trip I sent a postcard and kept him informed of my itinerary, but I never lost the nagging feeling with each new postcard that he might not live to read it. Fred, however, had never been short of guts and he was determined to live through my experience in New Zealand – it was almost as though, realizing he would never go himself, he wanted to savour as much as he could through me. As I prepared to board the homeward flight I saw a signpost at the airport – LONDON 13,000 miles. I wondered if I could make it in time.

On arrival in London my first thought was to dash straight on to Sandbach, where he was, by now, confined to his bed. It was a quiet reunion, with both of us glad simply to see each other again. His condition slowly worsened over the following few weeks and he finally, peacefully, died. Determined to the end, he had spent his last evening sitting up in bed filling out the wages slips for the men, who that week were once more performing in Hyde Park.

176

There was no chance that the funeral of this, the most respected and popular conductor of his day, would pass unnoticed by the band world. Representatives of literally hundreds of bands attended. The most poignant moment came when Foden's played the hymn which had always ended the victory celebrations on their return to Sandbach after winning a major trophy, and which was for ever associated with him, 'Beautiful Zion' – Fred's hymn.

Fred's death surely marked the passing of an era. Let me leave the last word to Bram Gay who, as a young man, came to live with the family. He wrote the following words about my father.

We bandsmen have a knack of forgetting our great men on the day they are lost to us. In a way this is natural and even good. Ours is a competitive art and, on the whole, one for young men. Such chaps are more interested in next year's results

Fred Mortimer

than in last year's faces, which is perhaps why so little has come down to us of the formative personalities in brass band history. What do we know, today, of the way Rimmer taught, or Owen performed? Perhaps only the curious middle-aged care.

Fred Mortimer would have been a hundred years old in 1980. There are, at most, a bandroom-full of people alive today who played for him. As a teenager in the middle forties I had the enviable experience of playing in that fabulous band at Foden's over which he reigned for more than a quarter of a century.

My view of the Old Man is more personal than most. I lived for a time at Rienzi in Clifton Road with him and Nannie Mortimer, and for a longer time with the next generation of his family. He became a kind of extra Grandfather, besides being provider of my musical education. Not that one got sentimentally close to him; never a chance. He expressed himself in few words. All the public got from him was performance, and those of us who were closest to him quickly came to realize that all he asked of us was music. For the rest, he was self-contained.

A forbidding character, then? No. Just the archetypal Yorkshireman, totally committed to his work, which in his case meant the fulfilment of an extraordinary musical instinct through the medium which he understood better than any other man I have met. It would be hard to find a man less like the conventional conducting musician. At sixty, when he first inspected me during one of my lessons with Harry, he was short, grey, pear-shaped, dressed in a dark blue suit which a bank-manager might have worn on his day off. On his head a soft hat; in his mouth a pipe. It rarely came out except when conducting. One got an instant impression of military bearing – not an obtrusive one, but there all the same. He was, of course, an old soldier, as so many of his generation had been. He stood as straight as a line. His eyes were clear and they looked straight at you. No beating about the bush with Mortimer. A quiet man, but one of absolute convictions, with a characteristic inability to change his mind once it was made up. I cannot imagine what it would have taken to get back into his good books once out of them. Fortunately for Foden's Band he was not often wrong. Being right is habit-forming: he was addicted to it.

The man and his band are for me one memory. He would have approved of that, since his performances were the only justification he ever asked. It could be said, and indeed it often was said by the older players at Foden's, that he did not build the band. That was the work of his teacher, Rimmer. But let's not forget that Rimmer's structure was complete in 1910, fourteen years before Fred arrived at Foden's and twenty years before he was allowed free rein with such astonishing results. In the meantime there had been others; Halliwell, especially, had been successful at Foden's as nearly everywhere else. But it was a Rimmer Band, and only in the hands of Rimmer's best disciple did it find its ultimate voice. Halliwell gave it up, as he told Harry, 'because they play better for your father than for me.' He was right.

By the time I arrived at Foden's the twilight years had arrived for Fred and for the band: the liveliest and most interesting coachload of ageing gentlemen one could hope to meet. Without exception they were still on top of their work, but the great strength of that band was in the accumulated experience of a combination which, with little change, had gone through twenty years of competitive success. Repertoire was *total*. There was simply nothing ever written for the brass band which they could not have put on record within four hours. They could, and did, play two weeks' touring performances, two concerts each day, without repetition and without rehearsal.

Virtuosi? Only if you define virtuosity as the dedication of technical and musical skills to the service of art. There were few, if any, star players at Foden's. Even Harry and Alex, the two balanced pivots upon whom the whole turned, contributed less in the way of solo performance than in ensemble control and style. Better cornetists than Harry, and better euphoniumists than Alex, there may arguably have been – though Fred would have chuckled at the suggestion – but better band-leading instincts have yet to emerge. They did well on their own account thereafter.

All this, you may think, must have involved a colossal technique on the part of the guiding genius. Well, so it did. But it was technique of a very unusual sort, and one never applied to the brass band before nor since. To Fred the problem was simple and all-embracing. He taught his musicians to do their own thinking and their own listening. He took aboard only men capable of it, and when they had learned the trick he stood back, gave them only such direction as was vital to cohesion, and enjoyed the result. When I arrived there in 1943 I was the only important arrival since 1932, I think. The latest arrival of the horn department joined in '28; the bottom horn, old Fred Sowood, was a Rimmer importation of '09, like the flugel, Hubert Shergold, with whom I shared a music stand for some happy years. So the Rimmer-Mortimer attitude was part of the air at Elworth, very much the essence of a going concern. Fred taught it to me. Since he was concerned, and rightly, about the effect all this excitement might have on a growing lad, he applied maximum pressure upon me to keep my eyes down and the mouthpiece on my lips. I was made to compete, in a way which seemed unbearably cruel at the time, with impossible models, technically. He knew that the band would teach me the music.

I vividly remember walking home with him after a rehearsal of Halliwell's arrangement (where is it today?) of the Introduction and Rondo Capriccioso of Mendelssohn, during which I felt I had achieved quite a lot. His conversation was of the music and its style at first, then reflective of the arranger and the players with whom such scores had become possible. Finally, 'Of course, to play a piece of that sort, you really need a cornet player like our Harry ...'

'Our Harry' and 'our Alex' he idolized. Alex, one felt, had let him down by taking up the tuba and the symphony orchestra. Harry was different because although he had 'given up' at Foden's he still had the band 'at heart' and would, by implication, one day come back. 'Our Rex' was of course still with us, and therefore taken for granted. His day was still to come, but the Old Man didn't know that.

Fred's stick technique was a minus quantity. It is not a question of whether he conducted well or badly. In conventional terms he did not conduct at all. This is true of some other great artists with whom I have played. All they need is an ensemble with ears and a common musical philosophy; not something you can teach in a day or two, but when it comes off there is nothing like it. He always made the band sort out the problem if he could. 'In that bar,' he remarked once during rehearsal, 'there are three different sizes of quaver going on. Make up your minds, can't you?' And off we went once more. No instruction given and none needed. Next time there was only one variety of note-value in evidence, and it was the Mortimer variety; the one which fitted the musical situation. Not a matter of counting or conscious decision, just the solution of twenty-five musicians listening together. Alas, there is no time for such things today. In 1980 we watch sticks and count beats, and are so much the poorer.

Fred's approach to the score was the simplest possible: he merely tried to get it 'right'. He never 'interpreted'. To him the score was as inviolate as a balance-sheet. It was an absolute, be it ever so bad music. Once committed to it, he could convince himself that it was worth doing. He could fool the band into thinking the same way, too. That, to him, was essential, since only a committed performance could ever succeed for him. Detachment was not an idea he would have understood, still less cynicism. Once everything was 'right' for him – which he never for a moment admitted – his direction was always with a feeling for the phrase, the line, the essentially vocal element of the brass band. A man of no formal musical education, raised among the operatic selections of Owen & Co., he believed intensely in the emotional content of melody. Given only three notes to play, our task was still to make them sing; somehow to 'sell' them. If possible to *move* the listener. He reacted badly to casual playing and still worse to complacency, a quality he could smell at a mile. 'That was very good,' he would say, 'in fact some people would think it was first-class. *But it is not good enough for Foden's Band.*' Nothing was ever good enough for Foden's Band, by half.

He held his stick – I will not say he conducted – in his left hand. Was he 'caggy-handed'? No. As a young bandmaster at Hebden Bridge he had no alternative to his left hand because he played solo cornet with his right. He filled his pipe (from a jar filled each week with tobacco lovingly rubbed out on to newspaper on the dining-room table) with his right hand, and a delight it was to watch; a remarkable one-handed feat possible only to a lifelong pipeman. He wrote, I think, with his right, at least, he filled in his football coupons and wrote manuscript with it. But he was a demon at the snooker-table with his left. So one can't be sure.

His beat was always a mile ahead of the band, and the miracle is that this tactic, an unconscious need to signal phrase and dynamic well before we arrived at the point of delivery, produced no bad ensemble. We could play together without him perfectly well, and in his increasing age and infirmity we often did. This was a

Fred triumphant, shown above on his seventy-first birthday, holding the National trophy which superseded the thousand guinea trophy at the National contest, and, below, with the Queen, then Princess Elizabeth, when she presented the prizes at the Albert Hall.

"COME AND PRACTICE YOUR CORNET"

chamber group, not a machine conducted by a policeman. I am grateful to him for teaching me a musical approach with which none of the greatest conductors I have since met have ever argued.

Fred was a total autocrat. Strange that the band world, so vocally democratic in its attitudes, should love such people – when they succeed. He once said that he liked the committee system, provided that the number involved was not more than three, and two of them deceased. He ruled with an iron hand at Foden's. Thinking back I realise that he could not have got away with it had the band not wanted it. They made polite (and always unseen) fun of him. His rather self-important walk when in uniform, his way of speaking, his sometimes obtrusively masonic handshake, all were copied with childish delight. He had a dozen names, some of them broad Cheshire like 'th' 'owd chap' or 'th' 'owd feller', or simply 'Old Mort'. But when he was about we called him Mr Mortimer, and we watched our p's and q's and everything else.

Band discipline was absolute. Attendance and punctuality were total. It was simply not 'on' to be elsewhere on band practice night. If some dire circumstance like a family funeral made attendance impossible (and he always gave the impression that only one's own funeral would be an acceptable excuse) then he would try to change the night. If that in turn produced an impossibility (which he never criticized, incidentally; the band owned us on Mondays and Thursdays only) then practice was cancelled. He would not knowingly rehearse 'a man short'. How right he was. Nothing spreads like accepted absenteeism.

Practice at Foden's had something of the ritual about it. There was little of the warm-up din found elsewhere. We were always seated at 6.55 p.m. on Mondays and Thursdays. The old man arrived at exactly that time. Some time during the next five minutes Mr William Foden arrived, driving himself in his ancient Rolls, and with him any member of the family he could dragoon into attendance. Mr Willie would sit in his personal chair, only the old coke stove between him and Charlie Cook. He would light his customary cigar in competition with the coke fume. And at seven o'clock the music started. There was absolute silence when the

182

band stopped playing and the minimum of time wasted. Concentration was total. Whether it was the National test-piece or 'Teddy Bears' Picnic', each bar was polished until it shone. Fred took an almost perverse delight in putting a superb finish on trivia. The most ordinary quickstep took on a life of its own. Nobody, absolutely nobody, would be able to better what we would do with it. Nobody could. Fortunately the records are still about, and we can still hear these performances and wonder at them.

He was a superb psychologist. Whereas every band competing at the National would run its own sweepstake on the result, our sweep was about the *second* prize. He was a rotten loser, having had little practice at it. 'The worst advertisement,' he once said, 'is *"Second prize, Foden's Band"*.' When, after the war, we began to lose through sheer anno domini, he remained convinced that we were playing the best performances. In a real sense we were. Youth was winning. We still made the best music.

At the end, of course, we began to wish for a younger and more energetic man. Yet none of those available compared with him. None commanded his band. Or perhaps it is more true to say that they commanded it where no command would do. Foden's Band, as we knew it, was his alone, and after him must come decline and rebirth. To do the same again would need a world now extinct, and twenty years of patient work. Banding is just not like that now. The world is spinning too fast for such things. How lucky I was to be there.

Thank you Bram. How lucky we *all* were!

Since those days, Bram has further followed in my footsteps. After Army Service in the Scots Guards (yes, he made it, even though I did not!) he eventually landed at my old trumpet desk with the Hallé before coming to London; not to the BBC, but to Covent Garden, where he is now Orchestral Director.

184   *The realization of a dream: Men o' Brass at the Festival Hall.*

9 Men o'Brass

My dream of a permanent massed band became a reality in 1952 when I formed the 'Men o'Brass', and Foden's, Fairey's and Morris were invited to fill the three places. Since those first days there have been one or two changes to the line-up, either because one or more bands were unavailable for a certain date or because of the odd internal wrangle. To be on the safe side the Men o'Brass ensemble is now a pool of four or five bands, and I simply ask any three, depending on availability, to fulfil concert or recording engagements. Sadly the concert dates are getting fewer and farther between owing to the escalating costs of mounting such a concert; no matter how large the hall, or how well packed it is, it is almost impossible to break even any more. It is not just the performing fees – you have to feed the brutes, an expensive business these days – bandsmen who often have to travel quite long distances to get to a concert are no longer content with a cup of tea and a bun. Recording is more easily arranged, but even so, a costly operation.

The question is often asked, 'Which is your favourite recording?', to which the invariable answer is 'Cathedral Brass'. This record, more than any other, epitomizes what Men o'Brass is all about. It was made on location at Worcester Cathedral with the resident organist, Christopher Robinson, joining forces with the band in some of the most moving music it was ever my pleasure to hear. Of all the tracks, I suppose the one I would choose for a desert island would be 'Jesu Joy of Man's Desiring' which, in the wonderful cathedral acoustics, had an almost ethereal sound. Although Sir Malcolm Sargent had conducted brass bands before, I think the atmosphere of that record opened his ears to a quality which, until then, he was not aware existed. So impressed was he that he immediately set about the task of arranging to conduct a whole Men o'Brass record himself as part of his seventieth birthday celebrations. We counted this as a great compliment. It is with great reluctance that I have ever invited another conductor to take Men o'Brass, but this was rather a special day and Sir Malcolm was rather a special man.

Another feature of brass banding I had the honour to share with Sir Malcolm Sargent was that we both got the sack from the National at the same time. Well, not the sack exactly, but the organizers of that time had developed a slightly inflated idea of their own importance and musical knowledge. It had for many years been the practice to leave the programme for the Festival Concert in the hands of those

Some of Sir Malcolm Sargent's arrangements for brass bands were planned on railway journeys we shared between Liverpool and London. He recorded them with Men o' Brass in his seventieth year.

of us who felt we knew something about the subject. In return we were quite happy to leave the detailed organization to them. It had also been the custom to engage the services of an eminent orchestral conductor to lead the massed bands. Like all good schemes it worked well enough for a few years. Sir Adrian Boult was amongst the first of such guests, whilst I filled the associate conductor role. As new regimes took over and found their feet they decided to impose their own ideas on what our distinguished guests should conduct, and inevitably the standard was in danger of falling to the level of popular, lightweight material. If Sir Malcolm and I did not think their choice was suitable, we would have to go.

It was some years later, when I visited him in his Kensington flat, that he casually asked, 'What happened to that competition next door in the Albert Hall? Does it still go on?'

'Oh, yes,' I said, 'very much so.'

'Well, I don't seem to have heard from them lately.'

'Perhaps it has slipped your memory,' I said, 'but you and I were dismissed on the same night.'

'Do you mean we were sacked?' he asked incredulously.

'Well, that's another word for it, certainly.'

'Oh, well,' he said, 'at least I was in good company.'

The footnote to that little story came when I visited the conductor's dressing room one night before the Festival Concert for a chat with my old friend and BBC colleague Sir Arthur Bliss.

'Ah,' he exclaimed by way of greeting, 'I want to see you. Can you tell me why you, of all people, selected such *undistinguished* music for me to conduct?'

I was glad to be able to say that I had nothing to do with it or the contest.

'But that's ridiculous,' he said, 'They can't run it without you.'

186

'But, Sir Arthur, they *can*, they *do*, and they will *continue* to do so!'

Sir Malcolm, like Tommy Beecham, is counted amongst the people for whom I have had the utmost respect and regard. Being two such opposites, it was hardly likely that they could get on together but, luckily, two great conductors rarely come into contact with one another. Sargent was too correct and gentlemanly for Beecham, and Beecham in turn was too unorthodox for Sargent, but it was a privilege to have worked with both of them. The only blot on Sargent's escutcheon in my book was at one of those Festival Concerts before we were both removed.

Having been to a Buckingham Palace Garden Party in the afternoon, he arrived at the concert wearing a morning suit and with no time to change. Leslie Woodgate, who was in charge of the choir, and I had, naturally, come prepared with our evening tail suits. The outcome was that I dashed home to get my morning suit and spent the rest of the concert changing jackets with Leslie Woodgate between items. To be honest it was not so bad for me, but Leslie was a few inches shorter and my coat almost reached the ground on his smaller frame.

In 1961 the opportunity came for me to take Men o' Brass to Canada. I had already been as a guest conductor to Toronto and London, Ontario, on my way to Australia in 1956 (about which I will say more shortly), and re-cemented many old friendships with some of the Canadian bandsmen who had served in the United Kingdom during the war. I was well aware that the Brigade of Guards bands were regular visitors to play at the Canadian National Exhibition in Toronto, and in 1956 had viewed, rather wistfully perhaps, the vast permanent site which it occupies on the shores of the lake in Toronto, wishing that we could bring a British *brass* band there. So when the invitation came, it was the fulfilment of long-held hopes. But which band to take? The twenty-five players plus two percussion, which is the normal British band, would have looked very forlorn in the middle of that huge bandshell – so it had to be three bands. And who else but my own Men o' Brass, who were accustomed to playing together as a unit? There was great excitement from the eighty-five players and officials concerned, but of course the three managements – Fairey, Foden's and Morris – had to be consulted for permission to take the bandsmen away for virtually four weeks. They co-operated by allowing them four weeks leave without pay, naturally, so my contract had to cover their wages. What fun we had, arranging for their respective wives to receive the weekly wages in the normal way in England, while I was responsible for the pay on tour. Some of the men (not many, I'm pleased to say!) were anxious that their wives should not receive more than they normally gave them, as they had never admitted to them their total weekly wage! Each bandsman was insured against illness, and most important of all, a BOAC aeroplane was booked for the trip; this was in the days before Freddie Laker and Pan-Am had the idea of cheap trips to America, and it was not only a costly business but, in the eyes of some of the older bandsmen, something of a hazardous one.

Unfortunately we were due to take off late at night, and the men had all the day –

188

We marched through Toronto, escorted by the Mounties, on our way to a civic reception.

Men o' Brass play in the Canadian National Exhibition bandstand, Toronto.

after parting from sweethearts and wives at their homes in the morning – to travel to London and take part in a sort of farewell broadcast from the Maida Vale studios of the BBC. Many of them had never been in an aeroplane before – and few had ever crossed the Atlantic – so it was with a great sense of relief that we counted heads on the waiting aeroplane and found that all had come – the prospect of a trip to Canada had proved too strong.

As was customary in those days there was a free bar on the 'plane, but I had asked the steward in charge to close it at 1 a.m. our time, in the hope that we might all get some sleep and be in good shape for our arrival. In fact, our Manager, Tommy Morcombe – a tower of strength on these trips, in spite of his small stature (and having by then lived down his indignant remarks to his bosses at Morris a few years before) – had even suggested, and arranged, a rehearsal on the CNE Bandstand at 2 o'clock on the afternoon of our arrival, after everybody had been settled into their various homes allocated by the CNE officials. But we had reckoned without Canadian hospitality. We were never sure whether the feast provided for us at the Hilton Hotel on arrival was intended as breakfast or a belated supper – our watches told quite different times from those in Toronto. Suffice it to say that having seen the rows of long tables set out for us, with an array of bottles of whisky, gin and brandy positioned like ninepins between each two or three men, and following a vast meal and the general cordiality of our hosts, we cancelled the 2 o'clock rehearsal!

But what happy memories we had of that trip! Some days were free, as we had to

189

Seventy-eight Men o' Brass competing with the deafening roar of Niagara Falls, 1961. Out front and inset on the right, my brother Rex.

play evenings only, which gave us all the opportunity for outings to Niagara and other beautiful spots, and to appreciate the warm welcome from many Canadian and English friends resident in Toronto, who were so kind in ferrying us all in various directions in their cars, and in arranging endless parties. Nevertheless, not one player was ever late on parade for our daily programmes, and looking back I cannot remember ever hearing finer playing before or since from three bands playing as one. Performing together for twenty-eight days – which would be impossible to repeat now, both financially and workwise – we became a tightly knit unit. And with only a single casualty – one player lost a tooth, which cost $2 to replace! We spent some happy days in that great bandstand.

All overseas visits to bands are milestones in a life of music. In 1956, my trip to Australia came about in rather special circumstances and in fact probably altered the remainder of my life.

I was still at the BBC, in my free time conducting as many as five bands at all the Championships, as had my predecessors Gladney, Halliwell and Rimmer. The results were very successful – Lady Luck was probably on my side – and anyway there were always five chances of a first prize in those days. But there came a time when the Controller, who was my chief at the BBC, summoned me to his office to tell me how much my work in the band world meant to the Corporation, congratulating me on my recent contest successes but making it clear that it was felt that my position as Supervisor of Brass Bands should put me on a higher plane, and that I should *not be competing at contests*. It so happened that I had been invited to go to Australia for their Championships in October, 1956 – a date which clashed with the National Contest in London. This was fortuitous, and there is now no doubt in my mind that my chief had wind of the invitation before he saw me. He enthusiastically recommended me to go, and mentioned that there were also some recordings in Canada and Australia which the BBC would like me to do.

So the decision was made. I would stop competing at contests. True, it had to come sooner or later, for if you are winning all the time, admiration at first from all your friends can often turn to envy. Mr Rimmer, as always, was right. While realizing that I would miss the dazzling excitement of the contest platform, I felt then, as I do now, that it was a better reward to retain one's friends than to continue to win competitions.

Fairey's were in victorious form at that time, and it was a wrench to leave them. Who to ask to take my place on the Albert Hall platform? We had won together at Belle Vue in September, and they were eager to pull off the double. I asked my old friend George Willcocks – Major Willcocks of the Irish Guards Band – if he would like to break into the brass band world and take Fairey's to the Albert Hall Contest. He had been a fine cornet player and was a distinguished conductor whose musicianship I respected highly, and I felt that his style would suit the band. He accepted, and it was with great pleasure that I telephoned from Australia on the night after the Contest to hear that Fairey's had won, and pulled off the double – even though with two different conductors. I was also amused to hear that one disgruntled losing competitor had been heard to say, 'There, he's 13,000 miles away, and he's still managed to fix it!' This was not only unkind, but totally untrue – winning as I had was the result of damned hard work, nights of travelling from band to band, sometimes three rehearsals in one day and, what is so essential, complete understanding from my players.

En route to Australia, this time accompanied by Margaret and our young son, we called in at Canada to renew old friendships, perform at a couple of concerts, and make some records for the BBC. On arrival in London, Ontario, I was alarmed to see a poster outside the concert hall saying, '*Hear* Harry Mortimer play – *see* him conduct!' Did they not realise that I had not performed in public for nearly ten years? I had not touched a cornet for some time, and certainly had not packed an instrument in my luggage. What to do? Eventually I borrowed a cornet and, joined by eight members of the Canadian Band, managed to scrape through 'Buglers' Holiday' and 'The Post Horn Gallop'. But Mr Rimmer would not have been pleased with the end result, I fear.

Looking back on the route taken by the Besses o'the Barn Band in 1906, we more or less followed their trail, by air instead of ship, of course, with a call in Honolulu for another visit to Waikiki and to the beautiful shell bandstand where the Municipal Band played. I do not know whether this still applies, but I understood from their conductor that his appointment was for only one year – every time they changed the Mayor they changed the band conductor as well! More a political than a musical appointment! There have been many bandstands which I have seen in

191

my life on which I have not been able to perform, but have gazed at, wishing I could. The bandstand in Honolulu was one of them, and another, very different, is the tiny wooden structure jutting out into the lake at Torre del Lago Puccini in Italy – the Tuscany home of Puccini for many years.

Fiji was Besses next port of call, and ours, but our stay was too short to make any enquiries about that long ago sojourn in the steamy heat of the island, a small speck in the ocean as we approached it from the air. And so to Sydney, en route for the City of Ballarat where the Australian Championships were to be held that year. Ballarat was a smallish city on a beautiful lake, which in 1956 was being prepared for the Olympic Games Yachting and Rowing competitions. All Australia was agog with excitement about two things – the Olympic Games themselves, the main events of which were to be held in the Melbourne Cricket Ground, and the coming of television to that country. The Band Contests in Ballarat, while an important national event, received radio but not TV coverage, since the actual opening of the ABC television network did not take place until the following week.

Meantime, Ballarat was alive with bandsmen from all parts of southern Australia. For a whole week the city resounded to the sound of bands – marching contests in the open air, solo championships and full band championships of all grades. In fact, like New Zealand, they do these things properly and make a week's banding of it, culminating in a memorable Champion of Champions concert on the last evening. Once again I was the subject of much supervision, segregated in the local hotel and not allowed to speak even to my family or to Frank Wright's sister, Laura, who still lived in his hometown of Ballarat, until the competitions were over. They were memorable days, full of variety and a wealth of music, marred only by the occasional shower which threatened to spoil the magnificent uniforms of some of the marching bands.

Back in Sydney, and the Championships over, it was possible to fraternize with some of the bands, and to continue my recording sessions for the BBC. It was good to meet once again one of the undoubted characters of the Australian band world, Albert (Bertie) H. Baille. He had caused a sensation at Belle Vue in 1924 by beating all our British bands with the Newcastle Steel Works Band. He was still conducting extremely successfully in 1956, and at the Ballarat Festival won almost everything with his new band, Melbourne Fire Brigade. Firemen in Britain do not as a rule take much interest in music, but this was a very busy and almost professional band, performing regularly on the famous racecourse in Melbourne. Alas, Bertie is no longer with us, but I was glad to have an opportunity of meeting once more in 1956, one of the outstanding conductors of Australia.

At the end of this trip I found myself with a whole suitcase full of reels of tape, all of which had to be edited on my return.

To give us a little breathing space after what had been an extremely hectic trip – it was still less than four weeks since we had left London – I had decided to take two weeks unpaid leave and with my family sail back from Singapore to Southampton on what was considered to be a very reliable and luxurious ship, the *Oranje*. She was a Dutch vessel, leaving Djakarta at a convenient time to call in at Singapore. We had been so busy during the previous few weeks that there had been little time to read newspapers or listen to the radio, and we were quite oblivious of the serious situation in the Middle East. A quiet sail through the Suez Canal would be a restful end to our trip ...

We set out from Sydney, and when our aeroplane touched down at Darwin we heard the first news of trouble. The British had attacked Egypt, the Suez Canal was closed, and how were we to get home? Darwin was not, in 1956, the most salubrious place in which to be stranded, and there seemed no alternative but to press on to Singapore as planned. This fascinating city provided all the distractions we needed for a few days. It was another and quite different world from the one we had just left, a busy, bustling place, full of the unexpected. After four anxious days and many trips to the shipping offices, banks and travel agencies, we managed to discover that our ship was at last about to leave Djakarta. Our route at that stage was decidedly sketchy. All we were told was that we would have to go back to Europe round the Cape – so our journey north to Singapore had really been a wasted one, since we had to travel south again. Our voyage on that ship took four long weeks and, in fact, we 'crossed the line' on that trip home no less than three times and became rather blasé about the accompanying ceremonies. The majority of passengers were Dutch, many returning from riot-stricken Djakarta with Indonesian wives and hosts of children, and our small clique of English passengers, with the additional support of a distinguished lawyer from Colombo who spoke perfect English, were the most unpopular people on the ship. It was, it seemed, our fault that our voyage was taking so long, that it was costing everybody so much in extra fares, and that unscheduled calls had to be made to pick up additional food, fuel and water for our extended journey. All the sins of Anthony Eden and the British Government in blocking the Canal were piled upon us. It was not exactly a pleasant voyage, but an interesting one in that it enabled us for a short while to see the glories of Colombo and, in my case, to revisit Cape Town exactly twenty years to the day (22 November) since I had last been there with Foden's, in 1936.

I had already spent a large proportion of our remaining supply of cash on cables, not only to the BBC but to various concert organizers and bands in England, explaining that the international situation prevented my return to duty on time. In all my long musical career I cannot remember having to cancel engagements to such an extent, but at last we left the sunshine behind and approached Southampton on a dull and cold December day. Before that trip the only date I could recall from my history lessons with any confidence was that of the Battle of Hastings. I could now safely add the Suez Crisis to my store of knowledge.

It was time to settle on a permanent contest conductor at Fairey's. I could take them for as many concerts as my duties would allow, but by BBC edict we needed a reliable contest man. I did not have to look far.

Smile you bugger, smile! Leonard Lamb.

Luckily there was at Fairey's a ready made contest conductor. When I had first accepted Sir Richard's blunt offer one of my first moves was to take a good look at the band as it was, and see where it might be strengthened. One of these structural alterations concerned my poaching, from the famous Oldham Rifles, a talented and serious-minded cornet player named Leonard Lamb. In a short space of time he became one of the most able bandmasters in the contesting field. He believed in my methods absolutely, and followed them to the letter. This is invaluable when you cannot attend every rehearsal, as it assures a continuity of standards. All too often you can find, when you only take a weekly rehearsal, that the bandmaster has, in the meantime, undone all your previous week's work by not being able to follow your line of musicality. I am not saying that the professional conductor is invariably right, or that the other chap is wrong. It is just that, when you are aiming for a standard or an interpretation, you need your bandmaster to pull in the same direction as you and not take the band off in another direction. Leonard Lamb was superb. I didn't have to tell him – he knew what I wanted. Consequently he was the ideal permanent contest conductor. He even liked to go along with my superstitions: for instance, I had a habit in those days of conducting with a long pencil – Leonard was most insistent that he had the same pencil.

The arrangement worked wonderfully. I rehearsed the band right up to the contest, and Leonard conducted on the day. In fact, he did so well that he went on and achieved a hat-trick between '61 and '63 at Belle Vue – a feat which had eluded me as a conductor for years.

If Leonard Lamb had any fault as a conductor it was that he could never break from his serious-minded inclination and be a bit of a showman on the conductor's rostrum. There has to be something of the extrovert about the man in the front – not too much, but enough to bring the best out of the band and to evoke a greater response from the audience. There are times when you need to look at a section to bring them in, and it is important to look at them in the right way. It would be nonsense to be all smiles in a tender passage, or miserable in a happy one. 'Life Divine' is a piece with which I have often been associated, and it so happened that this was the test-piece in 1963, when Leonard and the band were going for the difficult hat-trick. There is a trombone entry in the piece, and it had always been my practice to smile at the section when I brought them in. This set the mood for them, and they expected it. Try as I might I could not get Leonard to smile on the rostrum. In desperation, in the time between the final rehearsal and the contest, I 'borrowed' his score, and wrote on the top of the appropriate page the immortal words: 'Smile, you bugger, Smile!' He did. It worked. They got the hat-trick, and, as far as I know, the blemish remains on the score to this day.

Fairey's have been fortunate in their conductors over the years – Frank Smith, Elgar Clayton, Bob Mulholland, Jack Atherton, Kenneth Dennison and Walter Hargreaves have all added their own expertise to the band's fine record.

Although I am no longer anything to do with the musical management at Fairey's, I shall always feel part of the band. Since those first days in 1936 we have come a long way, and I am now promoted (or booted upstairs, if you prefer) to the position of Vice President. A happy memory will always be the visit of Prince Philip to the factory just prior to the contest in 1963. With his good wishes and my comments on the score we could hardly lose, could we? The Fairey band has always had a style of its own, which all successful bands must have. Some bands, like Foden's in the thirties, had an orchestral quality, others have a distinctive roundness of tone and some have a depth, but Fairey's always had brilliance – a sparkle – a shine. Forty-five years is a long time to spend with a band. It says much for them, and for me, that our association has lasted so long. Sir Richard Fairey would have been pleased, I think.

Then, all of a sudden, it was 1962 and I had to retire from the BBC, being past the age of reason, or so the rule book says. Retirement? What would I do? I hated gardening, had given up smoking a pipe and the dog had long since chewed up my slippers. Retirement was the last thing on the agenda. There was still so much to do, so many programmes still to make. It was hard to think of my department either belonging to somebody else or, worse, being amalgamated with a larger one. The evil hour was put off for two more years but in 1964 the day finally arrived when I would have to tidy my desk, clear out all those personal bits of nonsense which meant so much to me but would be merely a pile of junk to somebody else.

No more battles with programme controllers. No more 8.30 a.m. drives past the park and up through busy Oxford Street. No more irate telephone calls from band secretaries who felt slighted if their own band was not broadcast at least twice a week. In fact, nothing to laugh at at all. There was one consolation, though. In all those twenty-two years my grand title had remained unaltered. While the rank of Supervisor gradually disappeared from all the other departments mine stayed the same, and when I finally left there were, as far as I know, only two of us. The other was the canteen supervisor!

My brother Alex, conducting CWS Manchester, receives the
Belle Vue Challenge Shield from Eric Iles, and the Wills Cup.

10 Belle Vue:
Hail and Farewell

Since 1964 my idle hours between concerts have been spent with such trifles as running the British Open Championship-at Belle Vue, and the Spring Festival Contest for lower section bands. Here I must apologise.

Right from Chapter 1 it has been rather assumed that the reader knows all about championships and how they are run, which is something of an assumption. Let's try to put the matter right. The following is a blow by blow account of that most esoteric of occasions – The British Open Brass Band Contest, as seen through the eyes of a 'new boy' to the Brass world, my collaborator, Alan Lynton.

After 129 years of almost uninterrupted run, certain aspects of the contest are bound to have become something of a ritual. The first thing the uninitiated will notice in the backstage area at the start of the day is secrecy – positively cloak and dagger at times – whenever the adjudicators are in view. This, fortunately, is of short duration, for as soon as the courtesies have been observed the judges are spirited away to their box, where they will remain under lock and key for the rest of the day. Only the most trusted of stewards is allowed in their vicinity the whole time, and then only to bring them sustenance. Even the steps leading to their box are guarded. This is to ensure that they will have no idea of the identity of the bands who will be trying to please them all day. Although they know which bands will be appearing they have no idea of the order of play. In this way there is no question of favouritism or awarding marks on reputation rather than performance. A double-edged sword, it also has the advantage of forestalling any later accusations of skull-duggery from disgruntled supporters who were quite sure theirs was the best band of the day. It happens, you know.

For the judges in some contests the demands of nature are catered for by the presence of a plastic bucket. This most recent of technological advances has proved to be a modern boon – plastic being so much quieter than enamel – although at Belle Vue we go one step further and provide a really up-to-date chemical toilet, complete with seat!

After the judges are disposed of comes the next preliminary, the draw for order of play. If you have ever watched the dignitaries of the Football Association drawing the next round of the FA Cup, you will know what the band draw is like.

Belle Vue, just before the draw: the organizers, the bag and the balls.

Two cotton bags, both containing numbered balls for the number of bands competing: from the first is drawn the band number according to the printed programme, and from the second the number at which that band will appear. Thus, if number 9 band comes out of the first bag, and a number 14 comes out of the second, then band number 9 on the programme will appear fourteenth, and so on.

Poor Wingates Temperance – they have been drawn the dreaded number 1 for the second year running. The commiserations from all round fail to hide the relief felt by the others. You feel, rather than hear, 'Thank goodness, it's not us!'

To avoid delay on the platform while transporting percussion instruments for each band, two sets of timpani have been ordered – one the pedal type, and the other the old 'steam' type. It has to be decided which the various bands require so that the correct one can be ready when needed. A swift roll-call: 'Number one?' – 'pedal'; 'Number two?' – 'pedal'; 'Number three?' – 'ordinary' ... 'Number seventeen?' – 'I don't bloody know, but if it's different, we'll have it!' They all filter back to their respective bands carrying the good or the bad news, and in the Wingates room there is a bit of a rush. Who would have expected lightning to strike twice in the same place? Uniforms are quickly adjusted, ready to go.

H.M. has been here since before breakfast, and is standing like a twentieth century Canute holding back the tide which threatens, at any moment, to engulf him. Wave after wave of questions come at him, and the questioners are sent away more or less happy with the information they have been given.

I think it about time to make myself scarce, and decide to have a look at the trade stands in the other hall. After running across a wet car park in a force ten gale (so it is true, what they say about Manchester) I find myself in a gleaming Aladdin's Cave of brass and silver plating. Each manufacturer is showing his wares, and a beautiful sight it is, too. Mixed in with this radiant vision are stalls where you can buy anything from a full Wagner score to 'First Steps' in playing the cornet/ euphonium/E flat bass/trombone, etc.

And so back to the concert hall. It is fifteen minutes before the contest is due to start and all the programmes have been sold. Worse still, about five hundred people have had to be turned away from the unbooked seating as the hall is sold out. Whilst most contest organizers would be delighted at a sell-out, H.M. seems positively upset by it. 'Five hundred. That's an awful lot of disappointed people.'

The Stage Manager, Stanley Wainwright, is busy checking that everything is where it should be, and that the registration table is functioning correctly. Every player has to register with his band before they can take the stage. No 'borrowed men' these days! It is generally reckoned that this one has the best line up of bands for many years. All the big names seem to be here – Black Dyke, Besses, Brighouse & Rastrick, Carlton Main, City of Coventry, Cory, C W S Manchester, Ever Ready, Fairey, Foden's, Grimethorpe, G U S, Hammond's, Stanshawe, Wingates, William Davis, Yorkshire Imps, Desford Colliery, Ransome, Rochdale, Webb Ivory and the Spring Contest winners (the Irish Champions) Templemore, who include in their ranks some charming young ladies in glamorous long dresses. And they are *all* about to perform the same piece of music!

By five minutes to eleven the hall is packed – 5000 people wait expectantly for the day's contest to begin. Many of them will be brass players – some from lesser-known bands and some perhaps retired from the contest arena. One thing is sure – they are men and women who know their bands. In their own sphere they are at least as knowledgeable as any audience assembled at any of our great concert halls to hear a classical orchestra. Typical of the Belle Vue stalwart is Arthur Renshaw, now aged seventy-eight, whom I met when he was backstage looking up old friends. He started attending the Open when he was five, and has not missed a contest for seventy-two years. When he first came it was held on Wakes Monday, and he accompanied his father and grandfather who had attended for many years before that, so the Renshaws have been part of the contest fabric almost since its inception.

The ever enthusiastic BBC announcer, Robin Boyle, now introduces us to the day's proceedings. A telegram from Her Majesty The Queen – patron of the British Open Brass Band Championship – is read out. And the first band takes the stand – Wingates. 'They were drawn first last year an' all,' intones a voice from the row behind.

And so to the first notes blown in competition. If you imagine that hearing a piece twenty-two times in a day tends to strain the musical appreciation of even the most dedicated of audiences, you could be right. But when an outstanding band plays, you instantly know it. The audience reaction is one of total recognition. Apart from the biased ones, and it must be admitted that contest audiences have their fair share of these, the hall will erupt when they have been treated to a 'Champion' performance.

Warm applause as Wingates finish, and the wry comment from the wise sage in the row behind – 'You'll hear worse than that today'. I think it was intended as praise.

199

The third band to play are the defending champions – Brighouse & Rastrick – The Floral Dance Band, as they are referred to by the non-banding fraternity. When they appear in their traditional purple and gold uniforms there is that peculiar buzz which comes from an audience anticipating something special. They are followed by another famous band, Besses, who have not figured in the top prizes at the Open since 1959. They are directed by a celebrated conductor, Roy Newsome, formerly of Black Dyke, who has now taken on Besses. But what is this? Besses having performed, the band changes but the conductor remains the same. These days it is rare for a conductor to have two bands in one contest, and even more unusual for his second band – in this case Sun Life (Stanshawe) – to have drawn the number immediately following – although Harry Mortimer remembers this happening to him at the National when he, also, took more than one band.

After a 'purple patch', which includes many other favourites to win the title – Black Dyke, Grimethorpe, Foden's and Fairey's – eventually every band of the twenty-two has played, and now the long wait while the judges confer and announce a result. The partisans in the audience line up in their clans. Finally, the judges are ready to emerge from their day-long incarceration. Who knows, they might even make a few friends this time. Making friends, though, is the last consideration on the minds of William Relton and Albert Chappell (two very experienced brass band adjudicators), and Eric Wetherell (making his debut as a judge at the Open). They mount the platform, hand a white envelope to the controller who must announce the six who in their view gave the best performance, and these are announced in time-honoured manner – in reverse order. From amongst these six bands, the youngest cornet player and the youngest flugel player will receive a brand new instrument – a valuable prize. Additionally, of course, the six prize-winning bands receive magnificent trophies, and divide between them cash totalling more than £2000.

The first band to be announced (sixth) is Yorkshire Imperial Metals. There is a sort of double dread about being called out early in the prizes: too early and it means you are in the lower places, although at least you know you are placed *somewhere*. The first and second places must go through agonies, thinking, perhaps, that they will come nowhere. Yorkshire Imps look reasonably resigned to their sixth place, and relax.

Next (fifth) is Besses o' the Barn. That is two of the big boys out of the way.

Fourth is announced, and it is Black Dyke. I seem to remember reading in a *British Bandsman*, dated 1900, that Black Dyke supporters did not take kindly to their heroes being placed anywhere less than first. Seventy-nine years later, things haven't changed that much.

Third prize is received with much more enthusiasm, though, and Grimethorpe look pleased enough with their place.

Now, two places left, and who is to get them? Fairey's, surely, must feel that they have done it, but after a gap of fourteen years since they last got their hands on the trophy they must also be feeling nervous. Second place, and a section from somewhere up in the rafters of Belle Vue suddenly explodes into joy and merriment. It is Desford Colliery, and this young band has gone wild. Not without justification – they had competed with, and beaten, some of the best bands in the land, and done so with distinction.

And now the silence as we await the winners. The Fairey supporters cannot look. Seats are squirmed in and nails are rendered useless.

The announcement. The relief! Walter Hargreaves and the Fairey Band are the winners of the 1979 British Open. The two instruments both are awarded to two members of the Desford Colliery band – the cornet to Kevin Dye, and the flugel horn to Clive Burnell. One more treat for the audience, who remain until the last note is blown. The winners, Fairey's, now take the stand again to record a selection which is to be broadcast by the BBC later in the evening.

Walter Hargreaves in action

That was just one day at Belle Vue, typical of so many over the last hundred and thirty years. What a wealth of memories the old place has! It has always been noted for changes; from the day when it was first named 'Jennison's Gardens' in the 1820s the motto of the founder, 'Old John' Jennison, was 'Novelty, Novelty' – and there was always something new at Belle Vue.

Originally a public house named rather grandly the 'Belle View House', with a 36 acre thistle patch, John Jennison had the vision to see that this property could become the entertainment showpiece of the North, and he set about making it just that. The hard working mill girls and their male counterparts took to the idea as only an entertainment-starved population could. A pleasure garden with a lake, travelling jugglers, tumblers and acrobats and, best of all, a zoo – something unique at that time, the first elephant to appear in Lancashire took up residence in 1850 – all went to make Belle Vue the regular Sunday afternoon outing. There was even the joy of dancing to the sound of the Belle Vue Band which played all the popular waltzes, quadrilles, polkas and schottisches of the day. And, of course, the most popular of all, clog dancing. John Jennison pioneered the first greyhound track *in the world* in 1847; balloon ascents, Rugby football, speedway, boxing and wrestling followed. Belle Vue brewed its own beer, baked its own bread and buns, and even printed its own programmes and tickets. In short, it was a little world of its own.

By 1852 Jennison, who never stopped his search for a new idea to attract and entertain his crowds, hit upon a Drum and Fife Band Contest. This proved to be yet another success, and so the following year he organized a Brass Band Contest to be held on the first Monday in September to coincide with the local Wakes Week holidays. The British Open Championship was inaugurated and, apart from the one exception of 1859, it has been held at Belle Vue ever since. The lasting success of John Jennison's venture was finally assured when the London and North-Western Railway built a main line station called, appropriately enough, Longsight, close to the Pleasure Gardens. *Alight here for Belle Vue* was emblazoned across the platform, and alight they did, in their hundreds. Belle Vue now could serve not only the population of Manchester, but the eager folk from other towns, cities and villages as well.

The first such contest attracted eight bands and was won by Mossley Temperance. The rendering afterwards of 'God Save the Queen' is one of the earliest recorded massed band performances.

Some of the rules from these early days are still in existence. For instance, the rule that no professional player should appear, although the professional conductor was allowed, as he is now. No maximum limit of players was specified, but the minimum number required was ten. Rules governing the adjudicators were very strictly laid down and are still adhered to today. In 1853, though, it was an outdoor contest and the adjudicators were firmly placed in a tent from which they

Early passes to Belle Vue pleasure gardens were signed by the Jennisons themselves.

ZOOLOGICAL GARDENS, BELLE-VUE,
MANCHESTER.

WODSOM 70 YT

TEMPERANCE FIFE AND DRUM BAND CONTEST,
MONDAY, July 31st, 1854.

EAST LANCASHIRE RAILWAY.

A SPECIAL TRAIN leaves—

	a.m.		a.m.
PRESTON at	8-15	CHERRY TREE	
BAMBER BRIDGE	8-23	BLACKBURN	
HOGHTON	8-30	RISHTON	
PLEASINGTON	8-35	CHURCH	

Returning from BELLE-VUE STATION at 10-15 p.m., at the conclusion of the Entertainments and the BURNING of MOSCOW, with a gorgeous display of FIREWORKS, by BRUCE.

FARE, *There and Back,* which includes Free Admission to the Gardens, all Covered Carriages. **3s. 6d.**

The St. Mary's Flute and Drum Band, Preston, the Walton le-Dale Flute and Drum Band, and the Preston, High-street, Fife and Drum Band, accompany the Train.

For Bands consisting of Performers of any age. First Prize, **£10.** Second, **£5.** Third, **£2. 15s.** Fourth, **£1. 5s.**
The number of Performers not to be less than Eighteen, nor more than Thirty.

THE FOLLOWING BANDS HAVE ENTERED TO CONTEND FOR THE PRIZES:—

Name of Band. and Residence.	No.	Conductor's Name.
St. Mary's Flute and Drum Band, Preston	20	James Warren.
Borough Fife and Drum Band, Oldham	21	George Bardsley.
Walton-le-Dale Flute and Drum Band	19	Thomas Marginson.
Ashton Temperance Band of Hope, Oldham-road	30	John Hinds.
Preston, High-street, Fife and Drum Band	19	Thomas Marginson.
Oldham Temperance Fife and Drum Band	23	Benjamin Needham.
Manchester Sons of Freedom Temperance Fife and Drum Band, Peter-street	30	John Newland.
Leeds, Yorkshire, Woodhouse Fife and Drum Band	30	Peter Gilston.

To the best Band will also be given a Brass Side Drum, value £3. 3s. presented by Mr. HIGHAM, of Manchester.

At the conclusion of the Contest, and before the Judges give in their decision, all the Bands will join in playing the "British Grenadiers' March," and "Rule Britannia."

TICKETS are to be had at the Railway Stations on the previous Saturday night; and, to secure places, application at that time is desirable.

These Grounds cover an area of 36 acres, and are laid out as extensive PLEASURE GARDENS, with Ornamental Walks and Parterres, Arbours, Greenhouses, Hothouses, &c. An extensive ZOOLOGICAL COLLECTION, including many rare and valuable specimens, is maintained within the Grounds; and each season, a GRAND HISTORICAL OPEN-AIR PICTURE is produced, which, on Gala Days, and on special occasions, is exhibited with FIREWORKS at dusk.

DETAILED PROGRAMME OF ATTRACTIONS.

GRAND HISTORICAL PICTURE OF MOSCOW,
THE ANCIENT IMPERIAL METROPOLIS OF RUSSIA,

Painted by DANSON and SONS, of London, upon upwards of 50,000 square feet of canvas, and erected across the great Ornamental Lake. Viewed by daylight, its effect is impressive and surprising. In front stands the sacred KREMLIN; and in altitude, towering above all, rises the FAMED BELFRY of IVAN VELIKII. This gay and gorgeous scene exhibits a totally different aspect at dusk, when is represented that Conflagration which is said to have been more extensive, awful, and sublime than the world had perhaps seen since its foundation. Whole quarters of the city, hitherto standing, in a few minutes are seen in a blaze—the fiery contagion spreads far and wide—the up-turning of iron roofs—the roaring of the flames—the crash of tumbling edifices—the fire-wreathed skeletons of desolated dwellings, and the boom of artillery, make up a combination appalling to contemplate. At length the Imperial Palace becomes a prey to the insatiable flames, the Belfry and Arsenal are blown up, and in the walls of the Kremlin, toward the river, several breaches are effected by the springing of mines; and the towers, torn from their foundations, are hurled into the air. Amid the burning wreck of Houses, Shops, Stores, and Palaces, are seen TWO TRANSPARENCIES, 200 FEET LONG, illustrating the RETREAT OF THE FRENCH ARMY, in endless enfilade, from the scene of that plunder and devastation by which the venerable and imperial City of Moscow fell by the hand of insatiable ambition within the brief period of six days.

EXTENSIVE MENAGERIE OF ANIMALS AND BIRDS,

Including five African Lions and Lioness', Leopards, Jaguars, South American Lion, Bears, Bactrian Camel, from Turkey, Deer, Lamas, Yak, &c. BIRDS:—Pelican of the Wilderness, Condors from the Andes, Ostriches from Africa, Horned Cock, (the most curious bird alive,) &c. &c.; together with the largest, finest, and most varied collection of Macaws, Cockatoos, and others of the Parrot tribe generally, in the kingdom.—*Feeding Hour,* 5 o'clock.

MUSEUM OF STUFFED BIRDS, ANIMALS, REPTILES, INSECTS, PAINTINGS, &c.

Curious Fossils, Shells, Living Lizards, Serpents, and other extraordinary specimens of Nature. Also a varied Collection of objects of antiquity and curiosity; and MAKIN'S GRAND ORIGINAL PICTURE of OUR FIRST PARENTS IN PARADISE.—*Catalogues 1d. each.*

MONSTER MONKEY HOUSE, containing the largest stock of this playful tribe in England.
PLEASURE BOATS on the large Lake, covering an area of two acres.

MAZE, for the recreation and amusement of Visitors, in the centre of which is an elegant Aviary, in the Gothic style.

A MAGNIFICENT OCTAGONAL ORCHESTRA,

In the Arabesque style of decoration, designed by Messrs. DANSON and SONS, and in itself an elegant work of art, has recently been constructed, for the increased Band of Performers.

The TWO SPACIOUS DANCING PLATFORMS accommodate 1,000 couple at a time, without inconvenience.

The FIGURES and GROUPS OF STATUARY interspersed throughout the Gardens are numerous and varied, and include two imposing Stone Statues, on appropriate pedestals, of the Heroes of Waterloo and Trafalgar; Diana, Apollo, Solitude; the Bird's Nest, by Cardwell; Thorwalsden's Boy and Thorn; Canova's Dancing Nymphs; and other examples of Ancient and Modern Art.

For the convenience of Pleasure Parties, a LOFTY and SPACIOUS TEA-ROOM has been built, where Excursionists, for a merely nominal charge, are provided with Hot Water, Teapots, Cups, Saucers, and all other requisites. They can also be supplied, on reasonable terms, with every description of Refreshments for the Tea-table.

The CELEBRATED BELLE-VUE BRASS BAND will continue to play the most fashionable Dance Music during the afternoon.
Refreshments, including Tea, Wines and Spirits, Ale, Porter, Ginger Beer, Cakes, Salad, &c. at reasonable prices.

Excursionists, after visiting the various attractions in Manchester, will be admitted to the Gardens free up to 6-0 P M.
N.B.—Excursionists are requested not to appear in working dress.

Railway to and from London-road, Fare 2d.; and Omnibus to and from Market-street Manchester.

CAVE and SEVER, Printers, Palatine Buildings, Hunt's Bank, Manchester.

By 1865 the Black Dyke band, looking like frontiersmen, had converted entirely to brass instruments. In the fifties we played similar ancient relics. From left to right: my brother Alex plays the ophicleide, Harold Moss the sackbut, myself the keyed bugle and Jack Mackintosh the valveless trumpet.

could hear all and see nothing. The bands played two pieces of their own choice, which must have made for a varied day's listening, but a difficult task for the judges to decide between the bands.

Mossley Temperance obviously took this first contest very seriously indeed and were equipped with a complete new set of saxhorns – something of a novelty at that time. The first prize of £16 would not have gone very far, even then, towards that sort of outlay, so their public subscription methods must have been very effective. Their success was short-lived, however, and it is not until 1897 – forty-four years later – that we see their name once more in the list of winners. By this time, we note that the Temperance part of their name has gone.

Many of the first competing bands were still using ancient instruments which had probably been passed from generation to generation – instruments like the ophicleide. Gradually, though, as the years went on many of the old brass and reed bands were abandoning their clarinets and flutes and were acquiring the more modern brass instruments. One of the earliest bands to opt totally for brass was Black Dyke. The local mill owner took them under his patronage and, in 1855, equipped them with a complete set of brass instruments. It was not until 1862 that the name of Black Dyke appeared on the Champions' list, but once it made the grade it was a name which for generations of brass band enthusiasts has meant musicianship of the very best – as consistent now as at any time in the past, and as regular a winner as any band in the country.

Having organized his first contest, John Jennison looked for ways to improve the prizes, and hit on an idea which has recently been revived through the generosity of musical instrument manufacturers – that of awarding a brand new instrument to the winning band. No doubt it was the increased price of the instruments which led to the cessation of this practice for so many years. When Jennison started the custom in 1854 an E flat bombardon cost ten guineas, whereas now a similar instrument would cost nearer two thousand.

In 1855 came another innovation – the test-piece. This was to be played in addition to one piece of the band's own choice. The first test-piece was called 'Orynthia', composed by a local Manchester musician, James Melling. This formula – one test and one own choice – went along very well until 1867, when the own choice was dropped and we had the contest much as it is today. There was, of course, the year 1859 when there was no contest as only three bands entered. Perhaps the test-piece was too daunting, or maybe they were fed up with the Leeds bands and Accrington taking all the prizes (they had taken all but the first year.) Whatever the reasons, the contest was abandoned that year – something which two World Wars and one Boer War all failed to achieve.

The 1870s ushered in the age of the professional conductor, with John Gladney at the vanguard of a line which stretched through Swift, Owen, Rimmer, Halliwell and, in all modesty, a few Mortimers. John Gladney scored at every contest from 1871 to 1904, with an unequalled twenty firsts in addition to many seconds and thirds. He conducted no less than one hundred and ten bands in his career, winning sixty-nine prizes. With every top band clamouring for his services, we may think that this was not so very difficult to achieve, but when you think of the time span – over thirty years at the top – the feat takes on superhuman proportions. His only serious rivals were Swift and Owen, and in 1882 the three of them took all six places at Belle Vue – two each – which they no doubt considered their due. The rule allowing conductors to take any number of bands on to the platform has never been amended, despite the efforts of many well-intentioned reformists. In 1924, for instance, a great debate raged in the popular band press as to the legitimacy of the use and abuse of this custom. 'One Band – One Conductor' was the cry. The controversy was never resolved, and the rules remain unchanged today. However, it is not so common to see a conductor with more than one band nowadays, so you might say that the practice died from natural causes.

Nostalgia is the bandsman's malady and many look back through their National or Belle Vue programmes, which still, after all these years, meticulously tabulate all the winners from 1853 to the present, with all the conductors and test-pieces – even the judges are named. A glance through these lists reminds us of all those old bands, some of whom, like Black Dyke, are still at the top, and others who shone for a year and faded out of the limelight. Names like Mossley Temperance, Dewsbury, Bramley, Accrington – who won twice in the first six years of Belle Vue, as did Leeds Railway Foundry – Batley, Todmorden, Meltham Mills, Heckmondwike, Bacup, Stalybridge, Robin Hood Rifles, Saltaire, Linthwaite, Kingston Mills, Denton Original, Nelson, Wyke, Rochdale, Irwell Springs, our own Hebden Bridge, Shaw, Horwich R.M.I. – the list could go on ten times longer, and remember these were the Championship Section bands. There were hundreds more from the other sections, some of whom were to go on to become Champions and others who never made the top at all. But all of them testify to the origins of brass bands, particularly but by no means exclusively, in the North, where people would get together and give up their free time for the sheer joy of making music.

With these second section bands in mind a second contest was added to the calendar in 1886, when the July Contest (now the Spring Contest) was introduced. The winner of this would automatically qualify for the September Open, and in 1890 history was made (never to be repeated) when Batley Old won both competitions. It goes almost without saying that their conductor was the omnipresent John Gladney.

One adjustment to the rules governing conductors was made in 1874 by John Jennison's son, who had taken over the organization of the contest on his father's death. From now on, conductors could no longer conduct *and* play at the same time. This, as we said on the subject of my father, was common practice up to this time – a practice which bred many a left-handed conductor. Perhaps the organizers thought things had gone just a shade too far when, in 1872, one Joseph Paley (father of the more celebrated player, John), played cornet *and* soprano *and* conducted! This almost one-man-band, Saltaire, won second prize. Another rule added to the statute book was the four-mile rule, which stipulated that all players in a contesting band should be resident in, or at least no more than four miles from, the town from which the band was entered. Doubtless this was an early attempt to restrict the use of 'borrowed men', though I daresay that a convenient address could soon be found if the need was urgent enough.

The rules, then, formulated at the end of the last century are still, in essence, those of today. The strict adherence – almost religious devotion – to the ritual of 'the draw' to see which band plays at which position still has the same excitement and magic that it always had, and the secrecy which shrouds the judges is as fastidious as ever. In fact, little has changed in nearly a hundred years. Such is the tradition of banding.

Sadly, as I write, Belle Vue as we all know it is to disappear and is already a shadow of its former self. The Zoo Park is now an over-grown jungle out of which the moss-covered heads of the plaster prehistoric animals (similar to those at the Crystal Palace) loom pathetic and startling. The celebrated 'Bobs' ride, the helter-skelter and all the other amusements have disappeared; the lake has gone, and so has the

A poster for the 1928 Belle Vue contest.
The test-piece was 'Lorenzo', and with it
Fodens completed their first hat-trick.

great elephant house – although the Elephant Room at the back of the King's Hall (used for stabling the circus elephants at Christmas) up to this year has accommodated a series of rather reluctant bandsmen as an additional changing-room – aerosols supplied free of charge!

Standing in isolation in the middle of this vast eighty acres of nothingness (soon to become a shop and office complex, we are told) the King's Hall still rises in shabby grandeur. Such a variety of talent has appeared there over the years, reflecting constantly the life of the nation in war and peace. Open-air clog dancing by thousands was replaced by the changing dance-scene in the Coronation Ballroom, where the Beatles appeared at the height of their fame. In the splendid arena of the King's Hall countless bright-eyed North Country children were first introduced to the glamour and magic of the International Circus, controlled at the flick of a finger by the world-famous ringmaster, the immaculate George Lockhart, and accompanied by Fred Bonelli's full-time Belle Vue Orchestra, which played for firework displays and dancing as well. On a grander scale, the Hallé Orchestra and Sir John Barbirolli made it their home after the bombing of the Manchester Free Trade Hall and Benjamino Gigli made his last concert appearance here in 1955. In contrast, the Trade Union Congress Centenary celebrations – bursting with marching bands, politicians and television cameras – were held there. Teenagers went wild over Andy Williams; more sober citizens enjoyed Bingo and Old-Tyme Dancing. Bringing things almost up to date, we even had a bomb-scare in the middle of the British Open in 1978. Imagine five thousand people sitting quietly in the Hall, adjudicators writing away in their segregated box, and a band half-way through the test-piece, when suddenly a bomb alert and the police instruction to the unbelieving organizer (who happened to be me!): 'Everybody out!' And everybody – including the continually-guarded adjudicators – indeed did get out within five minutes, only to find that it was a hoax! Nevertheless, a shattering experience. That was just *another* day at the British Open Championship. Now Belle Vue is destined to go, and a new home is to be found for the 1982 Championship.

Since those happy days listening to Father conducting the men of Hebden Bridge and hearing the bandroom talk of past triumphs, Belle Vue has always been the magnet – the goal towards which the year's work was aimed. Other contests were but a curtain-raiser to the big event at Belle Vue.

What's in a name? The British Open Brass Band Championship will surely survive in another hall.

Well, I daresay it will, but to me and thousands of other, older, bandsmen, the magic of the name will be sadly missed. Not only the name, but the place itself. The very dust on the walls reeked of brass. To step up to the rostrum on contest day was a certain cure for any misplaced over-confidence on the part of a player or conductor, knowing, as one did, that for over a hundred years the legendary figures of the past had trodden the same route and triumphed – not once, but over and over again.

The feeling of a great loss is one which refuses to be shaken off and the memory of 1936 when we heard of the fire at Crystal Palace returns to haunt me all over again.

If this is merely nostalgia, then let it be so, but nostalgia is a strong part of a bandsman's life. I, at least, shall always remember the faded old Duchess known as Belle Vue with fondness, love and, perhaps most of all, gratitude. For 129 years she laid low vain ambition and made giants of men who had the talent to take her on.

I wonder if, in another 129 years, somebody will think similarly of an as yet unnamed building?

The atmosphere of the Open. Dear to the hearts of generations of bandsmen will be the memory of the King's Hall at Belle Vue, seen here in 1980.

210

11
So you, too, think you can conduct

From Prime Ministers to choirmasters, from impresarios to the persistent foot-tapper and head-nodder at the Festival Hall, the whole world thinks it can conduct. 'Stick-itch' is what we call it in the trade, and stick-itch is an indiscriminate affliction. I have seen straight-backed martinets whose concern is for tempo and nothing else, who would be unable to coax music out of a song-thrush. On the other hand I have seen the opposite. The writhing contortionist who tries his damndest to climb into the bell of the nearest euphonium in his misguided efforts at interpretation. Neither should be allowed within a quaver's distance of a band or orchestra.

I have described how Beecham worked, but do not try to emulate him because Beecham was Beecham and inimitable. As a matter of fact, don't copy anybody. Once you have learnt your basic technique you are on your own, and will sink or swim by your own personality, and only that. Conductors are not manufactured, they are born with a gift of imparting feelings and instincts. They are leaders who will be blindly obeyed by good musicians because they are instinctively right.

The knowledgeable critic will only blame the conductor when the end result is a bad performance, and will happily accept whatever the conductor does or does not do in achieving his end when the result is good. Unfortunately, not all audiences are discriminating critics and some like their conductor to perform somersaults and cover himself in sweat and glory. I had once, back in the Foden's days, been playing at the Lord Street bandstand in Southport, the home of William Rimmer. At the end of the concert I had to dash for a train as I was expected in Manchester for a BBC Northern Symphony Orchestra concert, and I bundled myself into a corner seat on one of those old-fashioned separate compartment trains. Sitting opposite was a gentleman who, judging by the programme clutched in his hand, had attended the afternoon concert. If you travel on the railways as much as I do you eventually forget your British heritage and actually speak to fellow travellers.

'I see you've heard the band today,' I said cheerfully enough.

'That's right,' he replied, without too much enthusiasm.

'Did you like it?'

'No.'

'Oh,' I said, somewhat taken aback, 'Why not?'

'Well, conductor didn't do owt.'

'How do you mean?' I asked, beginning to bristle a bit by now.

'Have you heard Besses o' the Barn play?' he asked patiently, as though I were in need of instruction in Bible texts. 'When they play loud, you see the conductor waving his arms and making a great show. And when they play soft he gets down and he's all quiet like and on tiptoe.'

'Well, what about the band this afternoon,' I said, 'They played loud and soft didn't they?'

'Oh aye,' he reluctantly agreed, 'Band did, but conductor didn't!'

You see what I mean?

On my first ever adventure into conducting in a contest, I came off the stand at the end of what I had imagined to be an exhilarating performance with my hair on end and my collar half way round my neck, and eagerly awaited Father's appraisal. 'Well,' he said, carefully filling his pipe, 'If it's for doing the splits and pulling faces at the trombones, you've got it in the bag.'

On the other hand a few score years later, a critic recently reviewed one of my Men o' Brass concerts and wrote:

'Harry Mortimer ... was once a fiery and active conductor. Nowadays he conducts with eyebrow and elbow!'

Personally I like to think that I have at last learned that it is not necessary to precipitate a heart attack every time one mounts the rostrum. Be that as it may, in the end there is but one sure method: a local up-and-coming conductor suddenly started to win every contest he entered. He could do no wrong. Even the older and wiser lads started to take notice. What's this chap got, then, that he wins everything? So they watched him. At every contest they were there to see what it was he had discovered that they had overlooked. Gradually it dawned upon them that, in the second or two before the band started to play, he took a piece of paper from his coat pocket, looked at it, put it back again, and started. This happened every time, so his rivals decided that they had to find out what it was that was written there. One evening they sneaked into his dressing room while the young man was at the bar and they looked in his coat pocket and there it was, 'How to win a contest – cornets on the left, trombones on the right!'

You see, it's as simple as that.

I think one of the most rewarding aspects of banding is the friendships which one makes, and this applies particularly to visits abroad. There is a peculiar comradeship amongst bandsmen which transcends all barriers of language, and it is sometimes rather confusing to have one's hand shaken unexpectedly in a street, or at a contest, by someone one has met three years before, a few hundred or thousand miles away. But it is always a pleasure to meet such enthusiasts, and I was particularly glad to have the privilege, three years ago, of greeting in London and chatting (often through a very beautiful Japanese interpreter) with a party of bandsmen from Tokyo. Their leader was a charming man called Takeo Yamamoto,

212

who obviously greatly enjoyed his short trip over here, and repeated it the next year to include a visit to the British Open at Belle Vue, this time accompanied by his wife. I was intrigued to hear from them of the great enthusiasm in Japan for brass bands, who play our British band music and even compose some of their own. They suggested that I ought to visit their country and meet some of their bands. Mr Yamamoto was as good as his word. At the beginning of 1980 I heard from him that he had invited the Leyland Vehicles Band to do a tour of Japan during the summer of that year, and hoped very much that I could go at the same time to do some seminars and to guest-conduct the band. This was eventually arranged, and for the first time in my long career of touring with a band I was merely the guest conductor, and had no part in the organization of the trip, which was handled with great efficiency (as one would expect of the Japanese) largely by Mr Yamamoto and his wife – who even appeared with the band at one concert when a percussion-player was taken ill – we had not realized until then that she was a Professor of Percussion, and she performed with great aplomb despite the language barrier. This tour, which included fifteen wonderful concerts and seminars in many fine concert halls and schools, was a revelation to us all from England. It was hot; it was a very tight and busy schedule; and none of us could speak the language. But with the goodwill of Richard Evans, the Musical Director of Leyland Vehicles Band, and the splendid playing and deportment of the band I felt that they were excellent ambassadors of British bands to a far-off country, and probably blazed a successful trail for other bands to go there – and, who knows, for bands from Japan to visit us. For there is no doubt that there is tremendous enthusiasm, matchless discipline and great talent there which cannot do anything but increase, for school bands abound everywhere. Takeo Yamamoto, to his great delight was made an honorary member of our National Brass Band Club during our visit – as President of the Club I was authorized to present this to him during a television programme which we made in Tokyo. The long nineteen-hour journey there and back is a costly one, in comparison with which America seems but a step away; but I am sure we shall hear much more of brass bands in Japan, as opposed to the American-type bands which until a few years ago were the more popular.

Coda

At the end of every piece of music comes the Coda. The word has been before me thousands of times on a score, and after spending many months looking back over almost seventy-five years of brass – years full of incident, progress and, above all, the infinite joy of listening to and making music – I find myself thinking of *this* Coda as a new beginning – not for me, but for the thousands of young players all over the world in school or junior bands. Some will put down their instruments with their school books, possibly never to return to them. Others will persevere and enjoy the unique thrill of making music all their lives. In either case something will have been gained. They are indeed fortunate. They are the children of the age when music teaching in schools has become the accepted norm – of an age when music ceased to be the preserve of the more fortunate schools and became part of a broader educational philosophy. I was fortunate in my musical education because I came from a family which organized its life around such matters. There was precious little teaching in the ordinary schools of the day, and yet, when Fred advertised for willing lads to come and try their hand at playing in a band the response was wonderful. It could be argued that the lack of other diversions encouraged them, but they were not there out of boredom but because they genuinely felt that they and music had something in common and, at last, somebody had the foresight to let them see what they could do.

Now in the enlightened eighties we are in danger of slipping back to those days. 'Good thing, too', did I hear somebody say? No, it is not a good thing. In the last thirty years numerous gifted men and women have given their time and talent to teaching in schools and seminars. The result has been a remarkable rise in the pool of talent available to bands and orchestras and, perhaps more importantly, a rise in the number of educated audiences. All education is of vital importance and if, as we are promised, the age of leisure is upon us, let us be quite sure that our children go out into the world with the knowledge of how best to use that leisure. To do less is surely to court danger.

How much poorer would have been the BBC's marvellous 'Young Musician of the Year' competition had it not attracted entrants from the brass band world? As it was, the fact that so many young players came from very ordinary walks of life was, in itself, a triumph. And how delighted I was that Michael Hext, the trombonist who won the first series, came from good brass band stock. His story and mine were not really so different as he, too, was taught by his father, Terry Hext, also a fine trombonist and conductor of the Bedford Town Band. I may add that Michael won his first prize without my help, despite the fact that I was on the final adjudicating panel. As the representative of the brass section I was not allowed to propose the winner. However, the verdict was unanimous. Equally pleasing to see was the fact that there were even more brass band players in the finals of the second series, with two girls, Elaine Wolff and Catherine Howells, on cornet and trumpet, and two euphonium boys.

Whilst I claim no direct credit for the growth of youth banding in the past thirty years, I like to think that I played my part in that great movement. During my early years at the BBC we ran a programme called, appropriately, 'Bandsmen of Tomorrow'. Despite the sexist title (no doubt a similar series today would have to be called 'Bandpersons of Tomorrow') it was a programme which went out to various establishments and recorded young musicians. The youngest contributor was a diminutive seven year old girl who played 'Drink to me Only With Thine Eyes', but more often the subject of the programme would be a youth band such as the one at Besses o' the Barn or a band of junior ratings like the one at HMS *Mercury*, a Naval shore base in Hampshire, where the Commanding Officer was a great character – a cricketer of fearsome repute and a Naval Officer – Commander C. B. Fry. Of the soloists who took part in the series I remember well a young boy called Denis Carr who, like his father, went on to become a conductor and adjudicator before joining the BBC in Leeds. Another promising player who also followed in father's footsteps (a good brass band tradition, this) was a young girl

Denis Carr in 1947, a 'bandsman of tomorrow'.

216

The National Youth Band at Ogmore.

called Betty Anderson who, a few years later, with her band, Ratby, became the first lady conductor to grace the platform of the British Open Championship at Belle Vue. Appropriately both Denis and Betty (as chairman) serve on the Council of the National Youth Band. This was formed in 1951 by Dr Denis Wright and, after his death, carried on by Geoffrey Brand and currently by Arthur Butterworth, but always with the advice and goodwill of Denis Wright's widow, Maud and, of course, countless hard-working tutors, many of whom are ex-members of the Youth Band themselves.

A third important factor in the musical development of the young is the Alexander Owen Memorial Scholarship. This has, over the years, produced a wealth of talent which in maturity has advanced brass music. Arthur Butterworth and Elgar Howarth are two such examples. Elgar Howarth, as a result of a commission which I was pleased to offer him to write a test-piece for the 1976 Belle Vue contest, produced one of the most important new works for brass to appear in

Elgar Howarth, orchestral conductor, formed the relationship between brass bands and the Proms at the Albert Hall.

the last quarter of a century. 'Fireworks' was a truly original score, as innovative then as was the work of Elgar, Holst and Bantock in the thirties. Elgar Howarth's musical career has taken him into the realms of the international orchestras and opera nowadays, but we are always pleased to see him back with brass when he can spare the time. He is another prime example of the musician with his roots in brass who can never quite bring himself to turn his back on his past – and thank goodness.

Would there were a few more composers coming on to the scene prepared to write interesting music with an occasional tune in it! We cannot forget the old classics of our repertoire, which exploited the unique tonal qualities of the brass band. Good band music need not consist merely of a long succession of notes. This was appreciated long ago by composers and arrangers of the calibre of Elgar, Ireland, Bantock, William Rimmer, Eric Ball and many other Salvationist composers, by Frank and Denis Wright, Peter Yorke, Gilbert Vinter, Derek Broadbent with 'Floral Dance' and by probably the most prolific arranger of them all, Edrich Siebert, a man who admits to and is proud of writing for the masses as well as the elite. The music of these men is still the backbone of our repertoire, and a judicious blend of the old with the vitality of the new is what is required – surely we shall find it in the years to come.

Although many fine contemporary composers of the calibre of Gordon Jacob, Malcolm Arnold, Edmund Rubbra, Joseph Horovitz and Edward Gregson have contributed to our repertoire in recent years, it is disappointing that others such as the late Benjamin Britten and Constant Lambert, Michael Tippett and Malcolm Williamson, have not taken the plunge.

The comradeship which I and countless others have enjoyed over the years is under an ominous threat. 'Comradeship', according to some, needs to be made official. The Musicians' Union which, for years, has not recognized brass band

218

A clutch of conductors. From the left: Eric Ball, Derek Garside, Stanley Boddington, Kenneth Dennison, Geoffrey Brand, Roy Newsome and myself.

activities, much less interfered with them, has recently taken an unwelcome look into our affairs. Brass bandsmen have always boasted of their working-men musician image, and have considered themselves as much an amateur movement as hundreds of choirs. John Henry Iles at his first Crystal Palace concert made reference to his 'working men's brass orchestra', and, although the cloth cap has long since been dead and buried, that description, for thousands of bandsmen, remains a valid one. Already some of our star bands have been constrained to join the union in order to appear in certain TV programmes; a rule which, on the face of it, is not unreasonable, but like so many rules and regulations, when strictly applied there is a farcical side to the do's and don'ts – in BBC Radio's 'Friday Night is Music Night' we have the ridiculous situation which allows the band and the orchestra to share the platform, but not to play at the same time, not even to play the closing signature tune together.

A situation which needs clarification is the fact that bands may appear in BBC TV programmes with impunity while, in recent years, the Union has demanded that the winners of the Granada 'Band of the Year' contest should join before their winning-band programme (part of the prize) could be transmitted. The argument that the bandsmen are paid in line with Union rates falls on deaf ears. Actual cards must be held by all bandsmen who, in all probability, are already fully paid up members of another union in respect of their full-time jobs.

To have all bands in the Union and demanding union fees would signify the end of the band movement as we know it, and as I have known it for the last eighty years. What would happen to the old Band Concert? Would we have to pay bands to appear in contests? Worse, are we in danger of creating an elite, who are in equal danger of pricing themselves out of all the things which go to make banding?

At the moment the situation is that the number of Union bands can be counted on the fingers of one hand, whilst hundreds of others are still content to *pay* to be a

Conducting Men o' Brass (City of Coventry, Fairey and Morris) in the television series 'My World of Music'.

member of a band, and contribute their weekly twenty pence, or whatever, to the general fund, just as we used to back in the Luton days. The day when such bands are forced into the position of second-class citizens while the top few take all the cream will be a sad one. Certainly there will always be the better-paid bands, but let them achieve their elevated position through their talent as has always been the case, not at the expense of their humbler colleagues who might find certain doors barred because they are unwilling, or unable, to pay Union fees.

Despite these gloomy prognostications I still believe the future can be a healthy one for young players. Things will change – that is the natural order. It is up to those now in a position to make their opinions felt, to make sure that the changes are for the better. Personally, I shall bow out with as much grace as I can manage, and leave the stage clear.

I was recently invited to be a guest on the Michael Parkinson Show, which I was to share with André Previn and the band of Black Dyke which Previn, like so many of his forebears, had recently conducted at the Royal Albert Hall. The conversation drifted towards the subject of retirement – obviously a thing to which André Previn had given little or no previous thought. I remarked that, although I had officially retired eighteen years ago, I felt very strongly that one should continue to work right up to the end, in my case suggesting that I would be content if that moment should occur in the middle of a marvellous piece of music such as *1812* or 'Resurgam' to ensure a fitting exit. Previn's face twinkled in a mischievous smile and he replied,

'Let's hope it's something the band knows well. Then at least they can finish the piece without you!'

I am sure they will.

With Margaret at EMI.

Index

Figures in italics refer to illustrations

Acknowledgements

My very grateful thanks to Alan Lynton for his patience in collating miles of tape and painstaking hard work in listening to my sometimes unclear diction, not to mention his many time-consuming journeys from Dorset to London. Starting as a 'new boy' at Belle Vue two years ago I like to think that he has now joined the ranks of converts to the brass band scene. Thanks, also, to Tony and Leslie Birks-Hay for their understanding and forbearance of a not always diligent author; and for their expertise in reproducing the pictures in this book, quite often under difficult circumstances.

The authors and publishers also gratefully acknowledge the considerable help with pictures and research provided from many sources, including Alphabet and Image; Austin Morris, Oxford; BBC Copyright Photographs; BBC Hulton Picture Library; Boosey & Hawkes; Boys' Brigade; *British Bandsman*; British and Commonwealth Shipping Company Ltd; L. Newborough, *British Mouthpiece*; Chetham Library, Manchester; *Daily Mirror*; Eastbourne Museum; L. Englesberg; Entam Ltd, Belle Vue; *Evening Sentinel*; Fairey Band; Bram Gay, Granada TV; Barrie Hall; John Keeling; Kneller Hall Museum; Allan Littlemore, Fodens; Luton Museum and Art Gallery; National Museum of Wales (Welsh Folk Museum); Bryan Ledgard, Northern Lights Recording Co; John Pope; Wyndham Robinson, *Daily Herald*; Salvation Army; *Staffordshire Sentinel*; *Yorkshire Evening News*.